AF600564

LEGITIMACY AND LEGITIMATION

THE CATHOLIC UNIVERSITY OF AMERICA
CANON LAW STUDIES
No. 138

LEGITIMACY AND LEGITIMATION

AN HISTORICAL SYNOPSIS AND COMMENTARY

A DISSERTATION

Submitted to the Faculty of Canon Law of the Catholic University of America in Partial Fulfillment of the Requirements for the Degree of

DOCTOR OF CANON LAW

BY

REV. GILBERT JOSEPH McDEVITT, A.B., J.C.L.
Priest of the Archdiocese of Philadelphia

THE CATHOLIC UNIVERSITY OF AMERICA PRESS
WASHINGTON, D. C.
1941

NIHIL OBSTAT:
CLEMENT V. BASTNAGEL, J.U.D.,
Censor Deputatus.
Washington, D. C., June 2, 1941.

IMPRIMATUR:
✠ D. CARD. DOUGHERTY,
Archiepiscopus Philadelphiensis.
Philadelphia, June 4, 1941.

PRINTED IN THE UNITED STATES OF AMERICA
BY THE WATKINS PRINTING CO., BALTIMORE

TO MY FATHER AND MOTHER

TABLE OF CONTENTS

FOREWORD

The Church, zealous defender of the sacrament of Matrimony, has seen fit to recognize the difference between legitimate and illegitimate children. Today when the sanctity of marriage is everywhere derided, there is a determined effort to destroy any distinction between children born of lawful wedlock and those born outside of honorable marriage. Consequently it has seemed advisable to present the Church's teaching on legitimacy and to discuss the modes of legitimation employed to ameliorate the condition of those unfortunate children who have been born outside of lawful wedlock.

Outside the Church there are many false notions in vogue regarding the status of children. These mistaken ideas, it is interesting to note, constitute in part the results of the contempt with which our age regards the holiness of marriage. There are, for example, nations which proclaim that the duty of woman, whether married or unmarried, is motherhood. Such nations are interested in increasing the numbers of children not so much as the fruit of chaste wedlock, but rather for the sordid purpose of furnishing more servants to do the bidding of the State. The organized effort which is being made in the United States to destroy all distinctions between legitimate and illegitimate children is based on a false humanitarianism. The proponents of the idea that legitimate and illegitimate children should be regarded as absolutely alike, seem to forget that God has ordained that the procreation of children is the right only of those who are united in lawful marriage.

The over-emphasized, sentimental regard for the unmarried mother and her offspring led Pope Pius XI to write, "We note with sorrow that not infrequently nowadays it happens that through a certain inversion of the true order of things, ready and bountiful assistance is provided for the unmarried mother and her illegitimate offspring (who, of course, must be helped in order to avoid a greater evil) which is denied to legitimate mothers or given sparingly or almost grudgingly." [1]

It need only be mentioned that the Church, of course, does not consider the illegitimate child responsible for its plight. Thus the restrictions placed upon illegitimates in canon law do not constitute a punishment. They constitute rather a denial of the rights which belong properly to those children who are born of lawful wedlock.

The study consists of two sections. The first section is an historical synopsis comprising a consideration of the legislation of Justinian on legitimacy and legitimation and a treatment of legitimacy, legitimation, and connected questions in canon law until the time of the promulgation of the Code of Canon Law. The second section constitutes a commentary on the present canonical legislation on legitimacy and legitimation together with a treatment of allied topics. Finally, an appendix embodying a summary consideration of the English common law and modern American law is included.

The writer takes this occasion to thank His Eminence Dennis Cardinal Dougherty, Archbishop of Philadelphia, for the opportunity accorded him for advanced studies. He wishes also to thank the members of the Faculty of the School of Canon Law of the Catholic University of America for their direction of the work. Finally, he extends his thanks to all those other persons who have aided him in any way in the preparation of the dissertation.

[1] Ep. encycl., *"Casti Connubii,"* 31 dec. 1930— *AAS,* XXII (1930), 539-592.

SECTION I
HISTORICAL SYNOPSIS

Chapter I

ROMAN LAW

Part I. *Legitimacy in the Legislation of Justinian*

The consideration of the legitimacy of children is necessarily connected with the institutions of marriage and the family. The discussion of these as natural institutions will be undertaken in the Canon Law section.

Since the Roman law section of this study is restricted to the consideration of legitimacy and legitimation in the legislation of Justinian it suffices to state that all children conceived and born in lawful wedlock were considered legitimate by this Emperor. On the other hand all children born of marriages unlawful for any reason, or of quasi-marital or extra-marital unions were deemed illegitimate. It can be said then that the following children were regarded as illegitimate: (1) those born of concubinage; (2) those born of *contubernium;* (3) those born of incest; (4) those born of marriage forbidden for reasons besides consanguinity and affinity; (5) those born of adultery; (6) those born of fornication; (7) those born of *stuprum.*

All illegitimate children were known in Justinian legislation by the general term *vulgo quaesiti* or *vulgo concepti.*[1] Illegitimate children were classified in various ways in the legislation of this Emperor depending on the status of their parents. Thus the Emperor decreed that if any persons violated the laws of marriage which he had enacted they were not to be understood to be husband and wife and any children born of such unions were not in the *potestas* of the father. They were in the same

[1] Inst. (1.4); (1.10) 12.

position as those conceived by the mother in illicit intercourse. The children of these prohibited marriages were regarded as spurious. Spurious children, it may be explained were not deemed to have a father because of the uncertainty of his identity. The law placed the children of prohibited marriages in the same category.[2]

Another class of illegitimates were known as "natural" children. This term in itself had no legal signification because the true father of such children was not necessarily their father juridically. The term had purely a natural and factual signification. In the case of these children the father was actually known but legally they were presumed to have no father and were therefore, classed with the *vulgo quaesiti.* The children born of concubinage belonged to this class.[3] Justinian decreed that children born of an offensive or a prohibited marriage were not even to be called "natural," nor were they to be partakers of any favor. As a punishment the parents were to know that the children born of their depraved lust were to have absolutely nothing.[4] Among these children to whom he denied the name "natural" the Emperor placed first those born of intercourse "for we do not call this marriage" which was infamous, incestuous, or prohibited. Such children were not to be supported by their parents nor were they to share in any benefits of the law for "natural" children.[5]

In conclusion it can be stated that all illegitimate children were known in Justinian's legislation by the general designation *vulgo quaesiti* or *vulgo concepti.* They were divided into "natural" and "spurious" children. The "natural" children were those born of parents who were free to intermarry, e. g., the partners in concubinage. As will be shown presently this class benefited most from legitimation. The "spurious" children were divided into various groups because of the reasons which kept their parents from intermarrying. They were "simply spurious" if their parents

[2] Inst. (1.10) 12.
[3] Inst. (1.10) 13; C. (5.27) 2-9; Nov. 38, 2, 4, 5; Nov. 75, pref. 1-3.
[4] Nov. 74.6; 89.1.
[5] Nov. 89.15.

contracted a marriage which was legally forbidden. If the parents were related within the forbidden degrees of consanguinity or affinity in the collateral line the children were deemed the fruit of incest; if the parents were related in the ascending and descending line the children were also regarded as the result of incest.

Part II. *Legitimation in the Legislation of Justinian*

The decrees and Constitutions of this Emperor contain very complete and definite legislation on legitimation of "natural" children. By the legislative activity of his reign Justinian incorporated, amended, expanded, and in some instances abrogated the laws of his predecessors.

In 528 he permitted the natural father, provided he had no legitimate children, to give his "natural" children and their mother one-half of his possessions.[6] He also permitted a grandfather to give to the "natural" children of his legitimate son and to the "natural" and legitimate children of his own "natural" son his entire possessions in the event that there was no lawful heirs.[7] In the same year he reiterated the principle that "natural" children offered to the *Curia,* though they were the legitimate heirs of their father, nevertheless did not become members of his *familia.*[8] Girard observes that the *oblatio curiae* differed in this respect from the other modes of legitimation because the latter allowed the legitimated child to become a member of their father's *familia.*[9] Justinian also decreed that even if a man had legitimate children he could nevertheless offer his "natural" sons to the *Curia.*[10]

He found it neccessary in the years 529 and 530 to clarify certain points on legitimation by subsequent marriage. He decreed that in order to effect the legitimation of "natural" children

[6] C. (5.27) 8.

[7] C. (5.27) 12.

[8] C. (5.27) 9; Nov. (89.4).

[9] Girard, *Manuel Elementaire de Droit Romain* (7. ed. Paris: Rousseau et Cie, 1924), p. 196.

[10] C. (5.27) 9; Nov. (89.3).

it was sufficient to execute the dotal instruments and to manifest the marital affection thereby changing the concubinage into a marriage.[11]

By the execution of the dotal instruments was meant in the most general terms the drawing up of a written document to prove the existence of the marriage. Any defect, however, in the drawing up of such a document did not affect the status of the children.[12] A child born before or after the execution of the dotal instruments was legitimate.[13] The qualification of "natural" children for legitimation was to be determined according to the qualification of the mother at the time of the child's conception or of birth. If the time of conception was more favorable in a particular case that time was to be considered.[14] Justinian eliminated the distinction between legitimated "natural" children and children born in lawful wedlock. He made them of equal status in all respects.[15] This must be interpreted, however, by keeping in mind the fact that children offered to the *curia* did not become members of their father's family.[16]

The changes of Justinian's legislation on legitimation between 528 and 534 may be summed up as follows.

1. He maintained that the absence of lawful offspring was necessary for the legitimation of "natural" children. He was to remove this restriction in 535.[17]
2. The dotal instruments had to be executed in order to change a concubinage into a lawful marriage.[18]
3. The concubine mother of the child to be legitimated did not have to be a free-born woman. It sufficed if she was free at the time of the conception or birth of the child.[19]

[11] Inst. (1.10) 13; C. (5.27) 11.2; Nov. (18.11).
[12] D. (1.5) 8.
[13] C. (5.27) 11, 3; Nov. (89.8) 1.
[14] C. (5.27) 11, 4.
[15] Inst. (1.10) 13; C. (5.27) 10.
[16] C. (5.27) 9; Nov. (89.4).
[17] Nov. (12.4).
[18] C. (5.27) 10.
[19] Inst. (1.10) 13; C. (5.27) 10, pref.

4. Justinian established the legitimation by subsequent marriage as a permanent mode of legitimation with retroactive force.[20]

Despite the legislative activity of the Emperor on this topic of legitimation his laws were inadequate to cover all circumstances. This is evidenced when he himself described the possibility of the case occurring in which a father would want to legitimate his "natural" children by marrying their mother but was actually prevented from doing so by her death.

In other words the deficiencies of the existing legislation prevented the legitimation of "natural" children whose mother had died, thus precluding the possibility of her marriage with the father who was anxious to have the children legitimated.[21] In 539 Justinian corrected and amended the legislation of the former Emperors as well as his own. These corrections, amendments, as well as new provisions are found in the Novels. The modes of legitimation as they were finally developed in the Novels of Justinian will be treated now.

Article I.—*Legitimation by Subsequent Marriage*

This method of legitimation had been first introduced by Constantine. In 476 it was renewed by Zeno as a temporary measure. It provided for the legitimation of children already born in concubinage at the time of the law's promulgation, but it was not to be invoked in future cases.[22] The Emperor Anastasius in 517 instituted it as a perpetual means of legitimation. In 519 Justin deprived it of its character as an enduring institution for legitimation having value for the future. Justinian decreed that if a man and a free woman married who already had children born of their union, the children born both before and after the execution of the dotal instruments were in all respects equal.[23] In 529 and 530 he extended the law permitting the legitimation of the freeborn when the concubinage had been converted into a marriage, to include the children of a *liberta* and a *libertina*. In 536

[20] Inst. (1.10) 13.
[21] Nov. (74. pref.).
[22] C. (5.27) 5.
[23] C. (5.27) 10.

he went further permitting the legitimation of children born in slavery and manumitted with their mother.[24] Slave children were legitimated as soon as their mother was manumitted and the dotal instruments drawn up for her marriage with the master.[25] In 539 the Emperor permitted Senators and other men of high rank to marry a *liberta* if they drew up the dotal instruments. Any children born before the drawing up of such instruments were legitimated.[26]

Justinian in 542 made a sweeping change in the legislation regarding the prohibition to men of high rank concerning women who were called abject by the law. Justinian permitted such marriages to Senators and other men of high rank provided that they drew up the dotal instruments. Other free men were not required to draw up such instruments when they married these women.[27]

All citizens now had in the *ius conubii* with all free women on the hypothesis naturally that they had not entered into unions with these women which could neither be regarded as marriage nor as concubinage. Unions not regarded as marriage were those prohibited by law on the grounds of relationship or public policy. Unions not regarded even as concubinage were those in which the parties were not free to contract marriage later or because the alliances lacked the stability which was demanded even in concubinage. The children of these prohibited unions were regarded as "spurious".[28] The unions referred to were infamous, nefarious, and forbidden unions.[29] Regarding such forbidden unions the Emperor observed that he was enacting laws not for the benefit of those living licentious lives but for those who were chaste.[30]

[24] Nov. (18.11).
[25] Nov. (78.4).
[26] Nov. (78.3).
[27] Nov. (117.6).
[28] Meyer, *Der Römische Konkubinat* (Leipzig, 1895), p. 150.
[29] Nov. (89.15).
[30] Nov. (18.15).

Article II—*Legitimation by Imperial Rescript*

There is no unanimity of opinion on the question as to which Emperor first introduced this form of legitimation. For instance, Moyle says it was permitted by Anastasius (491-518), forbidden by Justin (518-527), and Justinian (527-565) the latter however reintroducing it in the Novels. Girard says simply that it was admitted by Justinian. Meyer says that it was inaugurated by Justinian as a new mode of legitimation. Whichever Emperor introduced it, and the sources seem to favor Justinian as his legislation can be found there, Justinian enacted very definite and new legislation governing this method.

If a man had no legitimate children, but only "natural" ones, and desired to render them legitimate, and the mother of the children was dead; or, if she was living, had been guilty of any misconduct; or had disappeared, or was prohibited by some law from marrying the father, the Emperor authorized the man in these circumstances to confer upon his "natural" children the right of legitimacy in the new way now proposed by the Emperor. If the father had no surviving lawful offspring he was permitted to petition the Emperor to provide for his children, giving the reasons why he desired to have them restored to their natural and original free birth, and to have them legitimated. These children would remain in the power of the father and differed in no way from children begotten lawfully.[31]

Two conditions were imposed: (1) That the father had no "natural" children; (2) that the concubinage could not be transformed into a marriage or that the father would not enter into a marriage because of the unworthiness of the concubine.

Article III—*Legitimatio ex Testamento*

There was another mode of legitimation which was closely linked with the preceding. It was introduced by Justinian and was called *legitimatio ex testamento*. The father, if he had been prevented by circumstances during his life-time from legitimating his "natural" children in one of the ways already mentioned, and

[31] Nov. (74. 1-2), Nov. (89.9).

if besides he had no legitimate children, could extend the privilege of legitimation to his "natural" children by his last will. To make valid such a bequest the children had to petition the Emperor, draw up a statement of the fact, and produce the will. When these conditions were fulfilled the children obtained the gift of legitimation, at the same time from their father and the Emperor, or, as Justinian declared, both from nature and the law.[32]

Article IV—*Legitimatio per Oblationem Curiae*

This method of legitimacy as far as inheritance was concerned was introduced by Theodosius II in 442.[33] It was enacted primarily for the benefits that accrued to the various *Curiae*. As it was first introduced it was more correctly a provision for *legitima successio* rather than a method devised to effect legitimation strictly so called. In 539 it became a mode of legitimation and is expressly referred to as such by Justinian and is called in fact by the Emperor the first method of obtaining the right of legitimacy.[34] The restrictions placed on children legitimated in this way must be kept in mind as has been noted before.[35] The legal status of a "natural" son offered to the *Curia* remained the same as it had been under earlier legislation. The son came under the *patria potestas* and became capable of inheritance. It seems correct to observe at this point that the *oblatio curiae* effected the legitimation of "natural" sons directly while natural daughters had to be married to a *decurio,* thereby being legitimated indirectly. Justinian effected some changes in this method of legitimation.

1. "Natural sons could offer themselves to the *Curia* after the death of their father if he had no legitimate children.[36]
2. If the natural father was a member of the *Curia* or not, if he had both legitimate and "natural" sons or only the latter, he was permitted to offer some or all of the "natural" sons

[32] Nov. (74.2); (89.10).
[33] C. (5.27) 3.
[34] Nov. (89.2).
[35] C. (5.27) 9; Nov. (89.4).
[36] Nov. (89.2) 1.

to the *Curia,* even if at the time the sons had acquired a distinguished office, as long as the office was not one which released a man from the obligation of the *Curia.*[37]
The trend of this legislation to seek primarily the advantage of the State rather than that of the child is shown here by the fact that the father could offer some or all of his "natural" sons to the *Curia.* The insistence, too, that the son to be legitimated could not hold an office incompatible with the curial duties is also worthy of notice.

3. If the father was himself a member of the *Curia* and had no legitimate heirs he could, by offering his "natural" son begotten of a union with a slave, both manumit and legitimate him.[38]
4. The succession to the property of a person who had been offered to the *Curia* was determined as follows: (a) His own legitimate children succeeded him; (b) If the children were not decurions a legal share was to be given to the *Curia* and the Treasury, the remainder being given to the children; (c) If such a person died without issue three-fourths of his estate went to the *Curia,* one-fourth to the other legal heirs; (d) If such a person had only "natural" children he was permitted to appoint them heirs by offering them to the *Curia;* if the children refused this offer the *Curia* claimed three-fourths of the estate; but if they accepted the duties of decurions they received three-fourths.[39]

It may be said in conclusion that even in Justinian's law the *legitimatio per oblationem curiae* was employed as it had been before—for the interests of the State.

In conclusion it must be stated that legitimation owing to its consequences, e.g., *patria potestas, officium decurionis,* etc., could not take place without the child's consent. Justinian observed that if it was not allowed to dissolve *patria potestas* when the children were unwilling then it was certainly not permissible

[37] Nov. (89.2) 1.
[38] Nov. (89.2) 3.
[39] Nov. (89.5) ; (89.6).

to place an unwilling child under *patria potestas* either by offering the child to the *Curia,* or by drawing up dotal instruments, or by any other method.[40] The text of the law shows that as a rule (*generaliter*) the consent of the child was necessary. It does not seem unreasonable then to maintain that in some cases the child's assent was not necessary.

[40] Nov. (89.11) praef.

CHAPTER II

HISTORY OF THE CANON LAW OF LEGITIMACY AND LEGITIMATION

PART I—LEGITIMACY

Article 1.—*Legitimacy in the Natural Law*

It has already been observed at the beginning of the discussion of legitimacy in the chapter on Roman Law that it is impossible to consider this question apart from the institutions of marriage and the family. In the present article the writer prescinds absolutely from the requirements necessary for legitimacy in Canon Law. He intends only to show that the fact of legitimacy in the natural law depends on a valid marriage. The validity of the marriage must be judged only by the standards required by that part of the natural law which is proper to man alone. If legitimacy in the natural law must be considered in connection with marriage and the family it is necessary to show the basis in natural law for the existence of these two institutions.

St. Thomas observes that a thing is said to be natural in two ways. First, as resulting of necessity from the principles of nature; thus upward movement is natural to fire. In this way matrimony is not natural nor are any of those things which come to pass at the intervention or by the motion of the free will. Secondly, that is said to be natural to which nature inclines, although it comes to pass through the intervention of the free will; thus acts of virtue and the virtues themselves are called natural; and in this way matrimony is natural, because natural reason inclines thereto in two ways: first, in relation to the principal end of matrimony, namely the procreation of children, and secondly, in relation to the secondary end of matrimony, which is the mutual advantage enjoyed by the spouses in matrimony.[1]

[1] S. Thomae Aquinatis, *Summa Theologica* (Taurini: ed. De Rubeis, Billuart et Aliorum, 1932), Supplementum, q. 41, art. 1.

For a recent study of this question cf. Ostheimer, *The Family,* The

Treating the question of legitimacy St. Thomas shows that illegitimate children are such precisely because they are born outside the natural institution of marriage.[2]

The question of legitimacy in the natural law has been treated recently by Ciprotti who states that only children conceived in a valid marriage are legitimate according to the natural law.[3]

There have been canonists who did not distinguish between legitimacy in the natural law and legitimacy according to the positive law. Schmalzgrueber in answering the question how children begotten outside of marriage but born after the marriage of their parents could be considered legitimate said it depended on positive law which law he maintained made children legitimate.[4]

According to Schmalzgrueber's view there would be no distinction at all in the natural law between children conceived in a valid marriage and those conceived outside of such a marriage.

Joyce dissents from the view that the natural law considered apart from any positive law demands certain requisites for legitimacy. He would restrict the whole question of legitimacy

Catholic University of America, Philosophical Studies, vol. 50 (Washington, D. C.: The Catholic University of America, 1939), p. 7 ff.

[2] Ad primum ergo dicendum, quod quamvis illi qui nascuntur ex illicito coitu, nascantur secundum naturam quae communis est homini et omnibus animalibus, tamen nascuntur contra legem naturae quae est propria hominibus; quia fornicatio et adulterium, et huiusmodi sunt contra legem naturae. *Et ideo tales secundum nullam legem sunt legitimi.*—Supplementum, q. 68, art. 1 ad primum.

[3] Nunc autem si prolis legitimitas quae statuitur iure canonico comparetur cum iure naturae, haec dicenda sunt; omnem prolem ex matrimonio valido, non autem putativo, conceptam, esse ex ipso naturae iure legitimam; immo hunc esse unicum casum quo proles est ex iure naturae legitima; ad quod nihil refert utrum proles nata sit durante matrimonio, an post huius dissolutionem.—Ciprotti, Pius, "De prole legitima vel illegitima in iure canonico vigenti," *Apollinaris,* XII (1939), 337.

[4] ". . . quia quod aliquis legitime natus dicatur, non est effectus iuris naturalis; nam secundum hoc ius omnes aequales nascimur ex viro, et ex femina; sed est potius effectus legis (unde et legitimi dicuntur) et iuris positivi, quod alicujus nativitatem approbat, eique iura legitime natorum attribuit . . ."—Schmalzgrueber, *Ius Ecclesiasticum Universum* (Romae, 1845), Pars IV, tit. 17, n. 10.

to the civil law. Speaking of the Church's recognition of putative marriage Joyce observes: "The system has been criticised on the grounds that to style the children of unmarried parents legitimate is a contradiction in terms. The objection is due to ignorance of the meaning of the word. In ordinary speech, it is true, *legitimate* signifies born in lawful wedlock. But such is not its original meaning. *Matrimonium legitimum* signified a marriage which gave to the wife the right to bear children capable of inheritance: and *filii legitimi* were children with full rights of succession to the property and the status of their father. In strict accuracy the word has reference to the civil effects of marriage. Hence an eminent English jurist says very truly: 'Legitimacy is the creature of civil institutions, varying as they vary. It is a civil incident and therefore no test of a spiritual question.' "[5]

Joyce's restriction of the question of legitimacy to the civil law alone is patently incorrect. If, as he remarks, in strict accuracy legitimacy has reference to the civil effects of marriage why has ecclesiastical law for centuries embodied legislation on this question? Further, it seems reasonable to insist that even according to the natural law there must be some distinction between children conceived in a valid marriage and children conceived outside of such a marriage.

In conclusion it may be said that according to the natural law taken by itself, the conception of a child in a valid marriage is necessary for its legitimacy. This conclusion must be interpreted by keeping in mind that the writer has prescinded in this article from any consideration of legitimacy in canon law or civil law.

Article II.—Preliminary Notions of the Term *Filii Legitimi*

The word *filius* will be employed in this discussion because it is more precise in meaning than *liber*.[6] There have existed different acceptations of the term *filii legitimi* together with various divisions. The gloss to the word *repellendus* found in

[5] Joyce, *Christian Marriage* (London and New York: Sheed and Ward, 1933), p. 82.

[6] Cf. Schmalzgrueber, lib. IV, tit. 17, n. 1.

the chapter *"Tanta est vis matrimonii"* of Alexander III in the Decretals distinguishes various classes of legitimate children. Some are *filii legitimi tantum ut adoptivi sive arrogati.* Others are referred to as *filii legitimi et naturales ut nati ex legitimo matrimonio vero vel putativo, sive ab initio sive ex post facto.*[7] Ferraris calls the *legitimi tantum* such because he says they are made legitimate not by nature by by the law alone as in adoption.[8] Maroto says that a *filius naturalis seu corporalis* must be distinguished from a *filius adoptivus. Filii naturales seu corporales* are legitimate when they are born in wedlock.[9] Wernz-Vidal observe that these diverse acceptations of the term *filii legitimi* existed on account of the question as to what constituted a *matrimonium legitimum.*[10] Gradually the term *filii legitimi* came to signify in ecclesiastical law a child born of a marriage validly contracted *coram Deo* et *in facie ecclesiae* even though such a marriage might not be considered valid in civil law with regard to certain purely civil effects.[11]

The old law accentuated the capacity of the legitimate child to inherit. Every child that was a lawful heir of its parents was called a *filius legitimus.* Pope Innocent I (401-417), writing to the bishops Rufus and Eusebius as well as to the other bishops of Macedonia, decreed that a man after receiving baptism was not to dismiss the wife he already had and further that the children already born were capable of inheritance,[12] Freisen calls attention to this insistence of the old law on the capacity of legitimate children to inherit.[13]

[7] C. 6, X, *qui filii sint legitimi,* IV, 17.

[8] Ferraris, *Prompta Bibliotheca, Canonica, Iuridica, Moralis, Theologica nec non Ascetica, Polemica, Rubristica, Historica* (Parisiis: ed. Migne, 1860-1865), s. v. *"Filius, Filii,"* n. 1. This work will be referred to hereafter as: Ferraris, *Prompta Bibliotheca.*

[9] Maroto, *Institutiones Iuris Canonici ad Normam Novi Codicis* (Romae, 1919), I, 505.

[10] Wernz-Vidal, *Ius Canonicum ad Codicis Normam Exactum,* 7 vols in 9, Vol. V, *Ius Matrimoniale,* 2. ed. (Romae: Apud Aedes Universitatis Gregorianae, 1928), N. 609.

[11] Wernz-Vidal, *loc. cit.*

[12] C. 3, D. XXVI.

[13] "Die alte Zeit betonte hier namentlich die Erbfähigkeit, jedes Kind,

Article III.—*Matrimonium Legitimum*

In order to facilitate the study of the notion of *filii legitimi* it becomes necessary to discuss in some detail what was meant by a *matrimonium legitimum*. Since the promulgation of the Code the term still has two significations: 1. The technically strict meaning of canon 1015, § 3; 2. the wider signification of canon 1075, § 1, 1°. Canon 1015, § 3 states that marriage validly contracted between unbaptized persons is called *legitimate*. Canon 1075, § 1, 1°, states that there can be no valid marriage between those who during the same *legitimate* marriage have committed adultery and promised marriage to one another or attempted it, even by a merely civil act.[14]

In Roman Law the *ius conubii* was required for a fully legal Roman marriage.[15] The influence of Roman law on early ecclesiastical legislation is accountable for the different significations the term *matrimonium legitimum* had in the early ecclesiastical legal sources. In the first centuries of her existence the Church was unable effectively to exercise her exclusive authority over Christian marriage though she always insisted on her rights. As the number of Christians grew she gradually came to have more influence. This struggle necessitated some concessions to civil law, but the Church always urged her exclusive rights. She agreed in part to the regulations of civil law; in part she discarded them. In so doing the various meanings of the term *matrimonium legitimum* arose.[16] Sometimes the term was applied with its Roman law signification and sometimes it was used in the sense it had in ecclesiastical law.

I. Pope St. Leo I (458) was alluding to the Roman law when he wrote, "Nuptiarum autem foedera inter ingenuos sunt legitima."

welches das volle gesetzliche Erbrecht an die Eltern hatte, nannte man *filius legitimus*"—Freisen, *Geschichte des Canonischen Eherechts bis zum Verfall der Glossenlitteratur* (2. ed. Paderborn, 1893), p. 857.

[14] "Nota in textu Codicis voces *legitimo matrimonio* adhiberi cum significatione valide contracti matrimonii, etiam inter fideles."—Vermeersch-Creusen, *Epitome Iuris Canonici* (5. ed., 3 vols. Mechliniae: H. Dessain, 1933-1936), II, p. 247, n. 351.

[15] G. (1.56).

[16] Freisen, *Eherecht,* p. 72.

This, it may be explained, was a reference to the Roman *conubium* in the wider sense namely, that *conubium* existed between two free-born persons.[17] Pope Julius I (337-352) wrote that a marriage between a master and his freed-woman was legitimate, "Si quis ancillam suam libertate donaverit, et in matrimonio sibi sociaverit, dubitabatur apud quosdam utrum huiusmodi nuptiae legitimae videantur. Nos itaque, vetustam ambiguitatem decidentes, talia conubia legitima esse censemus."[18] The marriages alluded to by Pope Julius I were also mentioned in the legislation of Justinian.[19] Freisen observes that it is immaterial here whether the marriage was Christian or non-Christian marriage, beause the quotations used by Gratian employed the expression of Roman law.[20] With the idea in mind that a non-Christian marriage could be, in a sense, a *matrimonium legitmum* Pope Innocent I rebuked the bishops Rufus and Eusebius for holding the view that only Christian marriages could be such. He declared that children born before and after the baptism of a convert parent were legitimate and capable of inheritance, that the wife could not be dismissed after the baptism of the hubsand. The Pope argued that since marriage was not a sin it was not dissolved by Baptism, ". . . Nuptiarum ergo copula, quia Dei mandato perficitur non potest dici peccatum et quod peccatum non est, solvi inter peccata non debet; eritque integrum estimare aboleri non posse nomen prioris uxoris, cum non sit dimissum pro peccato, quod ex Dei voluntate sit completum."[21]

II. Other texts employ the term *matrimonium legitimum* in connection with the idea of *conubium* in the stricter sense. The stricter sense of the term was that *conubium* existed between parties between whom there existed no invalidating impediment. Just as in Roman law a person who entered an incestuous union was reputed legally to have no children, so too in ecclesiastical law those children who were born *ex incestuosis coniunctionibus* were

[17] C. 12, C. XXXII, q. 2.
[18] C. 3, C. XXIX, q. 2.
[19] C. (5.4) 26.
[20] Freisen, *Eherecht,* p. 72.
[21] C. 3, D. XXVI.

not even called *filii.*[22] Marriages within the forbidden degrees were characterized as *coniunctiones illicitae.*[23] In 506 the Council of Agde decreed in canon 61 that incestuous unions did not merit the name of marriage.[24] Pope Innocent I denied the legitimate character of a marriage entered into when the bond of a prior marriage still remained: ". . . statuimus fide catholica suffragante, coniugium illud esse, quod erat gratia divina primitus fundatum *conventumque secundae mulieris,* priore superstite nec divortio eiecta, *nullo pacto esse legitimum.*" [25] The words "priore superstite nec divortio eiecta" cause no perplexity when it is remembered that the Pope was referring not only to the invalidity of the second union in canon law but also in civil law.[26] For a valid Christian marriage it was necessary that the spouses be united according to the precepts of Christ.[27] *Matrimonium legitimum* at the same time is contrasted with concubinage, even when the latter is entered into for the procreation of offspring.[28] St Ambrose refers to the true wife as *legitima uxor* in opposition to all others, and observes that Christian spouses are equally bound to conjugal fidelity.[29]

III. There was another kind of marriage called legitimate with respect to the observance of prescribed formalities. As has already been seen, Roman law was not concerned with formalities in the sense that their observance or non-observance would affect the validity of marriage. The idea of prescribed formalities comes from the Germanic law. These formalities have been enumerated by Gratian as betrothal, settling of the dowry, and the celebration of marriage. Gratian notes too that it is not sinful if all these are not observed.[30] If these formalities were

[22] C. un., C. XXXV, q. 7.
[23] C. 2, C. XXXV, q. 8.
[24] C. 8, C. XXXV, q. 2, et 3.
[25] C. 2, C. XXXIV, q. 1, et 2.
[26] Joyce, *Christian Marriage*, p. 317.
[27] C. 2, C. XXXII, q. 2.
[28] C. 5, C. XXXII, q. 2.
[29] C. 4, C. XXXII, q. 4.
[30] C. 3, C. XXX, q. 5.

not observed a marriage was incapable of certain effects in Germanic law The Church took some cognizance of their observance and they are mentioned by St. Isidore of Seville (+636) by Benedict the Levite (ca. 847-857) and Hincmar of Rheims (+ 882).[31] The Church brought to bear more and more her own legislation on marriage. She abolished the Roman idea of *conubium* and disregarded the insistence of the Germanic law on formalities. Since this was so, the term *matrimonium legitimum* finally came to have its own distinct meaning in canon law, even if the former significations perdured for some time.

The *rubrica* and *dicta* of Gratian on the various significations of the term *matrimonium legitimum* may be inserted here. It is not intended at this point to evaluate his arguments regarding the question to be treated now. Asking the question, *"an coniugium sit inter infideles?"* Gratian cites texts from St. Paul, St. Ambrose, and St Augustine to show that they held there could be no coniugium among non-Christians. Then he cites other authorities, notably Sacred Scripture, to prove that there could be a *coniugium inter infideles.*[32] Later on, in a *dictum* he gives his own opinion regarding various classes of marriage. He distinguishes between *coniugium legitimum et non ratum, ratum et non legitimum, legitimum et ratum.* According to Gratian a *coniugium legitimum* is one entered into with the observance of legal formalities or according to the customs of the place. Such a marriage between non-Christians is not considered *ratum* because it is not of itself stable and inviolable. Among the fathful, however, a marriage is *ratum* because once entered into it cannot afterwards be dissolved. He observes further that a marriage among the faithful entered into without any ceremonies but simply with marital intent is not a *coniugium legitimum* but only *ratum.*[33]

The words *inter fideles* are to be taken attributively not predicatively. They mean that the marriage of infidels is not *ratum.*

[31] Freisen, *Eherecht,* p. 74.
[32] C. XXVIII, q. 1.
[33] c. 17, C. XXVIII, q. 1.

Only marriage among the faithful is *ratum* because once entered into it is indissoluble.[34]

It may be said then that according to Gratian *matrimonium legitimum et non ratum* is one contracted according to the laws or customs of the place. This marriage takes place only among infidels. Since it is not *ratum* it is therefore dissoluble. *Matrimonium legitimum et ratum* is the marriage of Christians fulfilling the requirements of both civil and ecclesiastical law. *Matrimonium ratum* is a valid Christian marriage entered into without any solemnities. It is *ratum* only in the internal forum.[35] This type of marriage cannot be called *matrimonium legitimum* in the external forum because every proof of the existence of the marriage is lacking in the external forum. Proof may, however, be supplied by both parties and if this is accepted the union, though lacking in form, is recognized in the external forum. To constitute a *matrimonium legitimum* among the faithful it is necessary further that there be no diriment impediments existing between the parties. *Matrimonium legitimum et non ratum* cannot exist between Christians because the observance of the formalities of civil law along with disregard of ecclesiastical law cannot result in a valid Christian marriage.

It is seen that Gratian distinguished two types of *matrimonium legitimum* viz., *matrimonium legitimum et non ratum* and *matrimonium legitimum et ratum*. The first, as has been already observed, is the marriage of non-Christians contracted lawfully; the second is the marriage of Christians entered into with the observance of both civil and ecclesiastical law. The division of Gratian is recalled by Benedict XIV.[36] A marriage of Christians before the civil authorities cannot be called a *matrimonium legitimum* ever since the Church has exercised her exclusive authority over

[34] Freisen, *Eherecht*, p. 77.

[35] C. 11, C. XXX, q. 5.

[36] ". . . quamquam hodie nomine matrimonii legitimi et non rati communiter intelligimus matrimonium infidelium, olim tamen a iuris canonici peritis etiam inter matrimonia fidelium fuisse hanc adhibitam distinctionem, ut alia dicerentur legitima et rata, alia dumtaxat rata et non legitima testis est Gratianus . . ."—*De Synodo Diocesana*, Lib. VIII, c. 12, n. 5.

marriage. At most, a marriage so contracted would be *ratum tantum*.

Peter Lombard held the view that clandestine marriage could be entered into legitimately as far as the validity of the sacrament was concerned. His sole requirement for such a marriage was the exchange of marital consent with the understanding, of course, that no diriment impediment existed between the contracting parties.[37] Rolandus Bandinelli (+ 1181) does not employ the term *matrimonium legitimum* in a strict sense. He along with Peter Lombard calls a marriage entered into without form a *matrimonium legitimum*. This is implied in his definition of marriage: "Matrimonium est coniunctio legitima viri et mulieris." The word *legitima* is to be understood as referring to the absence of diriment impediments.[38] Bernard of Pavia (+ 1216) in his *Summa de Matrimonio* adopts the viewpoint of Gratian, as he too argues for the solemnities connected with marriage, but he holds nevertheless that a marriage entered into without their observance could be a true marriage, even if it be not a *matrimonium legitimum*.[39] In his *Summa Decretalium* he refers to the solemnities of marriage, regarding them as being necessary for respectability, not however for validity. He concludes that *matrimonium legitimum* is a marriage contracted without any

[37] "In huius enim Sacramenti celebratione, sicut in aliis, quaedam sunt pertinentia ad substantiam sacramenti, ut consensus de praesenti, qui solus sufficit ad contrahendum matrimonium; quaedam vero pertinentia ad decorem et solemnitatem Sacramenti, ut parentum traditio, sacerdotum benedictio, et huiusmodi; sine quibus legitime fit coniugium quantum ad virtutem, non quantum ad honestatem Sacramenti."—*Libri IV Sententiarum* (2. ed., Apud Aquas Claras prope Florentinam; ed. P. P. Collegi S. Bonaventurae, 1916), II, lib. IV, D. 28, cap. 2, p. 926-927.

[38] Freisen, *Eherecht*, p. 80.

[39] "Notandum tamen, quia circa matrimonium duo considerantur, viz. et legitimarum personarum consensus et solemnitates contrahendi . . . Habito itaque respectu ad solemnitatem dicitur vel non esse matrimonium vel non esse legitimum, quod legitimis solemnitatibus non est subnixum, quod tamen respectu consensus matrimonium diceretur."—*Bernardus Papiensis Summa Decretalium* (ed. Laspeyres, Ratisbon: 1860), Appendix I, *Summa de Matrimonio*, p. 304, n. 14.

impediments and that the solemnities are not required for validity.[40] Tancredus (+ 1235) in his *Summa de Matrimonio* observes that a *filius legitimus* is one born in a *matrimonium legitimum* or in a marriage reputed *legitimum in facie ecclesiae*. He recognizes a marriage contracted without diriment impediments as a *matrimonium legitimum*.[41] The *glossa ordinaria* of the Decretum placed an intimate bond between *matrimonium legitimum* and the procreation of legitimate children. The legal status or capacity to beget lawful offspring is absent if a clandestine marriage is entered into with a diriment impediment. As has been observed already, Gratian classified a clandestine marriage as *ratum* but *non legitimum*. The gloss of *non legitimum* shows clearly that in such a marriage contracted with a diriment impediment the children were illegitimate.[42] On the authority of this gloss the legitimacy of marriage was to be judged no more by civil law, but by canon law.

It is beyond the scope of this study to treat in detail the history of clandestine marriage. It must suffice to observe that such marriages, even though forbidden under severe penalties, were always recognized, at least in the internal forum, as true marriages. In the external forum there existed a *praesumptio iuris* that such unions were illicit, and that the offspring was illegitimate. However, as has been shown before, the parties to such a marriage were permitted to advance proof that it has been their intention to contract a valid marriage. This state of affairs lasted until the promulgation of the decree *Tametsi* by the Council of Trent. Since that time the canon law regarding clandestinity has seen but little modification, the decree *Tametsi* being supplemented by the decree *Ne Temere* in 1908.[43]

[40] De illa clandestina desponsatione, quae solemnitatibus caret, illud notandum, quod illae solemnitates de honestate sunt potius quam de necessitate."—*Summa Decretalium* (ed. Laspeyres), Lib. IV, tit. 3, p. 141.

[41] Freisen, *Eherecht*, p. 82.

[42] ". . . Si enim probatum fuerit aliquod impedimentum in tali matrimonio rato tantum filii non erunt legitimi, ut extra de clandestina desponsatione cum inhibitio." *Glossa* ad c. 17, C. XXVIII, q. 1.

[43] Joyce, *Christian Marriage*, pp. 104, 122, 130, 136.

Though clanestine marriages constituted one of the greatest problems with which the Church had to deal in the Middle Ages, it must not be thought that Christians generally entered into marriage without any solemnities. It may be said that from the early days of the Church marriage was celebrated publicly, under the supervision of ecclesiastical authority. A very early example of such procedure is found in the letter of St. Ignatius of Antioch to Polycrap: "Decet vero, ut sponsi et sponsae de sententia epsicopi coniugium faciant, ut nuptiae secundum Dominum sint, non secundum cupiditatem. Omnia ad honorem Dei fiant."[44] Tertullian also witnesses to the fact that ceremonies were observed in the contracting of marriage between Christians.[45] St. Ambrose treating the question of marriage between a Christian and a pagan makes mention of the ceremonies of Christian marriage.[46] Pope St. Hormisdas (514-523) prohibited clandestine marriages and made mention of the priestly blessing which ought to be received.[47] These citations indicate that it was the mind of the Church that the sacrament of matrimony should be received publicly, with the solemnity due to its dignity.

The question of what constituted a *matrimonium legitimum* may now be summarized. At first the term was employed in the canonical sources in its civil law significantion with reference to the twofold signification of *conubium* in Roman law and with reference to the solemnities of Germanic law. However, at a very early date the Church laid claim to exclusive jurisdiction over matrimonial affairs and the civil law did not wish to comply. This conflict over matrimonial jurisdiction manifested itself in the

[44] De Journel, *Enchiridion Patristicum* (Freiburg im Breisgau: Herder, 1929), n. 67.

[45] ". . . Unde sufficiamus ad enarrandam felicitatem eius matrimonii, quod Ecclesia conciliat, et confirmat oblatio, et obsignat benedictio, angeli renuntiant . . ."—*Ad uxorem, Enchiridion Patristicum,* n. 320.

[46] "Nam cum ipsum coniugium velamine sacerdotali et benedictione sanctificari oporteat, quomodo potest coniugium dici, ubi non est fidei concordia?" —Ep. Vigilio (a. 385) *Enchiridion Patristicum,* n. 1249.

[47] "Nullus fidelis cuiuscumque conditionis sit, occulte nuptias faciat, sed benedictione a sacerdote publice nubat in Domino."—c. 2, C. XXX, q. 5.

canonical terminology. *Matrimonium legitimum* in canonical usage meant one thing; in civil law it meant another. The *filii legitimi* of canon law were *filii non legitimi* in civil law. This condition began to change as civil law complied to a greater degree with the authority of canon law. In general this harmony became an accomplished fact at the beginning of the thirteenth century. Since this time a *matrimonium legitimum* signified a true Christian marriage contracted in the absence of any diriment impediments. The other significations of the term disappeared. Together with this Christian marriage there existed at that time a *matrimonium legitimum* of non-Christians which had the same legal effects as the marriage of Christians in the sense that the children born in such marriages could inherit. It may be said again that both significations of *matrimonium legitimum* are still employed, but the expression has greater application in reference to the marriage of non-Christians than it has in reference to the marriage of Christians.[48]

Article IV—*Putative Marriage*

The undue extension of the impediments of consanguinity and affinity caused many marriages which were thought to be valid by the contracting parties to be null according to the law of the Church. Wahl observes that the extension to the seventh degree of the canonical computation (of consanguinity), which was equivalent to the thirteenth and fourteenth degrees of the Roman reckoning, caused much inconvenience and made the law very difficult to observe. Accordingly the fourth Council of the Lateran in 1215 approved the restriction made by Innocent III which made consanguinity a diriment impediment only as far as the fourth degree of the collateral line.[49] Before the restriction of the prohibited degrees by law, a provision to care for the marital status of the spouses and the legitimacy of the children of such objectively invalid marriages was found by

[48] Freisen, *Eherecht*, p. 82.

[49] Wahl, *The Matrimonial Impediments of Consanguinity and Affinity*. The Catholic University of America, Canon Law Studies, n. 90 (Washington, D. C.: The Catholic University of America, 1934), pp. 18-19.

canon law in the twelfth century, viz., through putative marriage.

A putative marriage in Canon Law may be defined as an invalid marriage contracted in good faith according to the ceremonies of the Church. It is sufficient if one of the parties is in good faith, the marriage remaining putative until both parties become aware of its nullity. According to the former law such a marriage had to be contracted *in facie ecclesiae.*

Gratian did not speak of putative marriage. However, in discussing the case of Jacob, Lia, and Rachel he observes that error regarding the fortune and quality of the other spouse does not preclude marital consent. In proving that Jacob really married Lia he distinguishes two possible types of consent, precedent and subsequent to the contracting of marriage.[50] In another place he says that relatives who have intermarried ignorant of their relationship are not to be separated.[51]

Esmein holds the view that the theory of putative marriage was clearly sanctioned by the law of the Decretals after the time of Alexander III (1159-1181). But, he observes, it was not the law which had introduced it. It was rather the result of doctrine and interpretation. It is, he continues, found for the first time completely developed by Peter Lombard.[52] Joyce expresses the same opinion that Peter Lombard set forth clearly the theory of putative marriage.[53] Freisen on the other hand says that even in the time of Peter Lombard the teaching was not as yet clear.[54] Because of the importance attributed to the teaching of Peter Lombard on this question his own words may well be incorporated here. "Et est sciendum quod Ecclesia inter praedictos septem gradus consanguinitatis separat. Si autem ignoranter coniuncti fuerint in conspectu Ecclesiae, et postmodum, probata consanguinitate, eiusdem iudicio separati, quaeritur, utrum copula

[50] C. XXIX, q. 1.

[51] C. 1, C. XXXV, q. 8.

[52] Esmein, *Le Mariage en Droit Canonique* (2. ed., 2 vols., Paris: Recueil Sirey, 1929-1935), II, 35.

[53] Joyce, *Christian Marriage,* p. 82.

[54] *Eherecht,* p. 858.

illa coniugium fuerit. Quibusdam videtur non fuisse coniugium, quia non erant legitimae personae; sed tamen de crimine excusantur per ignorantiam, et quasi coniugium reputatur, quia bona fide et per manum Ecclesiae convenerunt; unde et filii eorum legitimi habentur. Alii vero dicunt, fuisse coniugium licet non essent legitimae personae, quia talium coniunctiones vocant canones coniugia, ubi de personis agunt quarum testimonio consanguineorum sit dirimenda coniunctio."[55] The point that is of present interest is that Peter Lombard held the children of the unions he discussed to be regarded as legitimate.

In his *Stroma* Rolandus Bandinelli calls those children legitimate who are born of an invalid marriage contracted in good faith and *ex permissione Ecclesiae.* The words *ex permissione Ecclesiae* designated a marriage entered into before the Church.[56] When he became Pope Alexander III, Rolandus in a particular judgment insisted that the children whose parents had been divorced by sentence of an ecclesiastical tribunal were legitimate, since the parents had married publicly and *sine contradictione Ecclesiae.*[57] Celestine III (1191-1198) expresses the same view when he rules that a woman whose parents' marriage had been legitimately celebrated was to inherit after their death even though it was insinuated by others that she had been born illegitimately. The Pope decreed that the woman could inherit if the facts alleged were true.[58] Innocent III in the IV General Lateran Council (1215) restricted the prohibited degrees as has been remarked before. He also decreed that if both parents knowingly contracted a marriage within the forbidden degrees the children would be illegitimate, even if the marriage was celebrated *in conspectu Ecclesiae.* The Pope at this time demanded good faith and the publication of the banns for the contracting of marriage. He also renewed the prohibitions regarding clandestine marriages

[55] *Libri IV Sententiarum* (ed. P. P. Collegii S. Bonaventurae), Lib. IV, D. 41, cap. 3-4.

[56] Freisen, *Eherecht,* p. 859.

[57] C. 2, X, *qui filii sint legitimi,* IV, 17.

[58] C. 11, X, *qui filii sint legitimi,* IV, 17.

and laid down penalties for any priest who would assist at such marriage.[59] The term clandestine marriage was employed in more than one sense. It might signify a secret marriage for which no evidence was available save that of the parties themselves. It was employed for a marriage made in the presence of witnesses, but not *in facie ecclesiae.* After the IV General Council of the Lateran (1215) it was often used of marriages which had not been preceded by the publication of banns, as there prescribed.[60] That good faith and the publication of the banns were required can be gathered from the glosses of various chapters in the Decretum and the Decretals.[61] The publication of the banns signifies here the contracting of marriage *in facie ecclesiae.* The importance of contracting marriage *in facie ecclesiae* is shown by the decision of Innocent III who declared the child of a bigamist legitimate because the second woman, the child's mother, was ignorant of the fact that the man was already married and because the second marriage had been performed *in facie ecclesiae.*[62]

There was some discussion among the canonists as to the conditions necessary for contracting marriage *in facie ecclesiae.* Ordinarily the term signified the public celebration of marriage accompanied by the ceremonies of the Church which have already been alluded to in the discussion of the *matrimonium legitimum.* There were some places were it was customary to celebrate the wedding with a considerable gathering of people, but without the Church ceremony. Such marriages were regarded as having been celebrated *in facie ecclesiae.* Since the term *Ecclesia* has various significations, it might be taken to mean here an assemblage of the faithful. In such circumstances a marriage entered into with the usual celebration could rightly be said to have been solemnized *in facie Ecclesiae.* If it took place privately before a few selected

[59] C. 3, X, *de clandestina desponsatione,* IV, 3.

[60] Joyce, *Christian Marriage,* p. 107, footnote 2.

[61] C. 17, C. XXVII, q. 1, glossa: *non legitimum;* c. 3, X, *de clandestina desponsatione,* IV, 3; glossa: *ambo parentes,* c. 10, X, *qui filii sint legitimi,* IV, 17; glossa: *ignorantiam.*

[62] C. 14, X, *qui filii sint legitimi,* IV, 17.

witnesses, it would be clandestine if according to the custom of the place it should have been celebrated publicly.[63] The term was accorded a stricter meaning in the IV General Lateran Council (1215) in which it was decreed that the banns of marriage had to be published in the church by a priest before the celebration of the marriage.[64] The Council of Trent referred to this decree and renewed the obligation of the publication of the banns. It was also decided that the parish priest and two or three witnesses had to be present for the celebration of the marriage.[65]

The controversy among the canonists concerning the necessity of good faith and its efficacy when present in only one of the contracting parties was settled by Alexander III. Writing to the Abbot of St. Albans he recalled the law that people who had been guilty of adultery could not later marry.[66] However, the Pope denied the request of a bigamist who petitioned for a separation from his second wife after the death of his first wife on the grounds that he could not have validly married a second time while his first wife was still alive. The Pope denied the petition because the second wife had not known that the man was already married. It is not the intention of the writer to discuss the question of the validity of the second union. It can be said, however, that the Pope's express intention in not allowing the man to depart was to deprive him from gaining an advantage from the commission of his crime.[67]

Ignorantia affectata destroyed good faith and the children of a marriage contracted in such ignorance even if the parents had dared to contract it *in conspectu ecclesiae,* were deemed illegitimate.[68]

[63] Joyce, *Christian Marriage,* p. 109, footnote 3, p. 110.

[64] C. 3, X, *De clandestina desponsatione,* IV, 3.

[65] Sess. XXIV, *de ref. matrim.* c. 1—*Concilii Tridentini Canones et Decreta* (Paris, 1856), p. 281.

[66] C. 1, X, *de eo, qui duxit in matrimonium quam polluit per adulterium* IV, 7.

[67] C. 1, X, *de eo, qui duxit in matrimonium quam polluit per adulterium,* IV, 7.

[68] C. 3, X, *de clandestina desponsatione,* IV. 3.

Freisen remarks that in canon law illegitimacy is a punishment. This punishment however can be remitted if at least one of the parents is ignorant of an existing dirment impediment and marriage is contracted *in facie ecclesiae.*[69]

The discussion of putative marriage may be concluded by recalling that in Roman law no such provision existed. It is distinctly a contribution of Canon Law which disregarding the rigid provisions of Roman law, leaned to the side of equity to help both the parties to and the children of those marriages which were objectively invalid but nevertheless contracted in good faith and *in facie ecclesiae.* The various meanings of the words *in facie ecclesiae* during the different periods of Canon law must be kept in mind.

Article V.—*Qui filii sint legitimi*

After the discussion of *matrimonium legitimum* and *matrimonium putativum* the question of the legitimacy of children may be now more readily considered.

A *filius legitimus* may be defined as one born of a truly valid or at least a putative marriage, excepting however the case of anyone born of a valid marriage the use of which is denied to the parents. This happens e.g., when the parents already married make solemn religious profession or the father receives Sacred Orders. In these cases an impediment arises between the parties which does not nullify the marriage but which does absolutely forbid the use of the marriage.

Filii legitimi are classified as follows: (1) children conceived and born during the valid marriage of their parents, even if the marriage was contracted illicitly, but not if the use of the marriage has been denied to the spouses at the time of the child's conception: (2) children born during the marriage of their parents, even though their conception probably or even certainly took place at a time prior to the marriage of their parents. In this particular case there is a fiction of law, because strictly considered a child conceived outside of marriage ought to be called

[69] Freisen, *Eherecht,* p. 860.

"natural;" but such a child is legitimate in Canon Law because the presumption is that he who marries the mother is the father of the child born soon after the marriage is contracted. (3) Children of a widowed mother after the dissolution of marriage as long as there is present any possibility that the posthumous child was conceived of the dead husband. (4) Children conceived or born during the putative marriage of their parents.[70] (5) Children born of a morganatic marriage.[71] (6) Children born of a marriage of conscience.[72] (7) Adopted children are reputed legitimate by law.[73]

Some children are considered fully legitimate as to all effects both in canon law and in civil law; others, though legitimate, do not enjoy all the effects of legitimacy. The legitimate children considered according to the rights they enjoy are classified as follows: (1) those legitimate *plenissimo iure* as to all canonical and civil effects. (2) those legitimate *minus pleno iure* as to canonical effects alone, but not as to all civil effects, as for example the children born of a morganatic marriage.[74]

The question of the legitimacy of foundlings has been disputed among canonists. Before the reception of Holy Orders by such children it has been customary to issue a dispensation from the irregularity *ex defectu natalium ad cautelam.* Hinschius maintains that there exists no presumption of law for either the legitimacy or the illegitimacy of such children.[75] He disagrees with the opinion that foundlings reared by certain confraternities were regarded as legitimate in virtue of a Papal privilege. This privilege, he remarks, was granted in only one case.[76] In the

[70] De Becker, *De Sponsalibus et Matrimonio,* pp. 370-371.

[71] Wernz, *Ius Decretalium* (2 ed. 6 vols. Romae et Prati, 1906-1913), IV, n. 679.

[72] Benedict XIV, ep. encycl. "Statis vobis" § 11, Nov. 17, 1741, *Fontes,* n. 319.

[73] Ferraris, *Prompta Bibliotheca s. v., Filius adoptivus,* n. 1.

[74] Wernz, *Ius Decretalium,* IV, n. 679.

[75] Hinschius, *Das Kirchenrecht der Katholiken und Protestanten in Deutschland* (6 vols., Berlin, 1869-1897), I, 12.

[76] *Op. cit.,* p. 12, footnote 8.

case of such children he holds that nothing remains but to seek a dispensation for Holy Orders because the absence of the blemish of illegitimacy is not established.[77]

Some canonists hold that foundlings are to be considered illegitimate in view of the circumstances, because there is a grave presumption of fact against their legitimacy. Others hold that they ought to be regarded as legitimate, because a child is presumed legitimate until the contrary is proved. The fact that a child is a foundling does not necessarily mean that it is illegitimate. It may be said, then, that as long as there is any doubt the rule of Benedict XIV may be applied: "Iudex debet in bonum et commodum prolis propensus esse." [78] Reiffenstuel says foundlings are to be considered legitimate because in doubt the presumption is in favor of the child.[79] Gasparri observes that if the parents of a child are unknown the child is to be deemed legitimate because ". . . in dubiis inspicimus quod plerumque fieri solet ex R. 45, R.J. in VI°."[80] The question of the legitimacy of foundlings is practical in so far as the canonical effects of legitimacy are concerned. It is important today as regards the reception of Holy Orders and as regards eligibility for office in religious Institutes.[81]

The discussion of the question of the legitimacy of foundlings may be concluded by observing that among canonists the more common and more probable opinion is that these children are to be regarded as legitimate.[82]

[77] *Op. cit.*, p. 12.

[78] Benedict, XIV, epist. "*Redditae nobis,*" Dec. 5, 1744, *Fontes*, n. 350.

[79] Reiffenstuel, *Ius Canonicum Universum* (6 vols., Romae, 1831-1833) lib. IV, tit. 17, nn. 14-16.

[80] Gasparri, *Tractatus Canonicus de Matrimonio* (Edito nova ad mentem Codicis Iuris Canonici, 2 vols., Romae: Typis Polyglottis Vaticanis, 1932), II, n. 1114.

[81] Gasparri, *loc. cit.*; Cappello, *Tractatus Canonico-Moralis de Sacramentis* (Vol. III, De Matrimonio, 4. ed. Romae: Marietti, 1939), n. 749; canons 984, 1°; 504.

[82] Cappello, *loc. cit.*

Article VI.—*Filii Illegitimi*

Since the fact of a child's legitimacy is necessarily connected with the existence of a marriage between its parents, so the fact of illegitimacy is intimately connected either with the absence of marriage between the parents or the prohibition of the use of marriage by the parents at the time of the child's conception. The possibility or impossibility of marriage between the parents of an illegitimate child also affects its status. The fundamental classification of *filii illegitimi* divides them into two groups: *filii naturales* and *filii spurii*. This distinction is very important in reference to the question of the possibility of legitimation, as will be shown later. The term *filius naturalis* is to be understood here in the sense of *filius illegitimus*.

Filii naturales taken in this sense are children born of parents who were free to contract marriage at the time of the child's conception, during the period of gestation or at the time of birth.

Filii spurii on the other hand are those children whose birth is not merely illegitimate, but has a note of infamy added to it. They are, so to speak, base-born. These children are thus regarded because their parents could not contract marriage between themselves at the time of conception, during the period of gestation, or at the time of birth of their children.

It is evident that the distinction between a *filius naturalis* and a *filius spurius* has its basis in the fact that the parents of the former were free to marry while the parents of the latter were prohibited from marrying either at the time of the child's conception, during the period of gestation, or at the time of the child's birth.

Filii spurii are subdivided into various groups depending on the circumstances surrounding their birth. They are: (1) merely spurious; (2) adulterine; (3) children who are the fruit of sacrilege; (4) children who are the fruit of incest committed between persons related within the forbidden degrees of consanguinity or affinity in the collateral line; (5) children who are the fruit of incest committed by persons related in the direct line.

(1) "Merely spurious" children are those whose parents were hindered from contracting a valid marriage by such diriment impediments as age, disparity of worship, abduction, crime, public propriety, spiritual or legal relationship. Any diriment impediment which in its juridical effect will not place the children in any of the following groups will have the effect of branding the offspring as "merely spurious."

(2) Adulterine children are the result of the crime of adultery. They are born of parents one of whom or both of whom are already married to another.[83] Adulterine children are also known as *nothi*.[84]

(3) Children who are the fruit of sacrilege are those born of parents one of whom or both of whom are bound by solemn vows or whose father is in Sacred Orders from the obligation of which, there has not been a release, at the time of the child's conception. These children are the result of sacrilege. They are regarded as the fruit of sacrilege either if the parents are parties to a valid marriage the use of which has been denied to them before the children are conceived or if the parents have attempted marriage after at least one of them has been solemnly professed or the father has been ordained to the Subdiaconate.[85] It must be remembered that by special privilege the simple profession of Jesuit scholastics and lay brothers has a nullifying effect on a subsequent marriage.[86]

(4) Children born of persons related within the forbidden degrees of consanguinity or affinity in the collateral line are the fruit of incest.[87]

[83] Schmalzgrueber, lib. IV, tit. 17, n. 7; Reiffenstuel, lib. IV, tit. 17, n. 28.

[84] Hostiensis, Cardinalis (Henricus de Segusio), *Summa Aurea* (Venetiis, 1570), lib. I, *de filiis presbyterorum,* n. 3.

[85] Schmalzgrueber, lib. IV, tit. 17, n. 7; Reiffenstuel, lib. IV, tit. 17, n. 28.

[86] Gregory XIII, Const. "*Ascendente Domino*," 25 Maii 1584, § 22—*Fontes,* n. 153.

[87] Schmalzgrueber, lib. IV, tit. 17, n. 7; Reiffenstuel, lib. IV, tit. 17, n. 28.

(5) Children born of persons related in the direct line are also the fruit of incest.[88]

There are various other special designations of illegitimate children. Thus the children born of a public harlot are known as *manseres* or *manzeres*.[89] Bastards are the illegitimate children of a single woman who is neither a concubine nor a prostitute. Such are the children of a woman ". . . alias honesta, hic et nunc autem seducta est."[90] In canon law *filii spurii* have been called also *vulgo quaesiti* ". . . quasi de spuma rivalium, sive corrivalium nati."[91] Ferraris says that spurious children in civil law are the children of a public harlot. Such children are called *quaesiti*, because the father is unknown.[92]

There is yet another classification of illegitimate children considered as born *ex damnato coitu*.[93] Such are the children whose parents could not marry at the time of the children's conception or birth. In canon law these children are considered the same as "spurious" children.[94] Kutschker goes as far as to say that canon law regards every procreation of offispring outside marriage as a *damnatus coitus*.[95] Such a view seems extreme if the distinction between *filii naturales* and *filii spurii*, as cited above and admitted by canonists generally, is to be maintained. The view of Kutschker would seem to be true only in the sense that every procreation of children outside marriage is gravely sinful.

Children born *ex damnato coitu* are referred to by Hostiensis

[88] Leviticus, XVIII, 17; Schmalzgrueber, lib. IV, tit. 17, n. 8; Reiffenstuel, lib. IV, tit. 17, n. 28.

[89] Deut. XXIII, 2; *Summa Aurea*, lib. I, *de filiis presbyterorum*, n. 4; Reiffenstuel, lib. IV, tit. 17, n. 25; Ferraris, *Prompta Bibliotheca*, s. v. *Filius* (Manzer), n. 25.

[90] Reiffenstuel, lib. IV, tit. 17, n. 25; Ferraris, *Prompta Bibliotheca*, s. v., *Filius* (*Bastardus*), n. 27.

[91] Hostiensis, *Summa Aurea*, lib. IV, *qui filii sint legitimi*, n. 2.

[92] *Prompta Bibliotheca*, *Filius* (*Quaesiti*), n. 28-29.

[93] Reiffenstuel, lib. IV, tit. 17, n. 27.

[94] Reiffenstuel, lib. IV, tit. 17, n. 27.

[95] Kutschker, *Das Eherecht der katholischen Kirche nach seiner Theorie und Praxis* (5 vols., Wien, 1856-1857), V, 379-380.

as neither "natural" nor legitimate with respect to their father. He also calls such children "spurious." [96] In another place he remarks that concubinage, although permitted by ancient law, was absolutely forbidden in his day. He refers to it in the words, *"coitus omnino reprobatur."*[97] It can be said now that all children born of parents, barred from intermarriage at the time of conception, during the period of gestation, and at the time of birth are to be regarded as having been begotten *ex damnato coitu.*

As has been remarked before, knowledge of the various classifications of illegitimate children is very important with respect to the possibility of legitimation. These distinctions were emphasized by Clement III (1187-1191) referring to a particular question on legitimation.[98]

The discussion of *filii illegitimi* may be concluded by observing that these children were never regarded as responsible for their condition. Thus Gratian, quoting from the letter of St. Jerome directed against Rufinus, says that to be born of adultery is not the fault of the child but of the parents.[99] Again, quoting from St. Augustine, he says that the crimes of the parents must not be imputed to the children.[100] No matter how innocent such children are, their reputation is stained because their birth reflects in them the evil fruit and product of their parents' sin.[101]

Article VII.—The Irregularity *ex defectu natalium*

After the discussion of *filii illegitimi* the question of the irregularity *ex defectu natalium* may be properly introduced.

An irregularity according to canon 983 is a canonical impediment which *per se* primarily prohibits the reception of Orders and secondarily prohibits the use of them.

The notion of the irregularity *ex defectu natalium* was intro-

[96] *Summa Aurea,* lib. IV, *qui filii sint legitimi,* n. 2.
[97] *Summa Aurea,* lib. I, *de filiis presbyterorum,* n. 4.
[98] C. 10 (6) X, *de renuntiatione,* I, 9.
[99] C. 5, D. LVI.
[100] C. 3, D. LVI; *De Bono Conjugali,* C. 16.
[101] Hostiensis, *Summa Aurea,* lib. I, *de filiis presbyterorum,* n. 3.

duced at a rather late date in Canon law.[102] Vermeersch-Creusen assert that the term *irregularitas* itself was first employed by Rufinus, who wrote his Summa on the *Decretum Gratiani* about the years 1157-1159.[103] The reason for introducing the irregularity was to exclude illegitimate children from the reception of Holy Orders, from the acquirement of ecclesiastical benefices, and to prevent the succession by a son to the benefice held by his father. The laws in this regard were directed primarily against the *filii presbyterorum*.[104] Genestel holds that the origin of the irregularity may be traced to the legislation of the Council of Bourges in 1031. He admits, though, that this was a provincial council and that the Bishops assembled there could not oblige the whole church.[105] Hinschius states that this irregularity was introduced in the eleventh century against the *filii illegitimi presbyterorum* and was only later enforced against all illegitimate children. As evidence that the irregularity was not known before that time he cites the elevation of Arnulf, the "natural" son of Lothaire, King of France (956-986) to the Archbishopric of Rheims in 988.[106] Wernz-Vidal in commenting on this question say that the practice of admitting illegitimate children to Sacred Orders began to undergo a change in the tenth and eleventh centuries. They maintain that the first to be affected were the children who were the fruit of incest and sacrilege. They, too, cite the enactment in canon 8 of the Council of Bourges as an important step in the establishment of the irregularity *ex defectu natalium*. They posit as the reason for the legislation the deepest ignominy in which illegitimate children *laicorum* were held by the civil law of the Middle Ages. The Church in selecting her ministers naturally had to take cognizance of the status

[102] De Becker, *De Sponsalibus et Matrimonio*, p. 375.

[103] *Epitome*, n. 251; Van Hove, *Prolegomena* (Mechliniae-Romae: H. Dessain, 1928), p. 227, footnote 2.

[104] Genestal, *Histoire de la Legitimation des Enfants Naturels* (Paris, 1905), pp. 2, 5.

[105] *Op. cit.*, pp. 11-13.

[106] Hinschius, *Kirchenrecht*, I, 11 and footnote 4.

of such children in civil law.[107] Cappello on the other hand holds that the time of the introduction of this irregularity is uncertain. He claims that from the beginning the children born of sacrilege alone were repelled from receiving Sacred Orders.[108]

In connection with the question of the introduction of this irregularity it becomes necessary to touch on two other matters, viz., the law of clerical celibacy and the law which made Sacred Orders a diriment matrimonial impediment. The law which demanded clerical celibacy is evidently much more ancient than the regulation which made Sacred Orders a diriment matrimonial impediment.[109] Without any detailed consideration of the earliest history of the law of celibacy, it is sufficient for the purpose intended here, to remark that from the time of Pope Gregory the Great (590-604) the obligation of celibacy was imposed *ex iure communi* on all bishops, priests, deacons, and subdeacons of the Western Church. The obligations were never extended to those in Minor Orders. During the tenth and eleventh centuries the Popes found it necessary to reinforce the law with severe sanctions. Gregory VII (1073-1085) was the greatest reformer in this matter.[110] From early times the Church in the West had forbidden marriage to clerics in Major Orders, but it was not until the twelfth century that express mention of the nullity of the marriage of a man in Sacred Orders is mentioned, thus indicating that henceforth Sacred Orders would constitute a diriment impediment.

Such mention seems first to have been made in canon 7 of the II General Council of the Lateran held in 1139 during the pontificate of Pope Innocent II (1130-1143). Because of its importance the canon will be given in its entirety.

> Ad haec praedecessorum nostrorum Gregorii VII,, et Paschalis RR. PP. vestigiis inhaerentes praecipimus, ut nullus Missas eorum audiat, quos uxores vel con-

[107] *Ius Canonicum,* IV, n. 235.
[108] *De Sacramentis,* II, n. 461.
[109] Wernz-Vidal, *Ius Canonicum,* V, n. 282.
[110] Wernz-Vidal, *op. cit.,* II, n. 105.

> cubinas habere cognoverit. Ut autem lex continentiae et Deo placens munditia in ecclesiasticis personis et sacris ordinibus dilatetur, statuimus: quatenus episcopi, presbyteri, diaconi, subdiaconi,, regulares canonici, et monachi, atque conversi professi, qui sanctum transgredientes propositum uxores sibi copulari praesumpserint, separentur. *Huiusmodi namque coplationem quam contra ecclesiasticam regulam constat esse contractam matrimonium non esse censemus.* Qui etiam ab invicem separati pro tantis excessibus condignam poenitentiam agant.[111]

In the subsequent discussion, where it will be necessary to refer to the title *de filiis presbyterorum,* the distinction between the obligation of celibacy and the diriment character of the impediment of Sacred Orders should be kept in mind. It must also be remembered that the children of a lawfully married man who later receives Sacred Orders have always been legitimate. This can be gathered, for example, from canon 8 of the Council of Bourges in 1031[112]

It can be said that in general the Church did not legislate against illegitimate children with respect to the reception of Sacred Orders during the first ten centuries, even though the ordination of such children was looked upon as unbecoming. In reviewing the legislation on the irregularity *ex defectu natalium* particularly as affecting the *filii presbyterorum,* the modern viewpoint must be discarded and the situation considered in the light of the social conditions of the times. Today it is impossible for a man lawfully to receive the first Tonsure who does not intend eventually to enter the Priesthood. In the Middle Ages this was not so. Many men enrolled themselves in the ranks of

[111] Harduin, *Acta Conciliorum* (Parisiis, 1714), Tom. VI, pars II, p. 1209.

[112] Mansi, *Sacrorum Conciliorum Nova et Amplissima Collectio* (Parisiis, 1901-1927), XIX, 504; Hefele, *Conciliengeschichte* (2 ed., 9 vols., Freiburg im Breisgau, (1873-1890), IV, 691. These works will be referred to simply as Mansi, Hefele.

the clergy by receiving the Tonsure. They did so with the view in mind of obtaining an ecclesiastical benefice. Since they were not bound by the law of celibacy, many of them married, some publicly and some secretly. This abuse was attacked by Paschal II (1099-1118) who decreed that if such unions were not broken off the clerics were to be deprived of their duties and benefices.[113] What could happen in such cases has been described by Cardinal Otto, the Papal Legate at the Council of London, in 1237. In canon 15 he remarks that it has come to his attention that many clerics who were not yet priests had contracted a clandestince marriage and thereupon did not fear without putting away their wives to retain their benefices, to obtain new benefices, and even to receive Sacred Orders contrary to the Sacred Canons. He, moreover, adverted to the situation as one in which, after children had been reared from the matrimonial union of these clerics, it became readily possible for the clerics to prove by means of witnesses and documents that they had really contracted marriage. In view of this procedure they felt that they could likewise safeguard a recognized honorable status for their children.[114]

Although the irregularity *ex defectu natalium* did not appear until a rather late date, there are instances of earlier particular legislation directed against the ordination of illegitimate children. Thus the IX Provincial Council of Toledo in 655 in chapter 10 decreed that the illegitimate children of men in Sacred Orders, whether born of a free-woman or a slave, were incapable of inheritance and were to be condemned to perpetual servitude in the church of their progenitor.[115] With regard to this drastic enactment Genestal observes that in the seventh century the abuse against which the Council took action was particularly acute in Spain. Accordingly he warns that any generalizations must be guarded against.[116] The Synod of Chelsea in England celebrated in 787 decreed in canon 16 that illegitimate children were

[113] Harduin, Tom. VI, pars II, p. 1807.
[114] Harduin, Tom. VII, p. 297.
[115] Mansi, XI, 29; Hefele, III, 101.
[116] *Histoire de la Legitimation*, p. 5.

incapable of inheritence.[117] The Council of Meaux held in 845 legislated against a particular class of children. In canon 64 it declared that a child born of a subsequent marriage between the *raptor* and *rapta* was not to be promoted to any ecclesiastical dignity. Such children were not permitted to receive Orders unless they displayed high personal qualities.[118]

Since it has been shown that the irregularity *ex defectu natalium* was introduced in the eleventh century, examples of the legislation of that and later periods may be cited.

At a council held in the Lateran during the pontificate of Gregory VII (1073-1085) it was decreed that no illegitimate child could be ordained.[119] Genestal maintains that the rule barring illegitimate children from Orders was clearly established during the reign of Gregory VII. He says that in practice the rule met with great opposition.[120] Urban II (1088-1099) followed the traditional procedure. Thus he declared that a *filius presbyteri* might be elevated to the Episcopate if great virtues were found in him. It is to be noted that the Pope says this decision is not to be interpreted in the future as a general rule, as he intended it only as a temporary measure.[121] Gratian in his *dictum* seems to imply that the above decision must be understood to refer to a son born of the lawful marriage of a priest before ordination.

The Council of Poitiers held in 1078 ruled in canon 8 that illegitimate children could not be promoted to Sacred Orders unless they became monks, or joined a canonical congregation living according to rule. They were to be incapable of any prelatial dignity.[122] The Council of Melfi in Apulia celebrated in 1089 repeated the law of the Council of Poitiers in canon 14.[123]

117 Mansi, XII, 946; Hefele, III, 640.

118 C. 17, C. 1, q. 7; Mansi, XIV, 834; Hefele, IV, pp. 117-118.

119 "Filius presbyteri et adulteri, et quicumque bastardus non ordinetur."—Pflugk-Harttung, *Acta Pontificum Romanorum Inedita* (3 vols., Tübingen, 1881-1886), II, p. 125, n. 161.

120 *Histoire de la Legitimation,* p. 16.

121 C. 13, C. LVI.

122 Mansi, XX, 498-499; Hefele, V, 116.

123 Mansi, XX, 724; Hefele, V, 195.

The same legislation is repeated in canon 25 of the Council of Clermont which was held in 1095. In canon 14 of this council there is a prohibition directed especially against children born in concubinage. They are not to be promoted to Orders or to any ecclesiastical dignity.[124] It appears that Gratian did not consider illegitimate children barred from the reception of Sacred Orders. Citing the decision of Urban II already alluded to, he concluded that *filii presbyterorum* could not only become priests, but even bishops, if they were commendable men.[125]

The movement for reform in disciplinary matters certainly got under way in the eleventh century. An examination of the legislation shows, as has been asserted before, that the laws prohibiting the reception of Orders were directed primarily against *filii presbyterorum*. The enactment of these laws resulted finally in the establishment of the irregularity *ex defectu natalium*.[126] Esmein writing on the same question observes: "Il est en tout cás évident, que la condamnation des fils de pretres ne saurait etre considérée comme une application de la règle générale oui frappe les illegitimes. Les fils de pretres sont en effet exclus des ordres à une époque où le mariage des pretres, bien que condamné, etait encore considéré comme valable, et où par suite les enfants nés de ces unions étaient des enfants legitimes." [127] Esmein seems to be in error when he says such children were regarded as legitimate, as long as the marriages in question were admittedly valid, i.e., until the declaration of the II General Council of the Lateran in 1139. It has already been shown that to contract a *matrimonium legitimum* it was necessary that the marriage be celebrated *in facie ecclesiae* according to the particular meaning of that phrase during the various periods of the history of canon law. In view of the circumstances the marriages referred to would hardly be contracted *in facie ecclesiae* but if contracted could possibly be proved by witnesses.

[124] Mansi, XX, 817-818; Hefele, V, 223-224.

[125] C. 1, D. LVI.

[126] Genestal, *Histoire de la Legitimation*, p. 18.

[127] *Le Mariage en Droit Canonique* (1. ed. 2 vols., Paris: 1891), I, 291 et seq.

The corrective legislation was introduced not to punish the children but rather the parents, and to secure the best interests of the Church. One of the abuses attacked was the hereditary holding of benefices. Even *filii clericorum ex legitimo matrimonio* were to be excluded.[128] This did not, however affect such children in the Greek Uniate Church.[129]

At the Council of Westminster held in 1173 it was decreed, "Filii non succedant patribus in ecclesiis." [130] The same legislation was enacted in the IV General Council of the Lateran (1215) in cap. 31.[131] In 1216 Honorius III forbade such succession in a particular case.[132] A Synod of London in 1282 also prohibited such succession to a benefice.[133]

A Provincial Council held at Mainz in 1261 decreed in canon 32 that no illegitimate child could receive Sacred Orders, ecclesiastical dignities, or any ecclesiastical benefices, to which was attached the care of souls, unless such a person had been dispensed by the Bishop with respect to Orders, and by the Holy See with respect to dignities and benefices.[134] In the Council of Vienne celebrated in 1290 it was declared that no illegitimate could receive the first Tonsure.[135] The provincial Council of Padua celebrated in 1350 ruled in canon 6 that "spurious" children had to have a Papal dispensation to become Cathedral Canons.[136]

Though not directed primarily against illegitimate children, the legislation of the IV General Lateran Council (1215) on marriage may be mentioned here before concluding the present discussion, since it did ultimately affect such children. In canon 51 it was decreed that children born of parents related within the forbidden

[128] C. 11, X, *de filiis presbyterorum,* I, 17.

[129] C. 14, D. XXXI; C. 6, X, *de clericis conjugatis,* III, 3.

[130] Mansi, XX, 142.

[131] C. 16, X, *de filiis presbyterorum ordinandis vel non,* I, 17; Mansi, XXII, 1018-1019; Hefele, V, 892.

[132] C. 17, X, *de filiis presbyterorum ordinandis vel non,* I, 17.

[133] Hefele, VI, 222.

[134] Mansi, XXIII, 1091; Hefele, VI, 73.

[135] Mansi, XXIV, 1065; Hefele, VI, 259.

[136] Mansi, XXVI, 230; Hefele, VI, 694.

degrees of consanguinity and affinity, if the parties knew of their relationship, and the marriage had been contracted *in conspectu ecclesiae,* were to be regarded as illegitimate. Likewise children born of a clandestine marriage and of a marriage of persons related within the forbidden degrees who contracted marriage ignorant of their relationship were to be regarded as illegitimate.[137]

In concluding the treatment of the *irregularitas ex defectu natalium* it can be said that Gratian did not mention this irregularity. He would exclude no illegitimate children from Sacred Orders with the execption only of those who were *imitatores paternae incontinentiae.* Clement III (1187-1191) permitted the ordination of a man *in sacerdotio genitus* provided he was otherwise worthy.[138] The irregularity was definitely known in the time of Innocent III (1198-1216), who mentions that a man laboring under the irregularity may be dispensed if he has fulfilled his duties creditably.[139] Gregory IX (1227-1241) decreed that all illegitimate children had to obtain a Papal dispensation to be promoted to any dignity or to obtain a benefice to which was attached the care of souls.[140] Genestal observes that Innocent IV (1243-1254), who reigned after Gregory IX (1227-1241) was doubtful if the irregularity extended to all illegitimate children.[141] This observation seems strange in view of the fact that Gregory IX had expressly declared that all illegitimate children had to have a papal dispensation.

It can be stated that at the end of the thirteenth century the irregularity did extend to all illegitimate children. The term *defectus natalium* is used by Boniface VIII (1294-1303) as applying to all such children.[142] Hinschius concludes that the irregularity has been fixed since the end of the thirteenth century

[137] C. 3, X, *de clandestina desponsatione,* IV, 3; Mansi, XXII, 1038-1039; Hefele, V, 895-896.

[138] C. 14, X, *de filiis presbyterorum ordinandis vel non,* I, 17.

[139] C. 10 (6), X, *de renuntiatione,* I, 9.

[140] C. 18, X, *de filiis presbyterorum,* I, 17.

[141] *Histoire de la Legitimation,* p. 33.

[142] C. 1, 2, *de filiis presbyterorum et aliis illegitime natis,* I, 11, in VI°

when it prohibited not only the reception of Sacred Orders but also the reception of Minor Orders.[143]

Examples of legislation subsequent to the crystallization of the irregularity *ex defectu natalium* can be added here. In 1530 Clement VII in his constitution *Ad canonum conditorem* issued a severe prohibition against the abuse of the hereditary holding of benefices.[144] The same legislation was repeated by the Council of Trent.[145] The same Council also demanded that inquires be made concerning the quality of the birth of candidates for the Minor Orders, Subdiaconate, Deaconate,, and Priesthood.[146] Sixtus V in his constitution *"Cum de omnibus"* of November 26, 1587 forbade the entrance of children born of incest and sacrilege into the religious life, even if they had been legitimated by Papal, Imperial, Royal, or any other authority. He allowed such, however, to become lay-brothers or servants. They could never receive even Minor Orders.[147] The next year in reply to a question proposed he forbade the appointment of "spurious" and other illegitimate children as canons and prebendaries in the Church of Valencia even if they had been legitimated by any of the authorities cited above.[148] Gregory XIV by his constitution, *Circumspecta* of March 15, 1591, repealed the severe regulations of Sixtus V, which evidently had constituted an exception to the usual practice. Gregory XIV decreed that all illegitimates could be admitted to the religious life, in the same way as they had been admitted before the publication of the constitution of Sixtus V.[149] Clement VIII issued a constitution *"Cum ad Regularem,"* March 19, 1603, regarding the reception of novices. He declared that diligent inquiry had to be made by the superiors regarding the birth of the novice. No one who was not born

143 *Kirchenrecht,* I, 12.

144 *Bullarium Diplomatum et Privilegiorum Sanctorum Romanorum Pontificum* (25 vols., Augustae Taurinorum, 1857-1872), VI, p. 143.

145 Sess. XXV, *de ref.,* C. 15.

145 Sess. XXIII, *de ref.* C. 5, 13, 14.

147 *Fontes,* n. 162.

148 *Bullar. Rom.,* IX, 30-31.

149 *Fontes,* n. 170.

ex honestis parentibus was to be admitted.[150] The same requirement was insisted upon in his constitution *"Cum ad regularem"* of March 16, 1603.[151]

In conclusion it can be stated that the irregularity *ex defectu natalium* was introduced to combat those abuses which tended to subvert the exalted and sacred character of the clerical state and the high dignity of Christian marriage. The consideration of the Church in dispensing from the irregularity is evidence of her regard for those children who were affected by the irregullarity wholly without any fault of theirs. The extent to which the Church has dispensed in this matter will be treated more fully in the section on legitimation.

PART II—LEGITIMATION

Article I.—*Preliminary Notions of Legitimation*

The process of legitimation has been defined in various ways. Payen calls it "the juridic restoration of legitimacy."[152] Vermeersch-Creusen speak of it as "a benefit of the law or lawgiver by which some or all of the rights and honors of legitimacy are conferred on an illegitimate child."[153]

In the consideration of legitimacy in the natural law it was shown, according to the teaching of St. Thomas, that the conception of a child in a valid marriage is necessary for legitimacy. Positive law, can, however, declare a child who is illegitimate according to the natural law to be legitimate according to positive law, e.g., a child born in a putative marriage. On the other hand. positive law can declare a child who is legitimate according to the natural law to be illegitimate according to the positive law. e.g., a child conceived in a valid marriage by a man bound by the obligations of Sacred Orders at the time of the child's conception.

[150] *Bullar. Rom.*, X, p. 768.

[151] *Fontes*, n. 189.

[152] Payen, *De Matrimonio in Missionibus* (3 vols., 2. ed., Zi-ka-wei, 1935-1936), II, n. 2171.

[153] *Epitome*, II, n. 419.

Legitimation is governed by positive law both ecclesiastical and civil. It must be noted that the positive law cannot alter by any means the fact of illegitimacy according to the natural law. It can, however, by legal fictions regard the fact as non-existent in so far as it bestows upon illegitimate children either fully or partially the rights of legitimacy which it ordinarily denies to children born outside of lawful wedlock. St. Thomas in treating this question says that illegitimate children may be legitimated by positive law.[154] This is to be interpreted in the sense that since positive law has inflicted certain disabilities on illegitimates the same law has the power to remove these disabilities.

Positive law then can regard illegitimate children as if they were born of lawful wedlock. In so far as the positive law confers the status of legitimacy on such children it may be said that thus far the effects of legitimacy depend on positive law.

In considering the topic of legitimation in Canon Law it is of interest to note that the introduction of the irregularity *ex defectu natalium* and the revival of the study of Roman law took place during the same period. The similarity between the modes of legitimation in Canon law and Roman law is evident. It can be said that the Church has employed the power of legitimation since the introduction of the irregularity *ex defectu natalium,* the modes of legitimation being patently adapted, to a very large extent, from the provisions of Roman law.

Genestal says that legitimation is not at all an institution created under the influence of the Church and Christianity. This, he continues, explains why the Church did nothing in the Middle Ages to introduce it into Canon law until the renaissance of the study of Roman law led the Church, so to speak, to recognize legitimation.[155] The regard in which legitimation came to be held in the Church is illustrated by Panormitanus, who said that legiti-

[154] "Respondeo dicendum quod filius illegitimus potest legitimari, non ut fiat de legitimo coitu natus, quia coitus ille transivit, et numquam potest fieri legitimus, ex quo semel fuit illegitimus; sed dicitur legitimari in quantum damna quae illegitimus filius incurrit, subtrahuntur per legis auctoritatem."—*Supplementum,* Q. LXVIII, art. 3.

[155] *Histoire de la Legitimation,* pp. 132, 133.

mation is an honor from which it can be inferred that its opposite is ignominy.[156]

The purpose of the Church in granting legitimation is twofold: (1) to extend the benefits of legitimacy to illegitimates; (2) to encourage the subsequent marriage of unmarried parents. These two reasons are advanced by Schmalzgrueber in his treatment of legitimation by subsequent marriage.[157] Legitimation is purely a concession made by law to illegitimate children. It is evident that strictly speaking they have no right to such consideration.[158] Legitimation may be bestowed *plenissimo iure,* namely, when all canonical and civil rights are bestowed, or *minus pleno iure,* namely when some canonical and civil rights are withheld.[159] Since the introduction of legitimation into Canon law the following modes of effecting legitimation have been emploed: (1) Subsequent Marriage; (2) Radical Sanation of Invalid Marriages; (3) Papal Rescript; (4) Solemn Religious Profession; (5) Papal Dispensation.

It must be noted here that although Papal Dispensation and Solemn Religious Profession do not constitute legitimation in the strict sense they have, nevertheless, been regarded as legitimation in a wide sense. Hence they have been included in the list of the various modes of legitimation admitted in Canon law.[160]

Article II.—*Legitimation by Subsequent Marriage*

As has already been seen in the Roman law discussion, legitimation by subsequent marriage was first introduced by Constantine.

[156] Panormitanus, *Commentaria in Quinque Libros Decretalium* (Venetiis, 1588), Lib. IV, *qui filii sint legitimi,* 17, nn. 3-4.

[157] Lib. IV, tit. 17, n. 49.

[158] Vermeersch-Creusen, *Epitome,* III, 419.

[159] Wernz, *Ius Decretalium,* IV, n. 679.

[160] Le nom de légitimation n'est généralement pas pronouncé à propos de la dispense de *l'irregularitas ex defectu natalium* ou des avantages que procure à l'enfant naturel la profession religieuse. Les canonistes présentent la dispense et la profession religieuse comme des légitimations partielles dont les effets se limitent au domaine spirituel.—Genestal, *Histoire de la Legitimation,* p. 1.

After having been affected in various ways by the legislation of later Emperors it was finally established as a mode of legitimation by Justinian. The introduction of this form of legitimation into Canon law came about as a result of the revival of the study of Roman law. There is no mention of this means of legitimation in the *Decretum Gratiani.* According to Genestal, the Decretals of the Popes furnish no material on legitimation by subsequent marriage before the twelfth century.[161]

The doctrine of this mode of legitimation may be stated as follows. By the subsequent intermarriage of its parents a "natural" child is legitimated through a fiction of law retroactive in effect to the time of its conception or at least to the time of its birth. Thus it is seen that only those children may be legitimated in this way whose parents were free to contract marriage at the time of conception, during the period of gestation, or at the time of the birth of these children. The first instance of what may be said to be the recognition of such legitimation is found during the pontificate of Alexander III (1159-1181) in the reply to a question which had been proposed to him. The paternal uncle of a certain woman wished her to be disinherited. He claimed she had been born before the marriage of her parents. The Pope commanded that if the facts alleged were true, the woman might be adjudged legitimate. The uncle was to be ordered to refrain from molesting the woman about the inheritance.[162] The most celebrated text in this matter is derived from the same Pope's reply to the Bishop of Exeter. This decretal is known as "*Tanta est vis*" and is found both in the Decretals and in the appendix to the III General Council of the Lateran (1179).[163] From this text it is evident that the Pope expressly excluded adulterine chil-

[161] *Histoire de la Legitimation,* p. 137.

[162] C. 1, X, *qui filii sint legitimi,* IV, 17.

[163] "Tanta est vis matrimonii, ut qui antea sunt geniti post contractum matrimonium legitimi habeantur. Si autem vir vivente uxore sua aliam cognoverit, et ex ea prolem susceperit, licet post morten uxoris eandem duxerit, nihilominus spurius erit filius, et ab haereditate repellendus; praesertim si in mortem uxoris prioris alteruter eorum aliquid fuerit machinatus."—C. 6, X, *qui filii sint legitimi,* IV, 17; Mansi, XXII, 388.

dren from the benefits of this form of legitimation. Canonists have deduced from this text that all "spurious" children are excluded.[164] Benedict XIV in his letter *"Redditae Nobis"* of December 5, 1744, addressed to the Archbishop of San Domingo, writing—as he observes—in the capacity of a canonist, and not with the authority of his Apostolic Office, declared that only "natural" children could be legitimated by the subsequent marriage of their parents. He corrected the Archbishop's mistaken interpretation of the words of Alexander III, *"Tanta est vis. . ."* The Archbishop maintained that the Sacrament of Matrimony of itself could effect legitimation. The Pope denied this view and declared that it was the Church which had, because of the authority granted to it, instituted this means of legitimating children born outside marriage with the exception of adulterine children.[165]

To effect legitimation by subsequent marriage it is necessary that the parents be able to contract marriage either at the time of conception, during the period of gestation, or at the time of the child's birth. Thus children conceived in adultery or even in incest can be legitimated by the subsequent marriage of their parents if the spouse of the adulterous parent has died or the impediment to the marriage has disappeared before the birth of such children.[166] The reference to the possibility of legitimating adulterine children by the subsequent marriage of their parents must be understood in relation to the possible presence of the diriment impediment of crime which is not of immediate concern here. Reiffenstuel held that if the subsequent marriage was a putative marriage the children already born were not legitimated.[167] The common opinion of canonists though, was that a subsequent putative marriage did legitimate children already born provided that they were truly *filii naturales*.[168] The subsequent

[164] Wernz, *Ius Decretalium,* IV, n. 686, note 53; De Becker, *De Sponsalibus et Matrimonio,* p. 377; Gasparri, *De Matrimonio,* II, n. 1118.

[165] *Fontes,* n. 350.

[166] Gasparri, *De Matrimonio,* II, 1118, Cappello, *De Sacramentis,* III, n. 750.

[167] Lib. IV, tit. 17, n. 36.

[168] Schmalzgrueber, lib. IV, tit. 17, n. 57; Wernz, *Ius Decretalium,* IV,

marriage effected legitimation even if it was simply a *matrimonium ratum*. Such a marriage could be contracted even *in articulo mortis*. This was so because the legitimation was effected *non intrinseca vi matromonii sed Ecclesiae constitutione*.[169] The common opinion was that a *filius objective spurius* though *putative naturalis* was not legitimated by the subsequent marriage of its parents.[170] The consent of the parents or of the person to be legitimated was not required. Once the subsequent marriage had been celebrated the legitimation was *ipso facto* effected.[171] In conclusion it can be said that legitimation by subsequent marriage was regarded in Canon law as a legitimation which was conferred *pleno iure* and therefore accorded all the juridical rights of legitimacy. There was only one exception, viz., that a son legitimated by the subsequent marriage of his parents could not become a Cardinal. This restriction was decreed by Sixtus V in his constitution *"Postquam"* of December 3, 1586.[172] Wernz disagreed with the opinion of Putzer who held that sons legitimated in this way could not become Bishops nor be admitted to Seminaries.[173]

Article III.—*Radical Sanation as a Mode of Legitimation*

Concerning the possibility of a radical sanation in Roman law, Harrigan has this to say: "The consideration of the most common forms of legitimation in Roman law seems sufficient to lead one to believe that they did not bear any resemblance to legitimation by radical sanation in Canon law. In none of these instances are the children considered as if they had been born of a valid marriage in view of a radical sanation of the prior invalid mar-

n. 686, note 50; De Becker, *De Sponsalibus et Matrimonio*, p. 376; Gasparri, *De Matrimonio*, II, n. 1388.

[169] Wernz, *Ius Decretalium*, IV, n. 686; De Becker, *De Sponsalibus et Matrimonio*, p. 377; Gasparri, *De Matrimonio*, II, 1117.

[170] De Becker, *De Sponsalibus et Matrimonio*, p. 378; Cappello, *De Sacramentis*, II, n. 750.

[171] Wernz, *Ius Decretalium*, IV, n. 686.

[172] § 12, *Fontes*, n. 159.

[173] *Ius Decretalium*, IV, n. 686, note 52.

riage." [174] It can be said, then, that radical sanation is purely a canonical institution. The exact time of the introduction of radical sanation into Canon law cannot be determined accurately.[175] It is not intended here to trace in detail the history of the development of radical sanation in Canon law. It is sufficient for the purpose intended here to note the conclusion of Harrigan who says that by general admission it has been found acceptable to adopt the opinion that the first reported instance of radical sanation occurred in 1301 during the pontificate of Boniface VIII.[176] Esmein maintains that radical sanation originally furnished a simple expedient to the Pope to legitimate "natural" children. Then it became established as a principle and produced many results. In modern times the doctrine has been profoundly changed and radical sanation has come to be a new institution. It serves not only to assure *legitimatio plenissima* to the children, which in reality has come to be a secondary effect, but it concerns itself principally with the marriage and the spouses.[177] Harrigan observes that it was probably only at the beginning of the seventeenth century that this change came about. From that time the efficacy of radical sanation primarily as a method of convalidating invalid marriages has been emphasized.[178]

When the favor of radical sanation is granted the marriage becomes valid at the time the sanation is granted but as far as the canonical effects of marriage are concerned it becomes valid as to the past, i.e., from the time of the celebration of the invalid marriage.[179] Since one of the principal canonical effects of marriage is the legitimacy of children, it is evident that when radical sanation takes place the children already born of the invalid marriage are regarded by the Church as if they had been born

[174] Harrigan, *The Radical Sanation of Invalid Marriages.* The Catholic University of America, Canon Law Studies, n. 116 (Washington, D. C.: The Catholic University of America, 1938), p. 19.

[175] Wernz, *Ius Decretalium,* IV, n. 654.

[176] *The Radical Sanation of Invalid Marriage,* pp. 19, 20.

[177] *Le Mariage,* II, pp. 399, 406-407.

[178] *The Radical Sanation of Invalid Marriages,* p. 23.

[179] Cappello, *De Sacramentis,* III, n. 851, 1°.

of a valid marriage. This is made possible by the legal fiction of reaching back to the past in respect to the canonical effects of marriage.

The consideration of radical sanation may be terminated by observing that this favor has been granted since the time of Boniface VIII. It was granted very frequently particularly at the end of the eighteenth century. It has been granted not only in individual cases, but even for a whole diocese.[180] Finally it must be noted that the Sovereign Pontiff alone has the proper and ordinary power to grant radical sanation. He can and actually has delegated the faculty to grant this favor to bishops.[181]

Article IV.—*Legitimation by Papal Rescript*

In the Roman law section mention has been made of the *legitimatio per rescriptum Principis* which was introduced by Justinian. Canon law took over this mode of legitimation and made it its own. The power to issue such a rescript was vested naturally in the Supreme Pontiff and it has, therefore, been called correctly *legitimatio per rescriptum Pontificis.* It may be observed here that the Papal dispensation from the irregularity *ex defectu natalium* is to be distinguished from legitimation by Papal rescript. Genestal says that the former is a mode of legitimation *ad sacra* while the latter is a means of legitimation *ad temporalia.*[182]

Reiffenstuel characterizes legitimation by Papal rescript as a gracious act by which one who is illegitimate is made legitimate if it is possible thus to legitimize him.[183] According to Genestal the beginnings of legitimation by Papal rescript are found in the decretals of Innocent III (1198-1216). Genestal remarks that there are traces, not well defined, of some prior acts in this regard, but that they are of no consequence. Innocent III, he says, believed himself to be the first to effect legitimation

[180] Wernz, *Ius Decretalium,* IV, n. 654.
[181] Wernz, *op. cit.,* IV, nn. 655, 656.
[182] *Histoire de la Legitimation,* pp. 45, 181.
[183] Lib. IV, tit. 17, n. 46.

ad temporalia.[184] At the time of Innocent III the question of legitimacy of children was very important, because it was a requirement in both ecclesiastical and civil law for obtaining offices, dignities, and inheritances. As a result of the canonical legislation governing the legitimacy of children born of invalid marriages there was proposed to the Pope a very difficult question. He was petitioned to legitimate certain children in order to render them eligible to obtain certain temporal offices and successions in territories that were not subject to the temporal power of the Pope.[185] It can be noted here that although the possibility of legitimation by Papal rescript is not necessarily connected at all with the question of the marriage of the parents of the person to be legitimated, the first cases involving the granting and the refusal of such legitimation were actually cases of children born of invalid marriages.

The background of the question which was proposed to Innocent III is very interesting. Philip Augustus, King of France, married the daughter of Count Baudoin de Hainaut and niece of Count Philip of Flanders. One son, the future Louis VIII, was born of the marriage. The Queen, Isabella died on March 15, 1190, and the King married Ingeburge, the daughter of Waldeman I, King of Denmark, on August 14, 1193.

The marriage proved unhappy and Philip, in order to obtain an annulment, alleged that Ingeburge was related within the forbidden degrees to his first wife, Isabella. A sentence of nullity was rendered on November 14, 1193, by William the Archbishop of Rheims who was the King's uncle. The King of Denmark and Ingeburge petitioned Pope Celestine III to intervene, demonstrating the falsity of the alleged prohibited relationship. The Pope in the early part of 1195 sent Legates to France with a letter to the King ordering him to regard Ingeburge as his wife. The Pope also wrote to the Archbishop of Rheims declaring the judgment null. The Pope declared he was opposed to another marriage under the circumstances. The King, however, avoided

[184] *Histoire de la Legitimation,* p. 181.

[185] C. 13, X, *qui filii sint legitimi,* IV, 17.

a formal and judicial declaration of the validity of his marriage with Ingeburge and in June 1196 he married Agnes, the daughter of Duke Berthold III of Meran. In 1198 Celestine III died and was succeeded by Innocent III. The new Pope wrote directly to the King threatening him with an interdict. The interdict was declared in effect when the King refused to yield. In 1201 the King agreed to dismiss Agnes and the process regarding the validity of his marriage with Ingeburge was resumed. In the meantime Agnes died leaving two children, Marie and Philippe. At the death of Agnes the scandal disappeared. The King then petitioned the Pope to legitimate the two children, and the Pope complied with the request. The King finally accepted Ingeburge as his wife.[186]

The case which gave rise to the famous decretal *Per venerabilem* was that of William of Montpellier. In 1187 this man had put away his wife Eudoxie who had borne him one daughter. He formed a union with Agnes of Aragon who bore him many children. William petitioned the Pope through the Archbishop of Arles to legitimate the children born of Agnes. The petition cited the case of the children of the King of France. The Pope denied the petition declaring that there was no good faith present on William's part. This answer was given in 1202.[187]

The Pope's answer is important not so much because of the actual decision, but because it contains the claim of the Papacy to legitimate children *ad temporalia.* Innocent III carefully distinguished between the powers of the Church and State and showed the separation between them. The Pontiff declared that he could legitimate children in lands that were subject to the Church; but in other territories he could legitimize them directly only in respect to those things which were spiritual. In regard to temporal effects he added that he could legitimize only indirectly and as a consequence, as it were, of another action.

The language of the *glossae* regarding this decretal is not very clear.[188] Panormitanus refers to it as *"caput difficile et*

[186] Genestal, *Histoire de la Legitimation,* pp. 182-186.

[187] C. 13, X, *qui filii sint legitimi,* IV, 17.

[188] Freisen, *Eherecht,* p. 865.

multum famosum."[189] Canonists in attempting to explain the power which the Pope claimed in this matter excogitated no less than five variant opinions.[190] Some of them erred by excess in claiming for the Pope more power than he himself had claimed; others erred by defect in denying to the Pontiff what he had actually claimed. The Pope had declared that in territories outside his temporal jurisdiction he could legitimize children *ad temporalia* only indirectly and in consequence of another action. The "other action" referred to is the convalidation of invalid marriages. The best explanation of the Pope's power in this regard was given by Joannes Andreae. He held that it was necessary to make the will of the Pontiff extend back to the invalid marriage itself. If one could admit that the Pope, by granting a dispensation from a diriment impediment to the marriage, could efface the effects which the impediment had produced in the past, there would be given to the Pope an indirect but sure means of legitimizing children born of the marriage.[191]

This opinion, keeping intact the Papal power and without disregarding the rights of the temporal power, established a mode of action whereby the Pope could legitimize children directly, with respect to spiritual affairs and indirectly with respect to civil affairs. In this method of legitimizing the children of an invalid marriage, the invalid marriage itself becomes the object of the Pope's direct action, while the legitimation of the children would follow merely in view of the retroactive force which he intended to attribute to his action.

Reiffenstuel commenting on this question says that the Pope can legitimate children by rescript as to political effects, inheritance, honors, and civil dignities in his own territory. He observes that the Pope cannot ordinarily and directly legitimate children not subject to his temporal jurisdiction. He adds that the Pontiff can legitimate as to civil effects outside his temporal jurisdiction

[189] *Commentaria,* lib. IV, *qui filii sint legitimi,* 17, n. 1.

[190] Esmein, *Le Mariage,* II, p. 400.

[191] Joannes Andreae, *In Sex Decretalium Libros Novella Commentaria* (Venetiis, 1581), C. *Per Venerabilem,* n. 26 sq.

in extraordinary cases, e.g., whenever common necessity demands it.[192] The same doctrine is found in Schmalzgrueber. He maintains that the Pope can legitimate children outside his temporal jurisdiction as to civil effects and in two instances: (1) when there is a doubt as to the validity of the parents' marriage. If the Pope settles the doubt in favor of the marriage the children are legitimate; (2) when there is grave necessity for the legitimation. The reason that this is so, he holds, is because the Pope, in virtue of the general power which he has received from God, can do all things which are necessary and useful to govern the Church and to preserve therein the good of religion and of christian justice.[193] The Pope and the Pope alone could legitimate by rescript with respect to Sacred Orders, honors, dignities, and benefices to which was attached the care of souls.[194] The local ordinary or also the Cathedral Chapter if the See was vacant, could admit illegitimates to Minor Orders and simple benefices. This was done not through legitimation, but by virtue of a dispensation which had been granted to them. Therefore, a dispensation of this character did not have the effects of legitimation.[195] By Papal rescript not only "natural" children but also "spurious" children and those born *ex damnata coitu* could be legitimated.[196] To determine the extent of the effects of legitimation by Papal rescript it is necessary to examine the rescript issued in each case. It can be said that ordinarly by a *rescriptum simplex* the Pope does not intend to render an illegitimate capable of all ecclesiastical dignities.[197] A clause contained in such a rescript can limit the rights granted. The Pope is presumed not

[192] Lib. IV, tit. 17, nn. 48-50.

[193] Lib. IV, tit. 17, nn. 110-113.

[194] Reiffenstuel, lib. IV, tit. 17, n. 47; Schmalzgrueber, lib. IV, tit. 17, n. 103.

[195] Reiffenstuel, *loc. cit.;* Schmalzgrueber, lib. IV, title 17, n. 104.

[196] Reiffenstuel, lib. IV, tit. 17, n. 56; Schmalzgrueber, lib. IV, tit. 17, n. 93.

[197] Wernz, *Ius Decretalium,* IV, n. 687.

to grant legitimation in such a way as to prejudice the rights of a third party.[198]

Article V.—*Solemn Religious Profession*

According to Hinschius this mode of legitimation, widely so called, in Canon Law is as old as the irregularity *ex defectu natalium.*[199] This mode of legitimation *ad spiritualia* appears to have been adopted from the *legitimatio per oblationem curiae* of Roman Law. Solemn profession was regarded by law as having the power to heal the *defectus natalium* regarding the canonical effects of legitimacy. It has already been observed that one of the factors which contributed to the introduction of the irregularity *ex defectu natalium* was the fear that sons might be *imitatores incontinentiae paternae.* If, therefore, such illegitimate children entered religious orders to live a life of mortification and prayer it was thought that they had remedied their previous ignoble status in relation to which the law had maintained its attitude of acknowledged disaffection and implied distrust. By solemn profession, then, the irregularity which had been incurred by the fact of illegitimacy was removed. This legitimation, for it may be called legitimation in a wide sense, was not, however, *plenissimo iure.* This is evident from the Decretals, wherein it is stated that an illegitimate who has entered a monastery or joined a canonical congregation living according to rule, and has been promoted to Sacred Orders, may not be advanced to a prelacy.[200] In canon 504 it may be seen that the present law of the Church is the same in this regard as far as eligiblity for the office of Major Superiors is concerned.

The civil law took cognizance to some extent of the effects of solemn profession. It may be said that entrance into a religious order with solmen vows has been regarded historically by the Church as a spiritual rebirth. Hence it is easy to see how the church would permit solemn profession to heal the juridical

[198] Santi, *Praelectiones Iuris Canonici* (lib. V in 2 vols. 1 ed., Ratisbon, 1886), lib. IV, p. 166, n. 15.

[199] *Kirchenrecht,* I, 13, note 1.

[200] C. 1, X, *de filiis presbyterorum* I, 17.

defects attendant upon illegitimate birth as regards the reception of Orders. It must be noted here that if such a profession would be later declared invalid for any reason the *defectus natalium* would still remain. The contempt in which illegitimates were held in civil law has already been alluded to. It was only natural that some of these children, feeling keenly the stigma of the ignoble condition of their origin availed themselves of the advantages of solemn profession to enter the religious life with the express purpose of removing the stain of their illegitimacy. It is evident that such motives did not have the most desirable results. To correct the abuses which had arisen in the course of time in this regard Sixtus V issued some extraordinarily severe regulations. The Pontiff in his constitution *"Cum de omnibus"* of June 27, 1587 forbade the admission of children born as the result of incest and sacrilege to the religious life. All other illegitimates were to be admitted only after a diligent examination. Once admitted, these were not permitted at any time to be promoted to any dignity in their order, without a special dispensation of the Holy See. The Pope gave as his reasons for this severe legislation the fact that very often such children imitated their parents. They fled to the religious life, he observed, not for reasons of piety, but rather for temporal advantages.[201]

In his constitution *"Ad Romanum"* of October 21, 1588, the Holy Father declared that children legitimated by the subsequent marriage of their parents were not comprehended among those forbidden to enter the religious life.[202] The restrictions placed upon legitimation, widely so called, through solemn religious profession by Sixtus V were removed by Gregory XIV. The revocation of the drastic enactments of Sixtus V is found in the constitution *"Circumspecta"* of March 15, 1591. Gregory XIV decreed that illegitimates might be admitted to the religious life in the same ways in which they had been admitted before the promulgation of the laws of Sixtus V.[203] The present law

201 §§ 1-3—*Fontes*, n. 162.

202 § 3—*Fontes*, n. 164.

203 § 2 ad finem,—*Fontes*, n. 170.

distinguishes clearly between legitimation and Solemn Profession. Thus canon 984, 1°, states that illegitimates are irregular *ex defectu natalium,* ". . . nisi fuerint legitimati *vel* vota solemnia professi." Thus Schäfer holds that solemn profession is not strictly legitimation.[204]

Article VI.—*Papal Dispensation*

According to canon 80 a dispensation is the relaxation of a law in a special case. The first instance of Papal Dispensation from the irregularity *ex defectu natalium* is found in a letter of Paschal II written to Anselm, the Archbishop of Canterbury, in 1107. The Pope granted the Archbishop the right to promote illegitimate children to the sacred ministry (*sacra officia*) in so far as the necessities of the times and the utility of the Church demanded it.[205] The second instance is traced to the pontificate of Alexander III (1159-1181). No more exact date can be given. The Pope affirmed absolutely that a formal dispensation was necessary in the case of illegitimates who wished to be promoted to Sacred Orders and to acquire Benefices to which was attached the care of souls. The Pope distinguished between the reception of Sacred Orders and the acquisition of benefices. He declared that the reception of Sacred Orders was absolutely forbidden to illegitimates, implying that it was left to the bishop to decide regarding the conferring of simple benefices in such cases.[206] The same Pontiff answering the question of an English bishop involving the acquisition by an illegitimate of a benefice to which was attached the care of souls, decreed that the illegitimate, already a subdeacon, was not to be permitted to hold the benefice. The Pope ordered that a priest was to be appointed to the benefice within forty days after the reception of his letter. The subdeacon was not to be advanced to higher

[204] Schäfer, *De Religiosis ad Normam Codicis Iuris Canonici* (3. ed., Roma: S.A.L.E.R. Rappresentante della Casa Editrice Herder, 1940), p. 243 n. 115 b.

[205] Mansi, XX, 1063; Genestal, *Histoire de la Legitimation,* p. 58.

[206] Genestal, *Histoire de la Legitimation,* pp. 58, 59.

Orders, but to assist the priest at sacred functions. For these services he was to be permitted one-half of the fruits of the benefice.[207] Clement III (1187-1191) granted a dispensation to an illegitimate to embrace the clerical state and to receive a benefice. This dispensation appears to have been given only for Minor Orders, though some commentators assert that it was granted for Major Orders. The latter opinion, however, seems untenable from a consideration of the text alone, ". . . permittimus ipsum ordinari in clericum, et ad ecclesiasticum beneficium (unde commode sustentari valeat) promoveri." [208]

The discussion of this question may be terminated by observing that during the thirteenth century the necessity of a Papal dispensation from the irregularity *ex defectu natalium* had become clearly recognized. Thus Gregory IX (1227-1241), in writing to the Archbishop of Tours declared that illegitimate children who had been promoted to any ecclesiastical dignity, or who had acquired benefices to which was attached the care of souls, without having obtained a Papal dispensation, were to be removed without delay. The Sovereign Pontiff expressly forbade such promotions without Papal dispensation for the future.[209] Boniface VIII (1294-1303) decreed that a man laboring under the *defectus natalium* might, after having obtained an episcopal dispensation, be promoted to Minor Orders and could in such circumstances obtain a simple benefice. For promotion to Major Orders, and the acquisition of a benefice, to which was attached the care of souls the Pope demanded that a dispensation be obtained from the Apostolic See. He declared explicitly that Bishops could not dispense from the irregularity for Major Orders and for benefices having the care of souls.[210] The same Pontiff declared that if a man had been dispensed by the Apostolic See from the irregularity *ex defectu natalium*, and had been promoted to Sacred Orders and had been given a benefice with the care of souls, a second dispensation, obtained for two or more benefices, without

[207] C. 6, X, *de filiis presbyterorum*, I, 17.
[208] C. 14, X, *de filiis presbyterorum*, I, 17.
[209] C. 18, X, *de filiis presbyterorum*, I, 17.
[210] C. 1, *de filiis presbyterorum et aliis illegitime natis*, I, 11 in VI°.

mention of the *defectus natalium* was invalid.[211] The absolute need for a dispensation from the irregularity can be gathered from the fact that canonists treated this irregularity as part of the law *De Poenis*.[212] A dispensation from the irregularity *ex defectu natalium* did not constitute true legitimation.[213]

From what has been said regarding the various modes of legitimation in Canon Law it can be concluded that all illegitimate children can be legitimated. Disregarding legitimation widely so called by Papal dispensation and by Solemn religious profession, both of which are granted for a special purpose, it is obvious that the *filii naturales* benefit most. Thus they are regarded as if they had been born of a valid marriage if their parents, when the case demands it, have been granted a radical sanation. They can be legitimated by the subsequent marriage of their parents or by Papal rescript even if their parents do not marry.

Filii spurii on the other hand do not benefit by radical sanation if their parents' union was contracted in the face of a diriment impediment of the divine positive law or of the natural law. They cannot be legitimated by the subsequent marriage of their parents if they are already born when the marriage takes place These children must seek legitimation by some other means, e.g., by Papal rescript. With regard to this it must be noted that it is not customary for the Roman Pontiff to confer legitimation on children who are the fruit of incest or of sacrilege.

[211] C. 2, *de filiis presbyterorum et aliis illegitime natis,* I, 11 in VI°.

[212] Reiffenstuel, lib. V, tit. 37, nn. 71, 85-87.

[213] Wernz, *Ius Decretalium,* IV, pars II, n. 688.

SECTION II

CANONICAL COMMENTARY

CHAPTER III

LEGTIMACY AND LEGITIMATION IN THE PRESENT CANONICAL LEGISLATION

Part I—*Legitimacy*

ARTICLE I. INTRODUCTION TO THE COMMENTARY

The commentary will consist of two principal divisions: (1) legitimacy in the present canon law; (2) the modes of legitimation provided in the present canon law. An appendix showing in a general way the provisions of the common law and modern American law for legitimacy and legitimation will be included.

The importance of the questions of legitimacy and legitimation, not only for the individuals primarily concerned, but also for the social welfare of the community, has caused these questions to become objects of much legislation both ecclesiastical and civil. It is necessary, therefore, at the very outset to determine the respective competence of both Church and State to deal with these questions. The legitimacy of offspring is considered in canon law as one of the effects of marriage. The effects of marriage, in general, it may be noted, are understood to be all the goods and privileges, rights and duties of the spouses and the offspring which arise from the matrimonial contract and bond.[1] Legitimacy is considered in canon law to be specifically an intrinsic, essential and inseparable effect of marriage.[2] Not all theologians and canonists, as has already been shown in the historical synopsis, have described legitimacy as an inseparable

[1] Wernz, *Ius Decretalium,* lib. IV, Pars I, n. 49; Ottaviani, *Institutiones Iuris Publici Ecclesiastici* (2. ed., 2 vols., Romae: Typis Polyglottis Vaticanis, 1935-1936), II, *Ius Publicum Externum,* 211.

[2] Wernz, *loc. cit.,* n. 50; Cappello, *De Sacramentis,* III, p. 229, n. 475.

effect of marriage. While some have believed that it is merely a civil effect of marriage others have been not too precise in classifying it among the effects of marriage. The reason for the divergence of opinion is due, as Wernz remarks, to the fact that the theologians and canonists themselves have not always agreed on the terminology regarding the various effects of marriage.[3] Cappello observes simply that the opinion of the few authors who hold that legitimacy is not an inseparable effect of marriage is erroneous.[4]

It may be correctly stated that the common opinion of canonists is that legitimacy is an inseparable effect of marriage. Hence any question of legitimacy whose adjudication depends on the validity of marriage belongs exclusively to the ecclesiastical judge; for he alone is competent with regard to a declaration of the validity or nullity of marriage, and in deciding the principal question he should also decide the accessory question.[5]

While the solution of questions of legitimacy which are concerned with the validity or nullity of marriage is reserved solely to the ecclesiastical judge, other questions of legitimacy which are questions of fact rather than of law may be decided by a secular judge. Such questions as whether a marriage was actually celebrated or whether the husband is really the father of his wife's child may be said to be within the competence of a secular judge.[6] Cappello says that the question is controverted. He holds as his opinion, which opinion he claims is the more probable one, that a secular judge may decide these questions of fact under the following conditions: (1) when there is question of a mere fact; (2) when the proper subordination to the Church is observed; (3) when the decision does not touch upon legitimacy as such directly and immediately.[7] Wernz observes that many

[3] *Ius Decretalium,* IV, Pars I, pp. 69-69, note 125.

[4] *De Sacramentis,* III, p. 229, n. 475.

[5] Gasparri, *De Matrimonio,* II, p. 196, n. 1115; Santi, *Praelectiones Iuris Canonici,* II, p. 170, n. 11; Wernz-Vidal, *Ius Matrimoniale,* p. 715-716, n. 612.

[6] Gasparri, *op. cit.,* II, p. 196, n. 1115.

[7] *De Sacramentis,* III, p. 239, n. 754.

ancient authors did not exclude secular judges if the decision of legitimacy depended on a fact. He says, however, that this opinion was not without its difficulties in practice, because it is difficult to separate a question of fact from every question of law. Theoretically the competence of secular judges in a question of fact in this matter seems to be based not on a strict right of the civil power but rather on the tolerance of the Church.[8]

Questions regarding legitimation on the other hand, may bt properly decided by a secular judge. This is so because legitimation is a fiction of law having no direct connection with the question of the validity of marriage.[9] The legitimacy recognized in canon law should also be recognized in civil law, since it follows as a natural effect of marriage without any fiction of law and outside any positive disposition of the law. On the contrary, legitimation admitted in canon law need not be recognized by the State, *per se* but only *per accidens,* in so far as the same mode of legitimation is recognized in the civil law.[10]

The present discussion may be summarized in the words of Hannan:

> "The Sacrament of Matrimony is a good example of a supernaturalized institution that belongs exclusively to the jurisdiction of the Church as to its essence while certain temporal effects concern the State. . . . But the inseparable effects that are so closely bound up with the Sacrament as to be identical with it are regarded by the Church as being its exclusive concern independent of any right of interference by the State. Now such an effect is the legitimacy of children. Thus not only will the Church refuse to permit a State to deny validity to marriages valid under canon law, but it will

[8] *Ius Decretalium* IV, p. 593, note 42.

[9] Wernz-Vidal, *Ius Matrimoniale,* p. 716, n. 612; De Smet, *De Sponsalibus et Matrimonio* (4 ed., Brugis: Car Beyaert, 1927), p. 244, note 3. Cappello, *De Sacramentis,* III, p. 238, n. 752.

[10] De Smet, *op. cit.,* p. 244, note 3; Wernz, *Ius Decretalium,* IV, Pars II, p. 571-572, n. 664. Cf. also p. 572, note 46, where the question is given detailed discussion.

refuse the right to the State to regard the children of such marriages as illegitimate under the State law. Thus the Church would maintain that no State could deny such a child the right to share with his brothers under a general State law in the inheritance of his father, provided, of course, that the State law recognized such inheritance for legitimate children. However while the Church insists on its right in this regard, it is not blind to actual situations. . . . An effect of marriage that might at first sight seem to be an inseparable one is legitimation. However, it is a separable effect. Legitimation is a fiction. It means that by marriage after the birth of a child, the law regards the child as if it had been born after the marriage. Since this legitimacy is a favor granted by the law, it is no traspass on the validity of the marriage to deny legitimacy to such a child. So, although the Church might regard a child of parents thus marriad after its birth as legitimate for all spiritual purposes, it would find no fault if the State would refuse to find it legitimate for all temporal purposes." [11]

Article II. *Legitimacy according to Canon* 1114

Canon 1114—Legitimi sunt filii concepti aut nati ex matrimonio valido vel putativo, nisi parentes ob solemnem professionem religiosam vel susceptum ordinem sacrum prohibitus tempore conceptionis fuerit usus matrimonii antea contracti.

The fact of a child's legitimacy cannot be discussed apart from the question of the intermarriage of its parents. It has already been pointed out that strictly considered the conception of a child must take place during the marriage of its parents to render the child legitimate according to the natural law.[12] Canon law, of course, admits the legitimacy of such children, placing them first among legitimate children. In addition it admits the legitimacy

[11] "The Church's Province in the State," *AER,* XCIII (1935), 556-557.

[12] Chapter II, Part I, Article I, p. 11.

of those children born of a valid marriage although not conceived therein. Further, it recognizes the legitimacy of children conceived in or born of a putative marriage. The legitimacy of those children whose conception has taken place during the valid marriage of their parents is known as *natural* legitimacy. The legitimacy of all other children recognized in canon law as legitimate is known as *juridic* legitimacy.[13]

A. Requisites for Valid Marriage

. . . *ex matrimonio valido* . . .

It is beyond the scope of this dissertation to consider in detail all the requisites for the validity of marriage in canon law. A brief sketch of the requirements will not, however, be out of place here. The marriage of baptized persons is regulated not only by divine, but also by canon law the civil power remaining competent in regard to the purely civil effects of marriage.[14] The parties who wish to contract a valid marriage must not be hindered by any diriment impediment established in the present law of the Church.[15] When any diriment impediment does exist between persons contemplating marriage, then, if a *canonical cause* is advanced, a dispensation may be granted by the Church in cases over which it has the power to dispense and in which dispensations are accustomed to be granted.

True matrimonial consent must be given freely by each of the parties, both of whom must be cognizant of the nature of marriage.[16] Although the personal consent of each of the parties is demanded, it is not absolutely necessary for validity that both be present. The intervention of a proxy according to the regulations of canon law is permitted, or if necessity arises, an interpreter's services may be employed.[17].

The parties must contract marriage according to the form

[13] Cappello, *De Sacramentis,* III, n. 745.

[14] Cans. 1016; 87.

[15] These impediments are listed in canons 1067, § 1; 1068, § 1; 1069; 1070, § 1; 1072; 1073; 1074, § 1; 1075; 1076, 1077; 1078; 1079; 1080.

[16] Canons 1081; 1082, § 1.

[17] Canons 1088, §1; 1089; 1090; 1091.

prescribed by law. Canon law expressly states that only those marriages are valid which are contracted before the parish priest, or the local Ordinary, or a priest delegated by either of them, and at least two witnesses, in accordance with the rules laid down in the canons, excepting only the cases mentioned in canons 1098 and 1099.[18]

Of present interest is the consideration of those persons who are bound to observe the prescribed canonical form of marriage under penalty of nullity. The following are bound: (1) all persons baptized in the Catholic Church and those who have been converted to it from heresy or schism, even if the latter or the former have fallen away afterwards, whenever they contract marriage among themselves; (2) the above-mentioned persons, if they contract marriage with non-Catholics, baptized or unbaptized, even when a dispensation has been obtained from the impediment of mixed religion or disparity of worship; (3) Orientals when they contract with Latins, who are subject to this form.[19]

Orientals are, however, bound by the decree *Ne Temere* in some cases and by the decree *Tametsi* in others when they marry among themselves, and when they contract marriage with other Orientals, with heretics, or with schismatics. The Greek Ruthenians in the United States, Canada, and South America are governed by the decree *Ne Temere*. The Maronites are bound by the decree *Tametsi* whose binding force at the present will be determined by the principles of interpretation which formerly governed the decree *Tametsi*.[20] The following persons are not bound to observe the canonical form of marriage: (1) non-Catholics, whether baptized or unbaptized, who contract among themselves; (2) those persons born of non-Catholics, who although baptized in the Catholic Church, grew up from infancy in heresy, schism or [21] infidelity, or without any religion, if they

[18] Can. 1094.

[19] Can. 1099, § 1, 1°-3°.

[20] Carberry, *The Juridical Form of Marriage*. The Catholic University of America, Canon Law Studies, n. 84 (Washington D. C.: The Catholic University of America, 1934), pp. 126-127.

[21] Cf. can. 1325, § 2.

contract marriage with non-Catholics.[22] Oriental Uniate Catholics, with due regard to the exceptions already noted, are not bound to the Catholic form of marriage when they contract marriage with any other person not bound to the form.

There have been two important decisions handed down by the Pontifical Commission for the Interpretation of the Code regarding the canonical form of marriage and its binding force upon those persons who have been born of non-Catholics and baptized in the Catholic Church though not reared therein. On July 20, 1929, the Commission declared that the phrase *ab acatholicis nati* referred to persons one of whose parents was a non-Catholic, even when the latter had signed the formal promises demanded in accordance with canons 1061 and 1071.[23] The Commission later declared that the phrase *ab acatholicis nati* included also those persons who were born of apostate Catholic parents.[24] Gasparri holds that this decision refers to public apostates from the Church.[25] On July 25, 1931, the Commission in a reply to a query regarding the nature of its declarations of July 20, 1929, explained that the interpretation given was declarative, not extensive.[26]

[22] Can. 1099, § 2.

[23] *AAS*, XXI (1929), 573.

[24] *AAS*, XXII (1930), 195.

[25] *De Matrimonio*, II, p. 145, n. 1023.

[26] *AAS*, XXIII (1931), 388. Miaskiewicz maintains that one cannot believe that the term *declaratory* as used by the Pontifical Commission to indicate the nature of the previous interpretation, is the equivalent of the words *declaret tantum verba legis in se certa* of canon 17. There is all likelihood, he says, that *declaratory* is only to be taken in contradistinction to *extensive*. Evidently, the interpretation is not *restrictive*. Thus there remains the one possibility that it was meant to be *explanatory*. He states that the two interpretations of the Pontifical Commission were indeed *declaratory* but not purely such. He agrees with Nevin that these interpretations were not retroactive but would take juridical effect only upon due observance of the regulations of canon 9. He concludes that all marriages of the children of mixed marriages contracted without the observance of the form were valid in virtue of canon 15—*Supplied Jurisdiction According to Canon* 209. The Catholic University of America, Canon Law Studies, n. 122 (Washington, D. C.: The Catholic University of America Press, 1940), pp. 208-209.

Under certain conditions it may be impossible to observe the canonical form of marriage. In view of this possibility the Church provides for the valid celebration of marriage by what has been defined according to some authors as an extraordinary form of marriage.[27] Thus, if it is impossible without grave inconvenience to send for or go to a pastor or Ordinary or a priest delegated by either of these to assist at a marriage in accordance with the prescriptions of canons 1095 and 1096 marriage will be contracted validly and licitly in danger of death, in the presence of the witnesses only; and it will be the same outside the danger of death, provided it be prudently foreseen that this condition of things is to last for a month. In both cases, if another priest is at hand who can come, he should be called, and he should assist at the marriage together with the witnesses, but the marriage would be valid in the presence of the witnesses alone.[28] The extraordinary form will be employed more frequently in mission territories which cannot be visited every month by the missionaries. In other places a moral impossibility of approaching the parish priest may arise, e. g., during the time of persecution or war, when access to the pastor would be forbidden or fraught with grave danger.[29] It is worthy of note that in view of extraordinary circumstances the extraordinary form may, with the permission of the Holy See, be used also to validate marriages already contracted invalidly. This concession was made to the Ordinaries and the people of Mexico on December 22, 1927, through the Sacred Congregation of the Sacraments. The faculties were to be in force for two years if the extraordinary circumstances continued that long.[30]

[27] Payen, *De Matrimonio,* II, n. 1813; Vlaming, *Praelectiones Iuris Matrimonii Ad Normam Codicis Iuris Canonici* (3. ed. 2 vols. Bussum in Hollandia: Sumptibus Societatis Anonymae Olim Paulus Brand, 1921), II, n. 584.

[28] Can. 1098, 1°- 2°.

[29] Chelodi, *Ius Matrimoniale iuxta Codicem Iuris Canonici* (3. ed. Tridenti: Libr. Edit. Tridentum, 1921), n. 137.

[30] The Holy Father grants the following faculties which local Ordinaries can exercise either personally or through others specially delegated: (a)

It may now be observed that the marriage of baptized persons is valid: (1) when no diriment impediment of the divine law, natural or positive, or of canon law exists between the contracting parties: (2) when true matrimonial consent has been freely given; (3) when the canonical form of marriage has been observed provided, of course, that the parties are bound by the form. The marriage of non-baptized persons is valid; (1) when no diriment impediment of the divine law, natural or positive, or of civil law exists between the contracting parties; (2) when true matrimonial consent has been given (3) when the form, if any, demanded by the civil law, under pain of nullity has been observed. Although canon law does not generally legislate for the unbaptized, these are bound of necessity by the canonical form when they contract marriage with a Catholic bound by the form.[31] While it is admitted that the civil law has the right to establish diriment impediments for the unbaptized, it must be remembered that such a marriage is not null by the mere fact that it was contracted in violation of a civil law. To nullify such a marriage the civil law impediment must be diriment in character and it must also be reasonable and binding in character.[32]

There are actually few impediments of American civil law which render a marriage invalid or void. The majority of them, together with defects which prevent "real consent," render the marriage only *voidable*. By creating a *voidable* marriage civil law gives legal sanction to a status in which one or both parties have the right to void the marriage Until this is done, how-

as regards marriages invalidly contracted, to validate them, after dispensing from the impediments as hereinafter determined, by renewal of consent before two witnesses and a pastor or other priest, if they can be had, *otherwise before the witnesses alone*, . . .—Bouscaren, *The Canon Law Digest* (2 vols. and Supplement, Milwaukee: The Bruce Publishing Co., 1934-1938), Supplement, p. 4.

[31] Canons 12; 87; 1099, § 1, 2°; "Ad canonem 1099," *Ius Pontificium*, XV (1935), 323.

[32] Ayrinhac-Lydon, *Marriage Legislation In The New Code of Canon Law* (2. ed., New York: Benziger Brothers, 1936), n. 15.

ever, the marriage is considered valid Civil law rejects the theory that a voidable marriage is an invalid marriage until it is later ratified It adopts the opposite theory that the marriage is valid until it is disaffirmed.[33] If it be admitted that the civil law has power over the marriage of unbaptized persons even to the extent of establishing diriment impediments for such persons, the opinion of some authors, for example, Chelodi and Cappello, that the validity of marriage is determined solely by canon law, and further that the children of civil marriages must always be regarded as illegitimate, seems untenable.[34] Children of any valid marriage, whether the marriage be Christian or non-Christian, are legitimate.[35]

B. Requisites for Putative Marriage

. . . *ex matrimonio putativo* . . .

The Church extends the recognition of legitimacy to the children of parents whose marriage is putative A putative marriage is an invalid marriage which has been contracted in good faith by at least one of the parties It is considered putative until both parties become certain of its nullity.[36] Since the law expressly states that the marriage must be contracted in good faith, the opinion of Cappello, who maintains that supervenient good faith is sufficient, seems untenable.[37] Ciprotti notes that supervenient good faith may render an invalid marriage putative when such a marriage remains really invalid after it has been seemingly convalidated. The good faith must, of course, be present at the time of the apparent convalidation.[38] Since

[33] Brennan, *The Simple Convalidation of Marriage* The Catholic University of America, Canon Law Studies, n. 102 (Washington, D. C.: The Catholic University of America, 1937), p. 115.

[34] *Ius Matrimoniale,* n. 150; *De Sacramentis,* III, n. 746.

[35] Wernz-Vidal, *Ius Matrimoniale,* n. 607, note 2.

[36] Canon 1015, § 4.

[37] *De Sacramentis,* III, n. 746.

[38] "De prole legitima vel illegitima in iure canonico vigenti," *Apollinaris,* XII (1939), 332. Unless otherwise stated, all references made to Ciprotti refer to this article.

the legitimacy of the children of a putative marriage is effected by a fiction of law (the children of an invalid marriage are illegitimate according to the natural law), it is evident that one of the parties must be baptized if by ecclesiastical law an invalid marriage is to be recognized as a putative marriage.[39] An invalid marriage contracted in infidelity may, however, become putative by the subsequent baptism of one or of both parties.[40]

While all authors admit that at least one of the parties must be in good faith, there is no agreement as to the additional necessity of observing the canonical form of marriage if the parties are bound by it. This question has arisen since the promulgation of the Code; because it is certain that in the old law the celebration of marriage *in facie Ecclesiae* was regularly demanded to render putative a marriage that was otherwise invalid.[41]

The Holy See on various occasions has declared legitimate

[39] Payen, *De Matrimonio,* III, n. 2161.

[40] Cappello, *De Sacramentis,* III, n. 746.

[41] Putativum matrimonium appellatur, quod in se et obiective est nullum propter occultum impedimentum dirimens ab alterutra saltem parte bona fide ignoratum, sed specie tenus validum utpote coram Ecclesia in forma legitima contractum . . . Qua ex notione data consequitur matrimonium putativum esse matrimonium vera figura sive specie matrimonii praeditum; at non vicissim . . . Quare ubicumque forma ecclesiastica de matrimonio viget, tantum ille consensus matrimonialis fidelium in rigore habet speciem matrimonii, qui in forma ecclesiastica datus est; ubi vero forma ecclesiastica ad valide contrahendum non obligat, ea forma in exprimendo consensu matrimoniali ad eundem finem est necessaria, quae iure naturae requiritur et sufficit. Matrimonia vero ab infideli vel haeretico cum parte baptizata sive catholica sive acatholica invalide contracta etiam in locis, ubi vel ipsi haeretici forma ecclesiastica ligantur, fornicariis conjunctionibus non adnumerantur, sed figuram matrimoniorum habere dicenda sunt, si iuxta mores regionum vel infidelium vel haereticorum formam matrimoniorum tenent et legitima reputantur.—Wernz, *Ius Decretalium,* IV, Pars I, n. 29 and note 11; cf. IV, Pars II, n. 682 and note 35; Santi, *Praelectiones Iuris Canonici,* Lib. IV, tit. I, n. 76, 3°; Lib. IV, tit. XVII, n. 3; De Smet, *De Sponsalibus et Matrimonio,* n. 158 and note 3; n. 283 and note 6; Woywood, *A Practical Commentary,* I, n. 979; Cappello, *De Sacramentis,* III, n. 746.

the children of putative marriages which had been contracted either in accordance with the form demanded by the Council of Trent; or when the banns at least had been published (if in such a marriage the substantial ecclesiastical form was not required for validity) ; [42] or when the ecclesiastical form was not observed at all because it was not binding in the place where the marriage was contracted.

Thus in one case the children born of a marriage contracted in accordance with the form demanded by the Council of Trent were declared legitimate although the marriage was actually invalid, because of the presence of the impediment of affinity. The mother of the children knew nothing of the presence of the impediment.[43] In another case a marriage contracted in the presence of a military chaplain, who had obtained special permission from the local Ordinary to assist at the marriage, and three witnesses, was declared to be putative. The child born of the marriage was declared legitimate.[44] A case in which a local Ordinary refused to permit a man to receive Orders because he claimed the man was illegitimate was presented to the Holy See for adjudication. The man's mother had married his father some years after her first husband had joined the army. He was believed dead and when his death had been proved (as it was thought) from legitimate documents the wife married the second husband after the banns of marriage had been published according to the prescriptions of the Council of Trent. Soon after the second marriage the first husband returned and claimed his wife. The Holy See declared that the child born of the wife and the second husband was not illegitimate.[45] In regions where the Tridentine Decree had not been promulgated the observance of the canonical form was not required. Thus the Holy See declared that the children of a marriage contracted by two Lutherans in Brunswick, Germany,

[42] Cf. Wernz, *Ius Decretalium*, IV, Pars II, n. 682.
[43] S. C. C., *Tornacen.*, 24 maii, 1681—*Fontes*, n. 2859.
[44] S. C. C., *Mechlinien.*, 28 Ian, 1730, ad 1—*Fontes*, n. 3361.
[45] S. C. C., *Patavina*, 20 maii 1662, ad 1—*Fontes*, n. 2774.

where the Tridentine Decree had never been published, were legitimate. The father had contracted a prior marriage with another Lutheran without observing the form in Cologne where its observance was demanded. The second wife was ignorant of the husband's former union.[46] The invalidity of a putative marriage may be due either to lack of consent or to the presence of a diriment impediment. Thus the child of a marriage contracted through force and fear was declared legitimate by the Holy See when it annulled the marriage.[47] In another instance the Holy See declared legitimate the child of parents related within the forbidden degrees of consanguinity, because the parents had contracted marriage in good faith.[48]

The opinions of authors who have treated various aspects of the question of putative marriage after the promulgation of the Code may now be considered. According to Chelodi it does not matter whether the invalidity is due to a defect of the form or to the presence of a diriment impediment as long as there is present the *species matrimonii.*[49] The phrase *"ex defectu formae"* as employed by the author seems to signify the lack of form rather than any defect in the form when it is actually observed. This signification seems to be intended because in another place he remarks that it seems to be no longer necessary to celebrate a putative marriage *in facie Ecclesiae.*[50] If the phrase means the lack of form it is difficult to see how he insists on the necessity of the *species matrimonii,* provided, of course, that

[46] S. C. C., *Monasterien* seu *Paderbornen,* 5 sept. 1716—*Fontes,* n. 3158.

[47] " . . . nam puella novissime ab haeresi ad fidem conversa, probabilius leges de matrimonii impedimentis ignoravit, contubernium autem quattuor mensium neque voluntarium fuisse, neque pacificum erui ex tota factorum serie . . .", S. C. C., 17 maii, 1879 et 3 feb., 1880—*ASS,* XII (1880), 403-422.

[48] "Si ignorantia incestus facit, ut filii ex damnato coitu orti non incestuosi, sed naturales censeantur, eodem prorsus modo matrimonium irritum et invalidum legitimos facit liberos non minus quam matrimonium verum si ambo vel alter coniugum in bona fide versetur . . ." S. C. C., *Barcinonen,* 6 maii, et 16 dec., 1893, *ASS,* XXVI (1893), 407-423.

[49] *Ius Matrimoniale,* n. 9.

[50] *Op. cit.,* n. 150.

this latter term is employed in the canonical sense. The *species matrimonii* consists in the expression of consent when the substantial form of marriage is observed. Since the promulgation of the Code the substantial form of marriage for those baptized in the Catholic Church and for those converted to it is that given in canon 1094 and the following canons; for all others it is the expression of consent which is sufficient in the natural and civil law.[51]

Wernz-Vidal maintain that an invalid marriage can be putative only if the nullity results from an occult diriment impediment.[52] Their insistence on an occult diriment impediment seems unwarranted, for the law simply states that the existence of the impediment must be unknown to one of the parties. It does not seem necessary that the impediment be occult in the sense that it cannot be proved in the external forum.[53] As has already been noted, there is no agreement among the authors on the question of the necessity of the observance of the canonical form to render an invalid marriage putative. Some authors do not mention the question; others are of the opinion that the observance of the form is no longer necessary; others maintain that it is still required as it was required in the pre-Code legislation.

Gasparri makes no mention of the necessity of observing the form. He adds no comment to the words of canon 1015. § 4.[54] Vermeersch is silent regarding the necessity of observing the form. He merely restates the definition of putative marriage as it is found in the Code.[55] Genicot-Salsmans repeat the definition of the Code. There is no mention of the necessity of

[51] Gasparri, *De Matrimonio,* I, n. 47.

[52] *Ius Matrimoniale,* n. 22.

[53] Canon 1037. Cf. Payen, *De Matrimonio,* III, nn. 134-7, note 1, where the author remarks that those who say the impediment must be occult intend perhaps to signify that it must be occult as far as one of the parties is concerned.

[54] *De Matrimonio,* I, n. 46.

[55] *Theologiae Moralis Principia—Responsa—Consilia* (3. ed., 4 vols., Roma: Pont. Universita Gregoriana, 1933), III, n. 687.

observing the form.[56] Petrovits omits all mention of the form. He says that as long as the good faith of at least one of the persons concerned perseveres, the putative marriage, according to a long established rule, has all the effects of lawful wedlock, one of which is the legitimacy of the offspring.[57] Vermeersch-Creusen assert that the new definition does not require that a putative marriage have the *species matrimonii.*[58] Wernz-Vidal maintain that the *species matrimonii* is no longer required because it is not mentioned in the Code.[59] De Smet observes in one place that the juridical form is no longer required; in another he asserts that it does not seem to matter if the marriage was not celebrated *in facie Ecclesiae.*[60] Vlaming seems to imply that the observance of the form is required, Although he does not mention the necessity of the form specifically, when treating the question of putative marriage he does assert that an invalid marriage which lacks the *figura matrimonii* has no juridical effect.[61] The attitude of Prümmer has the same implication, for he says the Church will not recognize such a marriage unless it is celebrated publicly and with the approval of the Church.[62] Ayrinhac-Lydon maintain that Catholics who attempt marriage without observing the canonical form do not contract validly, but the union is not properly called an invalid marriage since it lacks the semblance of marriage.[63] They base their argument

[56] *Institutiones Theologiae Moralis* (12. ed. [5 post Codicem Iuris Canonici]. 2 vols., Louvain: Museum Lessianum, 1931), II, n. 456 bis.

[57] *The New Church Law On Matrimony*. The Catholic University of America, Canon Law Studies, n. 6 (Philadelphia: John Joseph McVey, 1919), n. 54—It may be remarked incidentally that the author is not altogether accurate when he attributes all the effects of lawful wedlock to putative marriage.

[58] *Epitome,* II, n. 277.

[59] *Ius Matrimoniale,* n. 22, note 14.

[60] *De Sponsalibus et Matrimonio,* n. 158, note 3; n. 283.

[61] . . . Matrimonium, ipsa matrimonii figura carens, omni effectu iuridico destituitur, adeo ut in foro ecclesiastico prorsus despiciatur."—*Praelectiones Iuris Matrimonii,* I, n. 56.

[62] *Vademecum Theologiae Moralis* (2. et 3 ed., Friburgi Brisgoviae: Herder et Co., 1923), n. 837.

[63] *Marriage Legislation,* n. 9.

that such a union is not to be considered even an invalid marriage on the response given by the Code Commission on March 12, 1929. The Commission had been asked: Whether by virtue of canon 1078 the impediment of public propriety arises from the mere so-called civil act of marriage between the persons mentioned in canon 1099, par. 1, independently of the fact of cohabitation. The Commission answered in the negative.[64] The impediment of public propriety arises from an invalid marriage, whether consummated or not, and from public or notorious concubinage.[65] Since the consideration of concubinage was expressly excluded from the question proposed, the response of the Code Commission that a civil marriage of persons bound to observe the form does not give rise to the impediment is interpreted by Ayrinhac-Lydon to mean that such a union is not even an invalid marriage. Hence, strictly taken according to their opinion such a union cannot be regarded as a putative marriage.

Cappello observes that nowhere in the Code is civil marriage referred to as a *matrimonium invalidum.* It is always designated as *matrimonium civile.*[66]

Payen holds that the opinion which demands the observance of the form is perhaps the more common opinion. He adds, however, that the other opinion is truly probable. It is, he states, based on the silence of the Code.[67]

Cappello says that the opinion which requires that the form be observed is *per se* and generally considered more probable and therefore to be observed in practice. He grants that in a particular case, on account of the peculiar circumstances of place and persons, there is no doubt that a marriage may be putative even if it is not celebrated *in facie Ecclesiae* He cites in confirmation of his opinion Chelodi, De Smet, and Wernz-Vidal, whose opinions have already been given.[68]

[64] *AAS,* XXI (1929), 170; Vermeersch-Creusen, *Epitome,* II, n. 361.

[65] Canon 1078.

[66] *De Sacramentis,* III, n. 543.

[67] *De Matrimonio,* III, n. 134-7.

[68] *De Sacramentis,* III, n. 746.

The arguments advanced in defense of the opinion requiring the observance of the form are according to Cappello: (1) a marriage to be putative had to be celebrated *in facie Ecclesiae* according to the pre-Code legislation; (2) the Code has seemingly made no change in this matter and according to the rules of canon 6, 2°, 3°, 4° and canon 23 the former law still obtains; (3) it is almost inconceivable that one or both parties bound to the form would not know of the nullity of a marriage contracted without observing it.[69]

With regard to the first argument there is no disagreement, as it is certain both from the decisions of the Holy See and from the works of approved authors already cited that according to pre-Code legislation a marriage to be putative had to be celebrated *in facie Ecclesiae.*

With regard to the second argument canon 6, 2°, affirms that those canons which restate old law in its entirety must be interpreted in accordance with the old law, and hence the interpretations already given by approved authors are to be followed in the interpretation of these laws of the Code. It seems obvious that if the new law (canon 1015, par. 4) were merely a restatement of the old law there would be no controversy.

Canon 6, 3°, states that those canons which agree only in part with the old law must be interpreted according to the old law in the part in which they agree with it; in the parts in which they differ from it, they must be interpreted according to the meaning of the words employed. Appeal to this provision of canon 6 seems futile because it appears that in it the legislator had in mind a law which agrees in part and disagrees in part with the old law. The new law certainly agrees in part with the old law, but it does not disagree with it in the sense contemplated in number 3, for the Code is silent regarding a provision which was certainly contained in the old law.

Canon 6, 4°, decrees that in case of doubt whether some provision differs from the old law, the old law must be followed. Recourse to this number is not generally admitted by the au-

[69] *Loc. cit.*

thors under the present circumstances because where there is a doubtful omission of any prior provision or only a doubtfully implicit insertion, then the continuity of such a provision must not be asserted on the grounds of canon 6, 4°.[70]. Canon 23 states that in the case of a doubt whether the former law has been revoked, the repeal of the law is not to be presumed, but the more recent law is to be as far as possible, drawn into the juridical orbit of the prior law and harmonized with it. It is admitted that the preexisting law enjoys the favor of the law; it is in possession and must be observed unless its abrogation is evident.[71] It has always been a legal maxim, too, that a change of the law and, what is more, its abrogation or revocation is a thing odious in law.[72]

The provisions of canon 23 taken by themselves would certainly strengthen the opinion which requires the observance of the canonical form for the existence of a putative marriage. However, in view of the silence of some authors, the denial of others, and the various degrees of insistence on the necessity of the form by those who require it, it does not seem unreasonable to suggest that there is a doubt of law regarding the necessity of observing the form. Even though canon 23 is employed to strengthen the opinion demanding the form, it must be noted that this canon can come under canon 15, which rules that all laws which contain invalidating and disqualifying clauses lose their binding force in a doubt of law.[73]

[70] Vermeersch-Creusen, *Epitome,* I, n. 56; Van Hove, *De Legibus Ecclesiasticis* (Mechliniae-Romae: H. Dessain, 1930), n. 65.

[71] Cicognani, *Canon Law* (Translation by Joseph M. O'Hara and Francis Brennan, 2. ed., Philadelphia: The Dolphin Press, 1935), 634.

[72] Ojetti, *Commentarium in Codicem Iuris Canonici* (4 vols., Romae: Apud Aedes Universitatis Gregorianae, 1927-1931), I, 160.

[73] Cicognani, *Canon Law,* 634; Van Hove states: "Non tamen ita urgendum est principium, (can. 23) ut sit retinenda lex antiqua quamdiu invicte non probatur ejus revocatio vel modificatio. Quamvis revocatio non sit absolute certa, potest habere pro se rationes tam momentosas, ut admitti possit, et proinde obligatio legis anterioris, quia dubia, fit nulla (can. 15)."—*De Legibus Ecclesiasticis,* n. 351.

With regard to the third argument offered by Cappello, it is difficult to see how any argument for the necessity of observing the form can be based on the almost inconceivable ignorance of one or both of the parties If the form is required, the obligation is created by the law and the observance of the form will be demanded, unless it is expressly declared otherwise, independently of the knowledge or ignorance of one or both parties.[74]

The conclusion seems justified, then, in practice that because of the doubt of law the canonical form need not be observed in order to render an invalid marriage putative, provided one of the parties is in good faith. It must be noted that the authors who do not require the form, do not at the same time presume good faith in those persons who, though bound by the form, contract marriage without observing it. Wernz-Vidal, for example, go as far as to say that in such cases bad faith is presumed. If a person bound to the form is inculpably ignorant of the necessity of observing it, he may contract a putative marriage without the observance of the canonical form for the contraction of a valid marriage.[75] On the other hand, Cappello, who maintains that the opinion demanding the form is more probable, says that in such a case the marriage *per se* would not be putative because according to canon 16 ignorance of the law is not presumed; *per accidens,* if and in so far as good faith is proved, the marriage can be putative.[76]

The assertion of Petrovits that a putative marriage is an invalid contract in which the pseudo-married parties are publicly reputed as husband and wife is misleading, if it is intended to mean that the parties must be publicly reputed as husband and wife to render a marriage putative.[77]

The common opinion relative to the marital status of the par-

[74] Canon 16, § 1.

[75] *Ius Matrimoniale,* n. 22, note 14; ". . . attamen aegre aderit bona fides apud catholicos, forman celebrationis negligentes . . ."—De Smet, *De Sponsalibus et Matrimonio,* n. 158, note 3.

[76] *De Sacramentis,* III, n. 746.

[77] *The New Church Law On Matrimony,* n. 54.

ties in an invalid marriage has no effect on the putative character of the marriage. Thus the invalid marriage of two parties in bad faith is not putative, even though the invalidity is unknown to everyone but themselves.[78] Finally, it, should be noted that the children who are conceived in or born of a putative marriage will always remain legitimate, even if in the course of time the good faith of both parties has ceased and the marriage itself has been declared null and void by the competent ecclesiastical authority.[79]

C. Marriage Enjoys the Favor of the Law

After this consideration of the requisites for a valid and putative marriage the favor of the law which marriage enjoys may now be noted The law expressly declares that marriage enjoys the favor of the law; therefore, in cases of doubt the validity of the marriage must be upheld until the contrary is demonstrated, except for such cases whose circumstances subject them to the regulation of canon 1127.[80]

It is not intended here to discuss this question in detail, since such a discussion would be beyond the scope of this study and, besides, the question has already been treated *ex professo* by Manning.[81] For the purpose at hand it will suffice to discuss the workings of the principle, "*in dubio standum est pro valore matrimonii,*" with regard to the question of legitimacy. Hence it may be said that all marriages which have the *species matrimonii* enjoy the favor of the law.[82]

The favor of the law operates either when there is a positive doubt concerning the fact of the celebration of a marriage

[78] Cappello, *De Sacramentis,* III, n. 746.

[79] Cappello, *op. cit., loc. cit.*

[80] Canon 1014.

[81] *Presumptions of Law in Marriage Cases.* The Catholic University of America, Canon Law Studies, n. 94 (Washington, D. C.: The Catholic University of America, 1935), pp. 53-67.

[82] Gasparri, *De Matrimonio,* I, n. 18; Vlaming, *Praelectiones Iuris Matrimonii,* I, n. 60 bis; Payen, *De Matrimonio,* III, n. 119-23; Manning, *op. cit.,* p. 59.

already "in possession" or when there arises a positive doubt regarding the validity of a marriage subsequent to its actual celebration.[83]

A marriage is said to be "in possession" when the parties in good faith think that they are living in a true and legitimate marriage and when no one is scandalized by the union because it is regarded as legitimate.[84]

In answer to a question proposed by the Vicar Apostolic of Central Oceania (Oceanica) the Holy Office on December 18, 1872, declared that a missionary would be wrong if he would apply the principle *standum est pro invaliditate matrimonii* to the marriages of infidels if it happened that such marriages were "in possession". Such marriages were to be presumed valid until the contrary was pròved.[85]

The favor of the law obtains until the second sentence of nullity has been handed down.[86] With regard to the status of the children of a marriage which is attacked on the grounds of invalidity the following may be noted: (1) If the invalid marriage was contracted in good faith by at least one of the parents, thén the children who were born or conceived of such a marriage before the good faith has ceased to exist are legitimate and will remain so always; (2) If both parents were in bad

[83] Vermeersch-Creusen, *Epitome*, II, n. 279; Cappello, *De Sacramentis*, III, n. 51; Wernz-Vidal, *Ius Matrimoniale*, n. 44; Chelodi, *Ius Matrimoniale*, n. 7.

[84] ". . . haereticorum matrimoniis applicabile esse principium, quod etiam in fidelium matrimoniis aptatur, scilicet: In dubio standum esse pro validitate matrimonii, praesertim quando constat matrimonium fuisse contractum. Imo etiam si hoc non constaret, sed matrimonium possessionem pro se ostendere posset, quod verificatur quando coniuncti bona fide putant se in vero et legitimo coniugio vivere, et ceteri nullum ex illa coniunctione scandalum patiuntur, quia arbitrantur eam esse legitimam: etiam in hoc casu praedictum principium valeret, et ab eodem recedere non liceret"—Instructio S. Officii 25 ian. 1877, ad Ep. Nesquallien (Seattle)—*Collectanea S. Congregationis de Propaganda Fide* (2 vols., Romae: Typographia Polyglotta S. C. de Propaganda Fide, 1907), II, n. 1465, 2°.

[85] *Collectanea*, II, n. 1392.

[86] Canon 1987.

faith from the beginning, the children will be legitimate, even though the bad faith is not occult, provided the parents cannot, because of lack of proof, establish to the satisfaction of the ecclesiastical tribunals the nullity of their marriage. Such a case will be extremely rare. Cappello says that the occult bad faith of the parents will not harm the legitimacy of the children in the external forum; and since the bad faith in such circumstances is always or almost always occult, it follows that on account of this the children will be regarded as legitimate in practice.[87] It is addmitted that in such cases the children would be regarded as legitimate in the external forum. The reason advanced by Cappello for regarding the children as legitimate seems to be incorrect. He bases the legitimacy of the children on the occult nature of the parents' bad faith. Canon 1014 would seem to offer the correct reason. In view of the same canon there seems to be no reason for excluding children of parents whose bad faith is not occult.

(3) Children of a marriage contracted in bad faith by both parents who later establish the fact of nullity are regarded as legitimate in virtue of the presumption of law of the validity of marriage. However when the fact of nullity is demonstrated, the presumption of law yields to the truth and the children must be regarded as illegitimate. This is so because they can claim none of the titles to legitimacy. (1) the valid marriage of their parents; (2) the putative marriage of their parents; (3) the presumption of law of the validity of their parents' actually invalid marriage. Once the nullity of the marriage is proved this presumption of law is no longer operative.

It may be noted here that a marriage which was not accused during the lifetime of both parties cannot be accused after the death of either party, or of both, but is presumed valid in law in such manner that against this presumption no proof is admitted, except when the question arises incidentally.[88]

According to Coronata the reason of the provision of this

[87] *De Sacramentis,* III, n. 746.

[88] Canon 1972.

canon is the protection of the legitimacy of the children and of their rights of inheritance, wherefore, although an attack on a marriage may be admitted with some difficulty after the death of either party, a cause which turns out in favor of the legitimacy of the chilldren is admitted with less difficulty.[89] Manning, after discussing the nature of the presumption contained in canon 1972 says it seems more correct to state that the legislator has inserted this canon only as a prohibition. It has, he maintains, the effect of the Anglo-Saxon estoppel, based apparently on the principle "De mortius nil nisi bonum." However, because it may be necessary indirectly to investigate a marriage dissolved by the death of one or both parties to determine legitimacy or succession, the law permits an investigation, or an incidental attack on an otherwise closed affair.[90]

The exception mentioned in canon 1014 is that in doubtful cases the law favors the privilege of the Faith.[91] The privilege of the Faith refers to the liberty enjoyed by the sincere convert in doubtful cases, i.e., when the conditions of the Pauline Privilege are not all certainly present, e.g., when it is doubtful whether the unbaptized consort has really departed, or whether the interpellations were validly made, or whether one of the consorts was really baptized on the occasion of his marriage with the infidel.[92]

The Holy Office has answered two queries on the subject of doubtful baptism. The questions proposed were: (1) Whether in a marriage contracted by two non-Catholics who are doubtfully baptized, in case of an insoluble doubt regarding baptism, either party upon conversion to the Faith may be allowed the use of the Pauline Privilege in virtue of canon 1127 of the Code of Canon Law; (2) Whether in a marriage contracted between a party who is not baptized and a non-Catholic party who is

[89] *Institutiones Iuris Canonici* (5 vols., [Vol. I-II, 2. ed.] Taurini. Marietti, 1933-1939), III, n. 1488.

[90] *Presumptions of Law in Marriage Cases,* p. 24.

[91] Canon 1127.

[92] Ayrinhac-Lydon, *Marriage Legislation,* n. 301.

doubtfully baptized, in case of an insoluble doubt regarding baptism, the Ordinaries can allow to either party upon conversion to the Faith, the use of the Pauline Privilege in virtue of canon 1127. The answers given were: (1) In the negative; (2) Recourse must be had to the Holy Office in each case.[93]

By the provisions of canon 1014 a marriage which is invincibly doubtful must be regarded as valid, as long as the favor of the Faith does not require that such a marriage be regarded as null for the purpose of permitting the convert spouse to contract a new marriage with a Catholic; on the contrary, because of canon 1127 that provision of law stated in canon 1014 yields to the favor of the Faith in so far as a doubtful marriage may be held invalid, if the convert spouse wishes to enter a new marriage with a Catholic.[94]

D. Legitimate Children According to Canon 1114

Legitimi sunt filii concepti aut nati ex matrimonio valido vel putativo. . .

Children are legitimate in Canon Law when they are conceived or born of a valid or putative marriage. Since the requisities for valid and putative marriage have already been considered, it remains only to investigate the questions of the conception and the birth of children from such marriages. It has already been pointed out that only those children are legitimate in the natural law who have been conceived in a valid marriage of their parents.[95]

Canon law, however, by a legal fiction extends the status of legitimacy to children who, although they are born of a valid marriage, have nevertheless been conceived outside of such a marriage. It also declares legitimate such children as are either conceived in or born of the putative marriage of their parents.[96] Those children who are born of a valid marriage

[93] S. Officium, *Decretum*, 10 iunii 1937, *AAS*, XXIX (1937), 305; cf. Cappello, *De Sacramentis*, III, n. 788.

[94] Cappello, *De Sacramentis*, III, n. 788.

[95] *Supra*, p. 13.

[96] Wernz-Vidal, *Ius Matrimoniale*, n. 610; Payen, *De Matrimonio*, III,

though they were not conceived in it, or also those who are conceived in or born of a putative marriage, are known not to be legitimate according to the natural law, but the legislator grants them the status of juridic legitimacy. The just cause which motivates the legislator is the good which accrues to the children, their parents, and society.

Canon 1114 states that the children conceived in a valid or a putative marriage are legitimate. It is evident, therefore, that the conception of such children must take place after the celebration of their parents' marriage and must be the result of the legitimate use of the parents' marriage. Hence, if any condition has been placed to the marital consent and not withdrawn, the right to use the marriage must be determined according to the provisions of canon 1092. The conception must occur during the marriage, not subsequent to its dissolution, as is also evident. If the conception occurs in a putative marriage it is necessary that the good faith of at least one of the parties persevere until the time of the conception. If the conception of a child occurs after both parties have become certain of the nullity of their marriage the child cannot be regarded as having been conceived of a putative marriage. If the conception has occurred in a valid marriage the child will be legitimate even if the conjugal life of its parents has been dissolved before the birth of the child for any reason, e.g., death, separation; and if the conception has occurred in a putative marriage the child is legitimate even though it is born after both parents have become certain of the nullity of their marriage and consequently are no longer living in a putative marriage.

The canon states further that the children born of—even if not conceived in—a valid or a putative marriage are legitimate. If the marriage of which the child is born is a valid marriage, then the birth of the child must occur during the marriage, and not after its dissolution. This is true if the child has been

n. 2160; according to the definition of Alciatus a legal fiction is a rule of law which assumes as true, for a just cause, something which is false, but not impossible.—Cicognani, *Canon Law,* 537.

conceived outside of marriage. If the marriage is putative, then the child must be born before the good faith of both parents has ceased to exist. This is true when the child's conception has occurred before the celebration of its parents' putative marriage.

According to Ciprotti the terms *"conceived"* and *"born"* complement each other: for children conceived during marriage may be born after the marriage has been dissolved; children born during a marriage may have been conceived before the celebration of the marriage.[97]

The legitimate status of children comprehended under the term *nati* in canon 1114 is assured in spite of the provision of canon 1115, § 2. which merely states that children born at least six months after the celebration of marriage or within ten months of the dissolution of conjugal life are presumed to be legitimate. It is evident that a child born during a marriage but within six months of the celebration of the marriage is not presumed legitimate according to canon 1115, § 2. However, if a child is born within six months of the time of the celebration of its parents' valid or putative marriage it is legitimate because it has been born though not conceived of a vaild or putative marriage. Its birth in such a marriage gives it a title to legitimacy recognized in Canon law. De Smet, therefore is incorrect in maintaining that children born of a marriage are illegitimate if they are born within six months of the time of the celebration of the marriage. It appears that he does not distinguish between what the law requires for legitimacy and the presumption which the law has created in canon 1115, § 2.[98]

Woywood in one place says it suffices for legitimacy that the child be born in legitimate wedlock. In another place, however,

[97] *Apollinaris,* XII (1939), 333.

[98] Plerique auctores censent, et nos ipsi hucusque censuimus, prolem haberi ab Ecclesia uti legitimam, modo nata fuerit matrimonii tempore: retracto scil. per fictionem iuris matrimonio, momento nativitatis existente, usque ad momentum conceptionis . . . Quam sententiam non possumus componere cum citato tenore can. 1115, § 2—*De Sponsalibus et Matrimonio,* n. 282, note 3.

he observes that there is some difficulty in determining whether a child is legitimate, if a married woman gives birth to a child within less than six months after her marriage.[99] He too fails to distinguish between the requisites for legitimacy and the presumption stated in Canon 1115 § 2.

The term *nati* must be understood also in, this sense, namely, that a child born of a valid or putative marriage, though conceived outside of such a marriage, is really legitimate, and not merely legitimated by the subsequent marriage of its parents, as Knecht maintains.[100]

If this opinion were true, then a child which was born of, but not conceived in, a putative marriage whose nullity resulted from a continued diriment impediment, would be illegitimate, because the requisites demanded to effect legitimation by subsequent marriage would be lacking.[101] Canon 1114 states simply that a child born of a putative marriage is legitimate.

It may be noted here that according to the general rule a child conceived in or born of a valid or putative marriage is legitimate even though the marriage is illicit.[102]

Ciprotti says that it is not clear whether a child conceived before marriage and born after the dissolution of marriage is legitimate. According to the provisions of canon 1114 it would seem that such a child whose father dies after the marriage has been celebrated but before the child is born is illegitimate. Such a child is neither conceived in nor born of a vaild or putative marriage. Neither can such a child be said to be legitimated by the subsequent marriage of its parents, as canon 1116 deals with

99 *A Practical Commentary,* I, nn. 1147, 1149.

100 . . . Nach diesem Rechte wird also, wenn z. B. der Gatte A. mit seiner Magd ein Kind C zeugt und seine Frau B. noch vor der Geburt des C. stirbt, durch die Ehe des Witwers mit der Magd das in materiellen und formellem Ehebruch erzeugte Kind C. legitimiert."—*Handbuch des katholischen Eherechts* (Freiburg im Breisgau: Herder and Co., 1928), p. 679, note 8.

101 The requisites for subsequent marriage and legitimation will be discussed in their proper place. Cf. pp. 125-126.

102 Gasparri, *De Matrimonio,* II, n. 1112.

children already born before their parents contract marriage.[103] Ciprotti is evidently correct in maintaining that it would seem that a child conceived and born in such circumstances is not legitimate according to the words of canon 1114. This, however, does not appear to be reason enough for hesitating to decide in favor of the legitimacy of a child when such circumstances are verified. Two considerations incline one towards a decision in favor of the child's legitimacy: (1) When the legislator makes a law he has in mind those cases which happen most frequently, and not those which are of rare or fortuitous occurrence. Since it is evident from human experience that the death of the husband is unusual soon after marriage, it can safely be deduced that the legislator has in mind those ordinary cases where marriage will continue for some time. (2) In the circumstances under discussion it seems necessary to have recourse to the intention of the legislator. The intention of the legislator relative to the whole question of legitimacy is well known. Everything possible is done to assure the legitimacy of children.[104]

In view of the extraordinary and unusual circumstances which are verified in the case under consideration, and because of the legislator's intention in the matter of legitimacy, it seems reasonable to conclude that, even though the terminology of canon 1114 would seem to exclude the child from legitimacy, in view of the spirit of the law such a child seems entitled to the status of legitimacy.

E. The Exception to the General Law of Canon 1114

. . . *nisi parentibus ob solemnem professionem religiosam vel susceptum ordinem sacrum prohibitus tempore conceptionis fuerit usus matrimonii antea contracti.* . .

This exception to the general rule states that children born of or conceived in a valid marriage are illegitimate if at the time of their conception the use of their parents' marriage, con-

[103] *Apollinaris,* XII (1939), 334.

[104] Cf. canon 18; Cicognani, *Canon Law,* 615.

tracted before, was prohibited because at least one of the parents had made Solemn Profession or the father had received Sacred Orders.

The Sacred Orders are Priesthood (including the Episcopate), Diaconate, and Subdiaconate.[105] A solemn vow is one that is recognized by the Church as such. Such a vow has the effect of invalidating acts which of their nature are in direct conflict with the import of the vow.[106]

The case contemplated will be extremely rare today, because unless a dispensation which is only rarely granted is obtained, a married person cannot be validly admitted to a novitiate while the other party to the marriage is still living.[107] The other party must consent in such cases before the dispensation will be granted. After a novitiate is completed it is necessary that temporary vows be taken for at least three years before Solemn Profession can be made validly.[108] As regards the reception of Sacred Orders it must be remembered that married men are impeded from receiving them while their wife is living.[109] In such cases the consent of the wife will be required. The necessity of invoking the exception contained in the canon will then be very rare, both because of the rarity of the concession of dispensations in such cases and also because of the time which must necessarily elapse before the making of Solemn Profession or the reception of Sacred Orders.[110] Should a dispensation have been granted, it seems that because of the circumstances the possibility of the use of the marriage would be slight.[111]

105 Canon 949.

106 Canons 1308, § 2; 579.

107 Canon 542, 1°.

108 Canons 572, § 2; 574, § 1.

109 Canon 987, 2°.

110 Non potest igitur iam esse locus inductae exceptioni, nisi quando quis professus est aut ordines suscepit ex dispensatione pontifica. Unde liquet parum in praxi attentendam illam exceptionem—De Smet, *De Sponsalibus et Matrimonio*, n. 283, note 7.

111 . . . etiam in hypothesi dispensationis desuper concessae, vix cogitari adhuc potest matrimonii usus elapso toto tempore illo, quod professioni

The question may be asked whether a child is illegitimate if the parents have been forbidden to use the marriage at the time of the child's conception because of a simple vow to which the Holy See has added the force of invalidating a subsequent marriage.[112]

It may be remarked that many canonists do not even mention this question. The only example of such a vow to which is attached the effect of nullifying a subsequent marriage is the simple vow of chastity taken by Jesuit scholastics after the novitiate of two years has been completed. This vow has the effect of invalidating marriage as long as the person bound by it is not legitimately dismissed from the Society.[113] Harrigan maintains that the simple profession of the Jesuits does forbid the use of a marriage previously contracted, in the same way that the use of marriage is forbidden to those who have made solemn profession i.e. that such use if conception results would render the child illegitimate.[114] Blat remarks that only Solemn Profession is comprehended in the exception. He excludes a simple profession which invalidates a subsequent marriage.[115] This exception of canon 1114 states that the child will be illegitimate if the parents were forbidden the use of the marriage because of solemn profession. It does not say nor does it seem correct to infer that it contemplates simple profession to which is attached the power of nullifying a subsequent marriage. The words *antea contracti* must be kept in mind. It seems reasonable to maintain that a simple vow which invalidates subsequent marriage does not affect a prior marriage except in the sense that

emittendae ordinive suscipiendo ex lege canonica necesse est praecedat—Vlaming, *Praelectiones Iuris Matrimonii,* II, n. 681 nota.

[112] Canon 1073.

[113] Vlaming, *Praelectiones Iuris Matrimonii,* I, n. 303; Creusen-Garesche, *Religious Men and Women in the Code* (3. Eng. ed. by Ellis, Milwaukee: The Bruce Publishing Co., 1940), n. 242.

[114] *Radical Sanation,* p. 63.

[115] *Commentarium Textus Codicis Iuris Canonici* (6 vols., Romae: Ex Typographia Pontificia In Instituto Pii IX, 1921-1927), III, Pars I, n. 522.

it renders the use of the marriage illicit. It does not follow, however, that the illicit use of the marriage will render a child illegitimate. It has already been stated that an illicit marriage does not render a child illegitimate.[116] It seems evident, then, that the illicit use of a marriage by persons having the vow of chastity will not render a child illegitimate, provided only that the use of the marriage has not been prohibited on account of solemn profession strictly understood. This view is maintained by Ciprotti, who bases his opinion on canon 19, which states that laws which decree a penalty or restrict the free exercise of one's right or establish an exception to the law, are subject to strict interpretation.[117]

To show further that the simple profession of the Jesuits, even though it invalidates marriage, is not regarded in law as solemn profession, it can be said that should a person who has made such profession attempt marriage, the marriage would certainly be invalid, but the person bound by the simple vow would not incur the penalties which a religious in solemn vows would incur should he attempt marriage. The case would, of course, be different if the person in simple vows should happen to be in major Orders at the same time.[118]

Finally, to constitute the exception the canon states that the use of the marriage must be forbidden at the time of the child's conception and not also during the period of gestation, or at the time of the child's birth.[119] On the other hand, the concession of a dispensation from the obligations of Holy Orders and Solemn Profession after the child has already been conceived in such circumstances will not render the child legitimate, as it is evident that a child conceived of the valid or putative marriage of its parents at a time when the use of their marriage was forbidden comes under the exception established by this canon.

Another question may possibly arise concerning this exception

[116] *Supra*, p. 87.

[117] *Apollinaris* XII (1939), 335.

[118] Canon 2388, § 1; Gasparri, *De Matrimonio*, I, n. 633.

[119] Cappello, *De Sacramentis*, III, n. 747.

to the general rule governing legitimacy, viz., whether the good faith of the parties would contribute to the legitimacy of a child conceived when the use of the marriage is forbidden. Chelodi is of the the opinion that even in such a case the good faith of one of the parties will benefit the child just as it does in a putative marriage.[120] Cappello is of the same opinion.[121] Payen insists that for the exception to obtain it is necessary that both the father and mother be in bad faith at the time of the child's conception.[122] Blat is evidently of the same mind because he holds that both parents must transgress the prohibition formally.[123]

It seems difficult to see how it is at all possible to have good faith regarding the prohibition to use the marriage in the case wherein one or both parties have been solemnly professed or wherein the hubsand has received Sacred Orders. It has already been shown that a married person must obtain a dispensation from the Holy See and must have the permission of the other party to the marriage before making solemn profession or receiving Sacred Orders. The mutual permission granted if both make Solemn Profession or if the wife makes Solemn Profession and the husband receives Sacred Orders or the permission of the party who elects to remain in the world granting to the other the option to make Solemn Profession or to receive Sacred Orders can reasonably be presumed to have been given with the realization that the future use of the marriage is absolutely forbidden. On the other hand, it is certain that the husband who makes Solemn Profession or receives Sacred Orders must swear that the obligations of the state of life chosen are known and understood.[124] In the case of the wife who wishes to make Solemn Profession the law demands expressly that she must know what she is doing when

[120] *Ius Matrimoniale,* n. 150.

[121] *De Sacramentis,* III, n. 747.

[122] *De Matrimonio,* III, n. 2161.

[123] . . . nisi parentibus, idest; utrique coniugi saltem propter formalem cooperationem transgressionis . . . *Commentarium,* III, Pars I, n. 522.

[124] *AAS,* XXIII (1931), 120; XXIV (1932), 74.

she binds herself by profession.[125] In view of all these factors it remains difficult to see how there can be good faith regarding the prohibition to use the marriage after one or both have made Solemn Profession or the husband has received Sacred Orders.

Ciprotti maintains that if the use of the marriage has been forbidden the good faith of the parents will not help the legitimacy of the child at all. This is evident, he remarks, from the words of the law, and especially because the exception is made not only regarding a valid marriage but also regarding a putative marriage: moreover, he says, the words of the law are general, neither do they distinguish whether the parents knew of the prohibition or were unaware of it. Therefore the favor set up regarding putative marriage cannot be extended by analogy because here the circumstances are not the same and therefore there is no basis for analogy.[126]

Ciprotti, however, fails to distinguish between the idea of the prohibited use of a valid or putative marriage *contracted before* and the idea of the possibility of a later putative marriage between a person in solemn vows or in Sacred Orders with a person who is in good faith. Continuing his argument Ciprotti says it also follows that a child begotten of a putative marriage which is null on account of the impediment of Sacred Orders or of Solemn Profession is certainly legitimate if it is conceived either after a dispensation from these impediments has been granted, provided also that the good faith of at least one or the other party has persevered, or, if the good faith has ceased, provided that the child is conceived after the convalidation of the marriage; but the child is not legitimate if it is conceived after a putative marriage has been entered into but before a dispensation has been granted even if it is born after the dispensation.[127]

One would presume that Ciprotti treating of the exception contained in canon 1114, would have in mind a putative marriage

[125] Canon 552, § 2.

[126] *Apollinaris,* XII (1939), 336.

[127] *Loc. cit.*

contracted before the making of a Solemn Profession or the reception of Sacred Orders. Yet he does not refer to a marriage contracted before, but rather to a putative marriage contracted after the making of Solemn Profession or the reception of Sacred Orders. He speaks of a putative marriage which is null on account of the impediment of Sacred Orders or Solemn Profession. It is evident that there cannot be a putative marriage which is null on account of either of these impediments in the case contemplated by the exception stated in the canon. The canon refers only to the use of a marriage contracted prior to either Solemn Profession or Sacred Orders. If the marriage is prior, it cannot be null on account of an impediment which doesn't yet exist in a given case. On the other hand, if the author means that a child conceived of a putative marriage which is null because of the impediments of Sacred Orders or Solemn Profession cannot be legitimate if the conception has occurred before a dispensation has been granted, one cannot agree with him. There is no reason why the good faith of an innocent party who unwittingly contracts marriage with a person bound by the impediment of Sacred Orders or Solemn Profession cannot render such a marriage putative and consequently effect the legitimacy of any children conceived, as long as the innocent party is unaware of the true status of the other party. The law nowhere states that the good faith of one party which renders an invalid marriage putative becomes ineffective when there is question of the impediments of Sacred Orders and Solemn Profession.

Ciprotti observes further that the time of conception of those children (i.e. those who are enumerated in the exception stated) which alone is given consideration in canon 1114 does not agree with the general rule regarding legitimate children, who as has already been explained, are such, even if they have been conceived before marriage, provided that they have been born after the marriage of their parents. It happens therefore that if children are conceived before their parents' marriage when the impediment of sacred Orders or Solemn Profession is present and in the absence of any dispensation to render a valid marriage possible, but are born after marriage, they are legitimate according to the general rule; for the exception of canon 1114 cannot be applied since their conception did not entail any violation of the prohibited use of a marriage earlier contracted for the obvious reason that at the time of the conception the marriage had not yet been entered. As a result a child which is conceived prior to marriage and in the absence of any dispensation that would have made a valid marriage possible for its parents enjoys a more desirable status than a child which is conceived in a valid or putative marriage at a time when the supervenient impediment prohibited the licit use of the marriage.[128]

For in the former case the child will be legitimate in the event that its birth takes place subsequent to the marriage of its parents, while in the latter case the effect of a legitimate status can be procured only by means of a properly authorized act of legitimation.

The author's observation that the consideration solely of the time of the conception of these children does not agree with the general rule seems to be of little importance, as the law makes an exception in their case. Exceptions to the general law of their very nature do not agree with the general law.

It may be concluded now that the following children are legitimate according to canon 1114: (1) children conceived of the valid marriage of their parents, though not born during the marriage; (2) children born at any time during their parents' valid marriage, although they have been conceived before such a marriage; (3) children conceived of the putative marriage of their parents, though born after the marriage has ceased to be putative; (4) children born at any time of the putative marriage of their parents, though conceived before the cele-

[128] ". . . Ita ut huiusmodi filii melius habeantur si ante matrimonium et dispensationem concipiantur, quam si, utique ante dispensationem, sed post matrimonium validum (si nempe impedimentum matrimonio supervenerit) vel putativum"—*Apollinaris*, XII (1939), 336.

bration of such a marriage. It is, of course, evident that children both conceived and born during a valid or putative marriage are legitimate.

According to the exception stated in canon 1114 those children who are conceived or born of a valid or putative marriage the use of which at the time of the children's conception is forbidden to the parents because of their assumption of the obligations of Sacred Orders or Solemn Profession are illegitimate. It seems that good faith regarding the prohibition to use marriage in such cases will not render the children legitimate. In view of what has already been said regarding such cases, it is necessary to insist on the distinction between that good faith which renders an invalid marriage putative, and that which might possibly, though not very probably, be present in the case of parties validly or putatively married, one or both of whom have made Solemn Profession, or when the husband has received Sacred Orders. The opinion of Ciprotti, who seems to maintain that a child conceived of a putative marriage whose nullity results from the impediment of Sacred Orders or Solemn Profession is illegitimate if its conception occurred before the concession of a dispensation, cannot be upheld if the marriage in question is really putative.

F. Artifical Fecundation and Legitimacy

The question of artificial fecundation has in recent years become the object of much discussion. It is interesting to note that the authors when treating this subject confine themselves solely to a discussion of the morality of the various means by which such fecundation is effected. None of them, with the exception of Wernz-Vidal mentions the question of the legitimacy of children whose conception results from artificial fecundation.[129]

It must be noted in the first place that artificial fecundation was condemned by the Holy Office on March 17, 1897. This

[129] *Ius Matrimoniale,* n. 231.

decision was approved and confirmed by Pope Leo XIII (1878-1903) on March 26, 1897.[130]

This condemnation has been interpreted by the authors to include only artificial fecundation strictly so called.[131]

On the other hand artificial fecundation widely so called is regarded as licit.[132]

Canon 1114 declares that children conceived or born of a valid or putative marriage are legitimate. Nothing is said in the law of the method employed to effect conception, but it may reasonably be presumed that the legislator had in mind that conception is ordinarily the result of the natural marital act To determine, then, whether children whose conception has been effected by artificial means may be regarded as legitimate the following considerations may be advanced: (1) The parents must be united in a valid or putative marriage. This absolutely excludes therefore the immoral impregnation of the wife by semen from anyone other than her legal husband. It can be noted here that if the diriment impediment of impotence is present and is recognized as such by the parties their marriage

[130] *ASS*, XXIX (1897), 704.

[131] Fecundatio artificialis *stricte dicta* praesupponit aut pollutionem, aut copulam onanisticam, aut utramque: pollutionem, si ex parvulo vase, post pollutionem at citra copulam, semen colligitur; copulam onanisticam, si, post viri retractum, ex involucro hauritur semen; utramque, si ex aliquo vase, post retractum et pollutionem, semen desumitur. Controversia est num sit fecundatio artificialis *proprie dicta*, si semen ex ipsis testiculis legitimi mariti directe a peritissimo medico colligitur—Payen, *De Matrimonio*, III, n. 2110.

[132] Fecundatio artificialis *late seu improprie dicta* neque pollutionem neque copulam onanisticam praesupponit. Colligitur semen: aut, post copulum rite consummatam, ex ipsa mulieris vagina, quin e vagina extrahatur, aut, licet ibi sit, ut dictum est, controversia, sine copula, et citra pollutionem et delectationem veneream, ex ipsis testiculis legitimi mariti.—Payen, *loc. cit.*, cf. Gasparri, *De Matrimonio*, II, nn. 1094, 1095; Wernz-Vidal, *Ius Matrimoniale*, n. 231; Cappello, *De Sacramentis*, III, nn. 380-384; Chelodi, *Ius Matrimoniale*, n. 70; Vlaming, *Praelectiones Iuris Matrimonii*, I, n. 268; *AER*, XC (1934), 434; Donovan, "Artificial Breeding of Human Infants" —*AER*, XCIV (1937), 423; Kelly, "The Morality of Artificial Fecundation"—*AER*, CI (1939), 109-118.

is neither vaild nor putative. Consequently, even if the conception of a child is successfully effected by means of artificial fecundation the child will not be legitimate.[133] However, it is possible even in a case where the diriment impediment of impotence is present that the good faith of one or both parties will render such a marriage putative. This would be true, it seems, especially in the case where a child has actually been conceived by means of artificial fecundation. (2) It does not matter whether the marriage has been consummated or not, as it is possible to beget children without consummation as it is understood in canon law. Thus the Sacred Roman Rota recommended the granting of a dispensation *super matrimonio rato et non consummato* in a case in which two children had been born of the marriage. It must be noted, however, that the Holy Father thought it inexpedient to grant the dispensation.[134] (3) Relative to the question of artificial fecundation it must be noted that conception properly so called is an act of nature as distinguished from the human act posited by the spouses.[135]

It is not intended here to estimate the moral value of the method employed to effect the conception. As has been observed before, the Holy Office has expressly condemned artificial fecundation strictly so called. The lawfulness of artificial fecundation properly so called is disputed. The lawfulness of artificial fecundation widely so called is generally admitted. The law of canon

[133] Impotentia antecedens et perpetua, sive ex parte viri sive ex parte mulieris, sive alteri cognita sive non sive absoluta sive relativa, matrimonium ipso naturae iure dirimit.—canon 1068, par. 1.

[134] *S. Romanae Rotae Decisiones. quae . . . prodierunt anno* 1909-1932 (24 vols., Romae: Typis Vaticanis, 1912-1940), XVII, 76-92; cf. Vermeersch, *Theologiae Moralis Principia,* IV, n. 67.

[135] Illa ergo coniunctio duplicis elementi spermatazoidis et ovuli est fecundatio seu generatio humana, in qua intervenit actio humana (hominis) et actio naturalis (naturae). In actione hominis principium activum est vir, quatenus per membrum virile in vaginam mulieris penetrat et in ea deponit seu effundit verum semen; principium passivum est femina, quatenus semen effusum recipit in vagina atque hic sistit actio hominis; quae deinde sequuntur sunt actio naturae, quae unice verificantur in muliere.—Wernz-Vidal, *Ius Matrimoniale,* n. 216.

1114 simply requires conception from a valid or putative marriage in order that children be legitimate. It can be concluded therefore that children conceived from a valid or putative marriage by means of licit or illicit artificial fecundation are legitimate. This conclusion seems justified unless the Holy See because of the peculiar circumstances defines the status of such children otherwise.

Article III. The Legal Presumptions of Paternity and Legitimacy

A. *The Legal Presumption of Paternity*

Canon 1115, § 1. *Pater is est quem iustae nuptiae demonstrant, nisi evidentibus argumentis contrarium probetur.*

§ 2. *Legitimi praesumuntur filii qui nati sunt saltem post sex menses a die celebrati matrimonii, vel intra decem menses a die dissolutae vitae coniugalis.*

It has already been shown that a child must be conceived in or born of the valid or putative marriage of its parents to be legitimate according to canon law. The fact that a marriage has been celebrated between the father and the mother can be proved from the marriage register of the parish where the marriage was contracted, or in the case of a marriage of conscience, from the book used to record such marriages in the secret archives of episcopal curia.[136] The record of the marriage contained in the matrimonial register is a public ecclesiastical document and constitutes proof of the fact which it attests.[137] If a record of the marriage does not exist, the fact of its celebration may be proved in other ways, e.g., by the deposition of the parish priest, the witnesses who assisted at the marriage, and other persons who are worthy of credence. It can also be proved through public repute together with the recognition of a child by the parents.[138]

[136] Canons 1103; 1107. Cf. also canons 379; 470.
[137] Canons 1813, § 1, 4°; 1816.
[138] Wernz-Vidal, *Ius Matrimoniale*, n. 613.

In view of the very nature of the relationship the mother of a child is always known. This natural truth was constituted as a principle in Roman law.[139] While it can be said with certainty in view of the record of the marriage and the knowledge of the mother that a child has been born of the wife during marriage, it is not always certain that the child's conception took place during marriage or that the mother's husband is actually the father of the child. It need only be mentioned that if doubts can arise regarding the conception and paternity of a single child, they can certainly arise concerning multiple births, as it is known that in such cases there exists the possibility of having more than one man as the father. To obviate the difficulties which might arise concerning legitimacy due to the time of conception and the paternity of children the law establishes the presumptions found in this canon.

The first of the legal presumptions invoked by canon 1115 is this: He whom the honorable wedlock itself signalizes for paternity is accepted as the father, unless evident arguments furnish contrary proof. Since it is impossible to have apodictic proof of paternity, because nature itself has shrouded the moment of human generation in secrecy, canon law has wisely established this presumption of paternity to safeguard the sanctity of marriage, the good of society, and the peace of families which would otherwise be disturbed.[140] It may be noted here that this presumption has been adopted from Roman law.[141] Since it admits direct contrary proof it is a *praesumptio iuris,* that is, a rebuttable presumption.[142]

The *"iustae nuptiae"* referred to is either a valid or putative marriage, as can be deduced from canon 1114. Hence, in the absence of a valid or putative marriage between the parents the presumption cannot be invoked.

[139] D. (2.4) 5.

[140] S. C. C., *Verulana*, 9 aug. 1884, *ASS*, XVII (1884), 382; *Fontes*, n. 4264.

[141] D. (2.4) 5.

[142] Canon 1826.

The presumption means that a child conceived during marriage is presumed to have been conceived from the use of the marriage, or, in other words, the hubsand is regarded as the father of all the children of his wife unless the contrary is evident.[143] It is not clear whether the legal presumption of paternity operates in the case of a child which had been conceived before its parents contracted marriage but was born during their marriage. Such a child is, of course, legitimate according to canon 1114 if the true father has married the mother.[144] Cappello, Payen, and Chelodi seem to infer that the child must be conceived in the marriage of its parents before the presumption can be employed. This is so because they use the terms husband and wife and not simply father and mother.[145] Gasparri says that a child born of a marriage is presumed to have been born of the use of that marriage, or, in other words, begotten by the husband of the wife.[146] Wernz-Vidal maintain that if the marriage of the parents and the birth of the child from the wife of the husband is evident, the presumption stands. They seem to mean that the child must be conceived during marriage, because when they speak of evident proof against the legal presumption they say that such proof is had if it is proved that the husband has had no relations with the wife during all the period of time necessary for the conception of the child whose paternity is questioned.[147] Ciprotti observes that the presumption refers certainly to a child conceived during marriage. Whether it refers to a child born during marriage but conceived before is not clear. He maintains that from a consideration

[143] Cappello, *De Sacramentis,* III, n. 748; Payen, *De Matrimonio,* III, n. 2163; Chelodi, *Ius Matrimoniale,* n. 150.

[144] Payen, incidentally, seems to err when he says that a child born, though not conceived, of a marriage is legitimate when the husband of the mother, though really he is not the child's father, does not repudiate the child.—At reapse est legitima, si maritus matris, sive est sive non est prolis pater, eam explicite vel implicite agnoverit—*De Matrimonio,* III, n. 2161.

[145] Cf. *supra.*

[146] *De Matrimonio,* II, n. 1113.

[147] *Ius Matrimoniale,* n. 613.

of both paragraphs of this canon it seems that there is no presumption of legitimacy for a child born though not conceived during marriage.[148]

It seems, however that a distinction must be made between the presumption of paternity and the presumption of legitimacy as found in this canon. In view of the fact that the legitimacy of children who are born of though not conceived in the valid or putative marriage of their parents is acknowledged in canon 1114, there must be some presumption (though not stated in the Code) that in the case of such children the true father of the child must marry the mother to effect legitimacy. It is unthinkable that the legislator would intend to rceognize formally the legitimacy of a child born during a marriage of its mother to a man not its father. The law does actually require that a child must be born *ex matrimonio* and merely not *in matrimonio,* to be legitimate if it was conceived before the marriage of its parents.

Manning maintains that any marriage which is "in possession" would indicate paternity, no matter how long or how short a time after the celebration of marriage a child is born. He says that according to the strict interpretation of paragraph 2 of this canon a child born in a marriage could be regarded as illegitimate, i.e., his legitimacy could be questioned. If he was born outside the time limits there stated, while the legal paternity could still be presumed.[149]

In view of the terminology employed and the meaning apparently intended according to the authorities cited it seems correct to say that the legal presumption of paternity can be applied only in those cases where a child has been conceived during a valid or putative marriage. With regard to the presumption of the paternity of a child born during a marriage but conceived before, it may be said that there is a weighty equitable presumption (*praesumptio hominis*), but not, as Maninng says, a strictly legal presumption (*praesumptio iuris*), that the husband of the mother

[148] *Apollinaris,* XII (1939), 340.

[149] *Presumptions of Law in Marriage Cases,* p. 90.

is the child's father. This conclusion seems justified because it can usually be presumed in such cases that it is actually the father of the child who marries the mother.

This presumption is concerned directly with establishing paternity, and not legitimacy. Proof of legitimacy, according to Wanenmacher, entails demonstration that the child derives from the named father and mother, and that the descent was legitimate. When there is no contrary proof, derivation from a husband is presumed, if the derivation from the wife is certain. Full or partial proof of this accrues from documents, witnesses, and from personal presumptions based on the sustentation and education of the child by the named hubsand and wife. Legitimate descent is shown by proof of a valid or putative marriage.[150]

It may be noted here that facts which are presumed by the law itself need no proof. The burden of proof is on those who attack the presumption.[151] In connection with the presumption of paternity it must be remembered that the law also declares that once the parties have lived together after marriage the consummation of the marriage is presumed until the contrary is proved.[152]

As has already been noted, the presumption of paternity can be overthrown by evident arguments to the contrary. It is generally admitted that the only conclusive proof which can be employed to destroy this legal presumption is the impossibility of marital relations between the husband and the wife during all the time when the conception of a child whose paternity is disputed might possibly have occurred.[153]

[150] *Canonical Evidence in Marriage Cases*, n. 160.

[151] Canon 1747, n. 2; cf. Whalen, *The Value of Testimonial Evidence in Matrimonial Procedure.* The Catholic University of America, Canon Law Studies, n. 99 (Washington, D. C.: The Catholic University of America, 1935), pp. 75-76.

[152] Canon 1015, § 2.

[153] Chelodi, *Ius Matrimoniale*, n. 150; Wednz-Vidal, *Ius Matrimoniale*, n. 613; Cappello, *De Sacramentis*, III, n. 748; Vlaming, *Praelectiones Iuris Matrimonii*, II, n. 687; Blat, *Commentarium*, III, Pars I, n. 523; Manning,

The legal presumption of paternity is so strong that it cannot be destroyed while there is any possibility at all that the husband of the mother is the father of her child. This was illustrated in a classical case werein the legitimacy of a child was upheld even though it appeared that the husband and wife had had no relations during the necessary period prior to the child's birth. The facts of the case may be given here, since they are illustrative of the arguments which may be offered for and against the presumption of paternity.

The presumed father and the mother were married in Rome on September 24, 1828. In 1831 the wife returned alone to Veroli while the husband remained in Rome. In 1837 the wife gave birth to a daughter. The child was baptized on February 8, 1837, and since the name of the father was not disclosed to the officiating priest he recorded the child as illegitimate in the Baptismal Register. The child was placed in an orphanage and sent subsequently to Civitella to be reared. Years later, on the occasion of her marriage, she learned the name of her mother, who disclosed to her in a letter of April 29, 1865, which also contained a picture of the presumed father, that the latter had tearfully inquired from a friend whether his daughter had received any education. It was testified that the father had left the Papal States in 1849 and settled in Pisa where he accepted a position as professor. He described himself as unmarried in the list of the professors. The presumed father died on July 24. 1865, and the mother died in 1877. In 1881 the woman gave the name of her mother's husband as her own to a census official in Rome who refused to accept it until the question of her paternity was settled by the ecclesiastical authorities. The woman appealed to the Vicariate of Rome, but apparently nothing was done. She then appealed to the Bishop of Veroli to be declared the legitimate daughter of her mother's husband. The bishop later brought the matter to the attention of the Pope (Leo XIII, 1878-1903), under whose authority an investigation

Presumptions of Law in Marriage Cases, p. 90; Wanenmacher, *Canonical Evidence in Marriage Cases,* n. 535.

was begun. On June 3, 1883, the Bishop of Veroli was ordered to make a more accurate inquiry of witnesses and relatives regarding the question. The bishop could find from a uncle of the petitioner only that the husband had never come to Veroli after the separation in 1831 and had never met his wife. The uncle also declared that the husband had remained outside the Papal States since 1831. This fact was declared untrue by others as far as an uninterrupted absence was concerned. The uncle thought the petitioner illegitimate because she had been baptized as an illegitimate child.

The Congregation declared that the following considerations were opposed to the legitimacy of the petitioner: (1) parochial books constitute proof of the facts which they attest; (2) moreover, as is evident, the baptismal register witnesses to the uncertain paternity of the petitioner and must be upheld until the contrary is proved; (3) the record clearly indicates the mother; (4) the uncle testified under oath that his sister who as though deserted by her husband had returned to Veroli had not been with him since; (5) no one asserted that the husband and wife ever saw each other after 1831; (6) the letter of the mother who mentions her husband as the father does not appear to create any difficulty. (7) the solicitude of the husband regarding his daughter seems strange, because he was so forgetful of his wife that in the authentic record of his death he is called an unmarried man (caelebs Communitatis Pisarum); (8) the presumption of paternity does not seem to help in this case for this presumption must be withheld if the husband has been absent for a long time.

On the other hand, the Congregation declared, the presumption of paternity has such force that it is impossible to retreat from it unless the contrary is proved by the most conclusive arguments such as that of the absence of the husband or his physical impotence. The Congregation declared that: (1) without doubt the petitioner was born during a legitimate marriage; (2) the burden of proof is not on the petitioner but on the person who denies her legitimacy; (3) the necessary proof against legitimacy, seems either to be lacking or to be precluded in this case; (4) the uncle at the time of the mother's return to Veroli was absent in the military service of the Pope and at his return could have heard false reports about his sister's conduct. She had remained away from her husband for a long time and was forced to conceal the birth of the child; (5) the husband demanded that the newly born child be placed in the orphanage before baptism so that no one would know that his daughter had been placed there; (6) the husband celebrated the marriage in Rome so that it would not be known at Veroli; (7) for this same reason he inscribed himself as single in the register of the Professors at Pisa; (8) despite this he used to send money to his wife: (9) he tearfully inquired of a friend regarding the condition of his daughter; (10) moreover it is not certain, and it is denied by some, that he remained always outside the Papal dominions after 1831; (11) the permanent separation of the spouses is not to be presumed because the journey from Rome to Veroli is short and easy and it is possible that the husband and wife met once; (12) finally, although the daughter may not be in the quasi- possession of legitimacy, nevertheless when she proves the marriage of her parents and her own birth (i.e. from the marriage) it must not be objected that she is legally incapable of laying claim to her legitimate filiation.

The Congregation decreed that the illegitimacy of the petitioner was not proved by the most conclusive arguments and held her to be legitimate.[154]

Evident proof against the presumption of paternity is not had from the simple fact that the mother has been unfaithful, for that alone does not prove that the adulterer rather than the husband is the father of the child. Moreover the solemn sworn testimony of a dying mother who is worthy of belief is not evident proof. The reason for this is that there is no case which can be decided by the testimony of one person and because a person admitting his fault in such circumstances is

[154] S. C. C., *Verulana,* 9 Aug. 1884—*ASS,* XVII (1884), 382; *Fontes,* n. 4264.

not to be believed. The same is to be said of the testimony of the adulterer or of both the guilty parties.[155] Gasparri holds the view expressed by the other authors just cited, but with this difference, viz., that if the mother at the time of death admits the adultery under oath such an admission may constitute evident proof against the presumption if the testimony she offers would suffice in the external forum.[156] Wanenmacher says that in cases of the legitimacy of a child Gasparri seems to deny that the joint testimony of a wife and her adulterer constitutes proof of adultery "quia non meretur fidem allegans turpitudinem suam". But it is plain, he maintains, that this principle of Roman law cannot be alleged as an absolute rule, and the judge may properly weigh the testimony of the adulterers according to his discretion.[157] This interpretation of Gasparri's words, however, seems unjustified. It must be remembered that he is speaking of evident proof against the presumption of paternity, and not about establishing the proof of adultery.[158]

According to Ciprotti it must be proved directly that the mother was not able to have relations with her husband during the time when the conception of the child occurred, or that she did not actually have relations with him during that time; or, finally, that she was not able to conceive the child of her husband because at the time of the child's conception the husband was impotent or sterile. Regarding the question of the unfaithfulness of the mother, he maintains, as do the other authors, that neither the fact nor its admission by the mother or also by

155 Canon 1791, § 1; Wernz-Vidal, *Ius Matrimoniale*, n. 613; Vermeersch-Creusen, *Epitome*, II, n. 420; Chelodi, *Ius Matrimoniale*, n. 150; Cappello, *De Sacramentis*, III, n. 748; Papen, *De Matrimonio*, III, n. 2163; Wanenmacher, *Canonical Evidence in Marriage Cases*, n. 535.

156 Imo nec est probatio evidens, si mater, fide dignissima, moriens iuramento id solemniter affirmaverit, *nisi talia profert indicia quae in foro exteriori satis forent.—De Matrimonio*, II, n. 1113.

157 *Canonical Evidence in Marriage Cases*, n. 201.

158 . . . Exinde deducimus nec esse probationem evidentem (i. e. contra praesumptionem) si etiam pater adulter id fassus fuerit.—*De Matrimonio*, II, n. 1113.

the adulterer will of itself destroy the presumption. It can, he says, constitute a weighty indication for eventual proof, but if it is to have full value as complete proof again the presumption in such a case it must be corroborated by unimpeachable evidence that the mother actually conceived the child in adultery and not as a result of the licit relations with her husband.[159]

It may be noted at this point that in a case regarding the legitimacy of a child the mother's acknowldegment of adultery and illegitimacy is not a confession in the judicial sense, since it militates against the rights of a third party, namely, the child.[160]

The Congregation of the Council declared expressly on various occasions that one or both adulterers admitting their crime were not to be believed. Thus in one case wherein it was alleged that the impediment of consanguinity existed between a man and the woman he wished to marry because the mother of the woman testified that she had conceived the girl as a result of the crime of adultery committed with the brother of the man who wished to marry the girl, the Congregation refused to accept the testimony.[161] In another case in which both the husband and wife maintained that a son had been conceived in adultery, and the child was publicly considered as having been conceived by the mother as the result of extra-marital relations, the Congregation in view of the legal presumption of paternity and of the fact that both the baptismal register and the civil record of birth described the child as legitimate, declared him to be such. It ignored the confession of the mother and the pretense of the father and gave no consideration to the public talk of the child's status, which talk, it observed, had been started by the parents.[162] On the other hand the

[159] *Apollinaris* XII (1939), 341.

[160] Canon 1750; Wanenmacher, *Canonical Evidence in Marriage Cases*, n. 170.

[161] . . . Idque adeo verum est, ut neque si mater ipsa, vel uterque parens in mortis periculo adseverent, quempiam ex filiis natum esse extra legitimum coniugii usum, ullatenus eis credit oporteat . . . S. C. C., *Bobien.*, 16 Feb. 1743; *Fontes*, n. 3547.

[162] S. C. C., 27 iunii, 1857—*ASS*, I (1865), 350.

Congregation did declare that the impediment of consanguinity existed between a man and the girl he wished to marry because the mother of the girl had confessed that the girl's conception resulted from the crime of adutlery committed with the man's maternal uncle. It was decided that the impediment existed because the mother had lived with the adulterer during the time when the girl's conception could have occurred.[163]

Since reference has been made to the decisions of the Sacred Congregation of the Council regarding questions of legitimacy, it may be remarked here that since the promulgation of the Apostolic Constitution *"Sapienti consilio"* the competent congregation in these matters is the Sacred Congregation of the Discipline of the Sacraments. The Sacred Penitentiary is competent in the internal forum.[164]

B. *Blood Tests for Paternity*

In recent years much discussion has arisen regarding the value of blood tests to determine paternity. It is obviously beyond the scope of this work to delineate technically the workings of such a test.[165] It may be said that such tests have a negative probative value, because they can prove that a particular man is not the father of a certain child. Even in such a case it has not yet been demonstrated that blood tests are infallible. On the other hand, such tests cannot prove that any man exclusively is the father of a particular child. At most, in such a case, they indicate that any man of a definite blood group may be the father. The Church has decreed nothing officially as yet regarding the admission of the findings of a blood test as proof in her courts. Civil law has not yet uni-

[163] *Thesaurus Resolutionum Sacrae Congregationis Concilii* (167 vols., Romae: 1718-1908), VI (*Pientina,* 20 Martii, 1734), 265-267.

[164] *AAS,* I (1909), 10, 85-87.

[165] Cf. Triebs, *Praktisches Handbuch des geltenden kanonischen Eherechts in Vergleichung mit dem deutschen staatlichen Eherecht* (Breslau: Ostdeutsche Verlagsanstalt, 1933), p. 663; Meister, "Die Bedeutung der Blutprobe fur die Seelsorge."—*Theologisch-praktische Quartalschrift,* LXXX (1927), 314-318. This periodical will be referred to hereafter as *LQS*.

versally accepted the results of blood tests as proof in paternity cases. In the United States only New York, Ohio, Wisconsin, Maine, and New Jersey have laws demanding such tests in paternity suits. It is interesting to note that in a recent case in New Jersey which has a law demanding the test, the court refused to order one.[166]

A blood test was employed recently in Washington, D. C., in an effort to establish paternity. The husband had been sued by his wife for support for herself and her child. The husband contended he was not the child's father. He indicated his willingness to submit to a blood test and although there is no law in the District of Columbia to compel the test the District Court ordered it. The wife refused to comply and the United States Court of Appeals later upheld the court order. The test was finally made and it was decided that it showed nothing incompatible with the husband being the father of his wife's child. The result caused the lawyers in the case to change their views regarding the probative value of the test. The husband's lawyer sought to have the results of the test stricken from the record while the wife's lawyer demanded that the findings be retained.[167]

It is evident from the two cases cited that even in civil law the blood test for paternity is not yet regarded as an established, dependable means of proving paternity. Its results are not accepted without dispute, especially by the party whom it affects adversely. In view of the attitude in civil law towards the reliability of this test, and because of the present inconclusiveness of the test itself, it seems unlikely that the Church would

[166] "In the first ruling of its kind since New Jersey passed a law recognizing blood tests as evidence in paternity litigation, Advisory Master Dougal Herr flatly refused to order one, in an opinion handed down in Elizabeth yesterday. The court, Herr said, has no more right to insist that a person's blood be taken against his will, than it has to order that his appendix be removed. It is 'assault and battery and clearly an invasion of personal privacy,' Herr wrote."—*Times-Herald,* Washington, D. C., October 31, 1940.

[167] *The Washington Post,* Oct. 30, 1940; Nov. 7, 1940; Nov. 14, 1940.

recognize the results of such a test, at least, until such time as science has demonstrated its probative value beyond dispute. It is not the policy of the Church to admit to its jurisprudence legal proofs which do not have a sound basis and which have not stood the test of time. Manning, too, maintains that *ex silentio* it might be concluded that the Church does not accept the results of a blood test for paternity as conclusive proof against the legal presumption of paternity.[168]

The consideration of the presumption of paternity may be concluded by observing that it must be upheld when there is a valid or putative marriage existing between the presumed father and the mother. Further, it seems that the presumption as stated in the canon applies only in those cases where the child has been conceived during the valid or putative marriage of its parents. All the authors consulted, with the exception of Gasparri and Ciprotti, maintain that evident proof is had against the presumption only by the demonstration of the lack of marital intercourse between the husband and the wife during the time necessary for the conception of the child whose paternity is questioned. It seems that the authors when they speak of the absence of relations between the husband and the wife include the case where the husband is impotent. Cappello, Ciprotti, and Manning mention this expressly. Ciprotti mentions also sterility on the part of the husband.[169] That impotence is an evident argument against the presumption is patent. In such a case it must be supervenient impotence, otherwise there would be no valid or putative marriage, if both parties recognized the impediment, and hence there could be no application of the presumption. It is very likely, too, that sterility, as claimed by Ciprotti, if proved would be admitted as an evident argument. This can be gathered from a decision of the Congregation of Council.[170] Gasparri's assertion that the sworn testimony of

[168] *Presumptions of Law in Marriage Cases,* p. 90.

[169] Cappello, *De Sacramentis,* III, n. 748; Ciprotti, *Apollinaris,* XII (1939), 341; Manning, *Presumptions of Law in Marriage Cases,* p. 90.

[170] Constans enim est iuris praesumptio (nisi contrarium doceatur per

the mother who at the time of her approaching death acknowledged her unfaithfulness, constitutes evident proof if the testimony she offers would suffice in the external forum seems correct theoretically. In view of the legal presumption of paternity and the presumption of the consummation of marriage it would appear to be extremely difficult to offer full proof in the external forum by the sworn testimony of the wife alone. The author is silent regarding the nature of the proofs which would suffice in the external forum in such a case. It might be said that the mutual aversion and hate of the parties, which are indications of the non-consummation of marriage, could be extended by analogy to apply to the case in which marriage has actually been consummated in the past, but in which the husband and wife, though living together, have no relations during the time necessary for the conception of a child whose paternity is questioned. If in such a case the wife confesses her unfaithfulness and proves the conditions which existed between her husband and herself the case contemplated by Gasparri would seem to be verified.

The observation of Ciprotti that in case of the unfaithfulness of the wife it is necessary to prove that the child was conceived as the result of the crime of adultery to destroy the presumption is, of course, true. The author implies that the adultery is committed at the same time the wife is cohabiting with her husband. Since this is so, it seems extremely difficult if not impossible in practice, to prove that a child has been conceived of adultery and not of the licit use of marriage.

From all that has been said it is evident that it is extremely difficult to prove that the child of a married woman who is living with her husband is not the husband's child.

C. *The Legal Presumption of Legitimacy*

The second paragraph of canon 1115 states that children are presumed legitimate if they are born at least six months

manifesta, vel diuturnae absentiae aut impotentiae viri *vel alterius similis causae*) . . . S. C. C., *Bobien*, 16 Feb. 1743—*Fontes*, n. 3547.

from the day marriage is celebrated or within ten months of the day of the dissolution of conjugal life.

Since the legal presumption of legitimacy is based on the legal presumption of paternity it may be said that the second paragraph of this canon complements the first. The presumption of legitimacy is simply a legal presumption and therefore it yields to evident proof of the contrary truth. The meaning of the presumption is that a child who is born within the time limits stated, is presumed to have been conceived during marriage. Hence, when a child is born within the indicated time limits it is presumed legitimate because the husband of its mother is presumed to be its father according to canon 1115, § 1. The presumption takes into account both the shortest and the longest possible periods of gestation. Ordinarily a child is born after nine months of gestation.[171]

The time element of this presumption is important. The Code states that if a period of time consists of one or more months and the *terminus a quo* is explicily or implicitly set in law then the months must be computed as they are found in the calendar. The *terminus a quo* is explicitly mentioned in this presumption as coincident with the day of the celebration of the marriage.[172] Most authors in considering this presumption refer to the period of six months as one of 180 days and the period of ten months as one of 300 days.[173] Blat seems to regard the time period in the same way, though he refers expressly only to the period of 300 days when discussing the question of the birth of a child at that time after the death of the mother's husband. Manning too mentions expressly the time period of 180 days.[174] Some

[171] Totum tempus quo foetus in utero sistit, praegnatio dicitur, et transcurrit ordinarie spatio novem mensium vel circiter 280 dierum (i. e. decem mensium lunarium)—Merkelbach, *Quaestiones de Embryologia et de Ministratione Baptismatis* (2. ed., Liege: La Pensée Catholique, 1928), p. 11.

[172] Cf. Canon 34, § 3, 1°.

[173] Gasparri, *De Matrimonio,* II, 1113; Wernz-Vidal, *Ius Matrimoniale,* n. 613; Cappello, *De Sacramentis,* III, n. 748; Chelodi, *Ius Matrimoniale,* n. 150; De Smet, *De Sponsalibus et Matrimonio,* n. 282, note 2; Ayrinhac-Lydon, *Marriage Legislation,* n. 279; Petrovits, *New Church Law on Matrimony,* n. 539.

authors simply mention the periods of six and ten months without any reference to the number of days,[175] Payne says that if a month is computed as having 30 days the time limits will be the same in the new law as they were in the old law, viz., 180 and 300 days. While he does not state so expressly, Payen seems to adopt the common opinion.[176] Vermeersch-Creusen maintain that the months must be computed according to the calendar.[177] Linneborn computes the periods of six months and ten months as periods of 181 and 302 days respectively. He remarks that a little difficulty arises as a result of the provision of canon 34, § 3, 1°.[178]

Wanenmacher says that the Code seems to require that the periods of time be calculated according to the calendar. This would bring, he observes, the actual number of days somewhat higher, and the number would vary according to the period of the year from which the term is calculated. Hence this change in the method of calculation is not without its difficulties, and most authors hold that the calculation of canon 34 is not meant to apply to this case, and that the terms of six and ten months must be calculated as formerly.[179]

The conclusion of Wanenmacher—that most authors hold that the calculation of canon 34 is not meant to apply in this case

[174] Blat, *Commentarium,* III, Pars I, n. 523; Manning, *Presumptions of Law in Marriage Cases,* p. 92.

authors simply mention the periods of six and ten months without any reference to the number of days.[175] Payen says

[175] Vlaming, *Praelectiones Iuris Matrimonii,* II, n. 688; Leitner, *Lehrbuch des katholischen Eherechts* (3. Auflage, Paderborn: Druck und Verlag von Ferdinand Schöningh, 1920), p. 373; Augustine, *A Commentary on the New Code of Canon Law* (8 vols., St. Louis: Herder), Vol. V (5. ed., 1935), 334.

[176] *De Matrimonio,* III, n. 2163.

[177] Codex vero, sumendo nunc sex et decem menses, mirum hoc habet consectarium, quod duorum puerorum qui per idem tempus gestati sunt, alter praesumetur legitimus, alter vero non . . . *Epitome,* II, n. 420.

[178] *Grundriss des Eherechts nach dem Codex Iuris Canonici* (2 und 3 Auflage, Paderborn: Druck und Verlag von Ferdinand Schöningh, 1922), pp. 361-362.

[179] *Canonical Evidence in Marriage Cases,* n. 536.

seems unwarranted in view of the fact that very few of them even mention the provisions of that canon. It seems more correct to say that most authors *de facto* hold that the two periods of time consist of 180 and 300 days respectively. Triebs, Schonsteiner, and Ciprotti hold that the periods must be computed according to the calendar. Ciprotti adds that this rule is certainly very troublesome, but that, unless the legislator changes it or gives an authentic interpretation regarding it, his words, in accordance with canon 18, must not be given another interpretation.[180]

It appears that according to the strict interpretation of canon 34, § 3, 1°, the six-month and the ten-month periods must be taken as they are found in the calendar. On the other hand, there are at least five considerations which incline one to favor the opinion which maintains that the two periods may be interpreted to contain 180 days and 300 days respectively: (1) it is the common opinion; (2) it employs the same calculation of the respective periods as did the old law; (3) it is more just because it gives to every child, no matter at what time of the year he is born, the same opportunity to vindicate his legitimacy. It does not seem reasonable that the legislator intended to favor a child born at a certain time of the year more than another child born at a time of the year when the arrangement of the months would militate against the presumption of his legitimacy if the presumption were strictly interpreted according to the norm of canon 34, § 3, 1°; (4) the mind of the legislator in the matter of legitimacy is to favor the child in every possibe way. Hence it does not seem likely that he would intend formally to set up a norm which as Ciprotti observes is very troublesome; (5) it is the calculation employed by the Sacred Roman Rota.[181]

The question of the applicability of the presumption of

[180] Triebs, *Handbuch des kanonischen Eherechts,* p. 667; Schönsteiner, *Grundriss des kirchlichen Eherechts* (2. Auflage, Wien: Verlag der Buchhandlung Ludwig Auer, 1937), p. 785; Ciprotti, *Apollinaris,* XII (1939), 345.

[181] Cf. S. R. R., 29 novembris, 1930, dec. LVI—*Decisiones,* XXII (1930), 632.

legitimacy to children born of a valid or putative marriage before six months have elapsed from the day of the marriage or after ten months have expired since the dissolution of their parents' conjugal life may be considered here. If a child is born within six months of the day of its parents' marriage it is, of course, legitimate according to canon 1114. It appears, however, that such a child is not entitled to enjoy the benefits of the presumption of law set up in canon 1114, § 2.[182] Since such a child is legitimate according to canon 1114 but the presumption of canon 1115, § 2 cannot be invoked in favor of its legitimacy it seems that the word *"legitimi"* has not precisely the same meaning in both canons. In canon 1114 a legitimate status is conferred on children who are born of their parents' valid or putative marriage although the conception of such children has occurred prior to their parents' marriage. The presumption of canon 1115, § 2 goes further and declares that children born within the time limits mentioned are presumed legitimate in this sense, namely, that it is presumed that children born at least six months after the day of their parents' marriage or within ten months of the day of the dissolution of the parents' conjugal life are presumed to have been conceived during the parents' marriage.[183] When a fully developed child is born within six months of its parents' marriage it is evident that it has not been conceived of their marriage. According to Gasparri and Cappello, if, in such a case, the husband was unaware of his wife's condition, or repudiates the child immediately, it is presumed that it was conceived of another man and it is illegitimate, otherwise it is presumed that the child was conceived of the husband before marriage and it must be regarded as legitimate.[184] Some authors say that in such a case the child is simply recognized as the husband's unless he repudiates it immediately.[185] Another says that in such a case the child is

[182] Vermeersch, *Theologiae Moralis Principia,* III, n. 751.

[183] Vermeersch, *loc. cit.*

[184] *De Matrimonio,* II, n. 1113; Cappello, *De Sacramentis,* III, n. 748.

[185] Chelodi, *Ius Matrimoniale,* n. 150; Payen, *De Matrimonio,* III, n. 2163.

presumed to have been conceived in pre-nuptial relations with another man unless the husband by acknowledging the child as his own, contravenes the presumption.[186] Ciprotti expresses his view thus: In the case here contemplated one cannot point to any legal presumption as militating definitely for one of the three possibilities to the exclusion of the two remaining ones. The three envisioned possibilities are: the child's conception during the marriage; the child's conception of the mother's present husband prior to the marriage; the child's conception of some other man before the time of the marriage. Accordingly, if the husband acknowledges the child as his own there is no reason why it cannot be regarded as legitimate. On the other hand, if the husband repudiates the child, it must be considered illegitimate.[187]

From the views of the authors cited here, it is evident that none of them admits that the legal presumption of paternity operates in the case of a child born before six months have elapsed from the day of marriage. They all admit that such a child is legitimate if not repudiated immediately by the mother's husband. On the other hand, they do not agree regarding the natural presumption of paternity in such cases. The assertion of Ciprotti that in such cases presumption favors neither the possibility that the child has been conceived of the mother's husband, nor the possibility that it has been conceived of some other man, seems beyond comprehension. It is evident that a presumption for one or the other eventuality must be brought into play. If the law itself does not expressly stipulate any legal presumption, then by the norms that underlie and support a fair conjecture men must arrive at the positive presumption of fact which the circumstances of the case insinuate for them.

It seems that the designation of the time-limit which the law requires before the legal presumption can militate in favor of the child's conception during marriage, will also obtain in the case, wherein for medical reasons, the child's birth has been

[186] Vlaming, *Praelectiones Iuris Matrimonii,* II, n. 688.

[187] *Apollinaris,* XII (1939), 344.

hastened so that it occurs before the expiration of six months from the date of marriage. The statement of the law is made without condition. Therefore such a child's legitimacy in the sense of canon 1115, §2, that is, its conception during the marriage, must be called into question in view of the law's established presumption to the contrary. However, in the supposition that the actual fact is not in harmony with the legal presumption, this fact of the child's conception during the marriage can be proved far more easily than in the case of a child which after a natural period of gestation was born before the lapse of six months from the date of the marriage, for the latter case of premature birth is rather uncommon in its occurrence.[188]

If a child is born more than ten months after the dissolution of conjugal life it is evident that the legal presumption of legitimacy does not apply. However, the time limit in such event is not so absolutely set by law that proof becomes inadmissible against the presumption. Thus, if it is proved that the pregnancy lasted more than ten months and that therefore the child was conceived during the time when the husband and wife were cohabiting, then the child must be recognized as legitimate, that is, as the child of the mother's husband, unless direct evidence and full proof to the contrary are furnished.[189]

The dissolution of conjugal life may occur through death, through a sentence of nullity against the marriage, through legal separation, through mere absence, or through any other similar cause. The dissolution of conjugal life does not have to be perpetual.

If a husband should return to his wife after an absence of

[188] Fetus regulariter ante *septimum* gestationis mensem completum seu 30 hebdomadas, extra uterum maternum *vivere nequit.* Attamen ubi haberi potest *artificialis incubatio,* probabilitas haberi potest infantem iam a sexto mense completo extra uterum alendi—Genicot-Salsmans, *Institutiones Theologiae Moralis,* I, n. 375.

[189] Gasparri, *De Matrimonio,* II, n. 1113; Cappello, *De Sacramentis,* III, n. 748; Wernz-Videl, *Ius Matrimoniale,* n. 613; Vermeersch-Creusen, *Epitome,* II, n. 420.

more than ten months and she gives birth to a child within six months of his return there is no legal presumption in favor of the child's legitimacy. If the law of canon 1115 § 2, presumes the legitimacy of a child as long as it is born *after six months*, which presumption can be overthrown by full proof of a contrary fact, then it must also be admitted that canon 1115 § 2, implies by way of presumption—and not in view of evident fact—that a child is to be regarded as illegitimate (that is, as not conceived of the marriage) if it is born *before six months* from the date of the husband's and wife's resumption of conjugal life, which presumption also yields to contrary proof, though it is readily admitted that such proof can be furnished only most rarely.[190]

If a woman after the dissolution of conjugal life gives birth to a child immediately, and later bears another, though both are born within ten months of the dissolution of conjugal life, it is evident that the second child cannot be presumed legitimate, since its conception in all likelihood must have occurred after the dissolution of the mother's conjugal life.

Ciprotti mentions the case of a woman who contracts a new marriage within four months of the dissolution of her first marriage. After six months have elapsed from the day of the second marriage but before ten months have elapsed since the dissolution of the first, she bears a child. According to the general tenor of canon 1115 § 2, the child could be presumed the legitimate son either of the first or of the second husband. But an equal insistence on both presumptions simultaneously

[190] Manning says that while such a child would be born apparently "*ex matrimonio valido*," yet in the face of the incontrovertible argument of non-copulation it would not be legitimate.—Cf. *Presumptions of Law in Marriage Cases, p.* 92—In view of the fact, however, of the husband's absence for more than ten months and the child's birth within six months of his return to conjugal life, it appears more correct to say that the child in this case is born "*in matrimonio*," not "*ex matrimonio*," as is required for legitimacy in canon 1114. The phrase "*ex matrimonio*" presupposes that the child's conception resulted from relations between the husband and the wife even though such relations have occurred before marriage.

would, of course, lead to absurdity. Hence the only conclusion deducible from canon 1115 is that one of these two optional presumptions must be adopted in favor of the child's legitimacy, that is, in favor of the assumption that the child was conceived of honorable wedlock. Canon 1115 does not specify which of the two presumptions for the child's paternity is to be invoked. This delicate question can be settled only by the aid of the pratical human presumptions of fact which a judge will glean from the relevant issues and circumstantial factors in which the particular case is framed. The greater or lesser stage of development and maturity of the child at the time of its birth is a factor of primary importance for deciding whether the child is the offspring of the earlier or later marriage.[191]

It is evident that the legal presumptions for a child's legitimate conception *"ex matrimonio"* and its correspondingly connoted paternity cannot be applied in the case of foundlings. Such children, however, are commonly regarded as legitimate, despite the fact that there may be a strong indication that they have been born of an unmarried mother. If the mother is known to be unmarried the case would, of course, be different and the child would have to be regarded as illegitimate.[192] As long as it is not proved that such a child is really illegitimate, the rule, "Iudex in dubio debet in bonum et commoda prolis propensus esse," must be applied.[193]

Gasparri and Cappello observe that the question of the legitimacy of foundlings is practical today as far as the canonical effects of legitimacy are concerned, namely, as far as the irregularity resulting from illegitimacy (Canon 984, 1°) is concerned.

[191] *Apollinaris,* XII (1939), 346.

[192] Gasparri, *De Matrimonio,* II, n. 1114; Wernz-Vidal, *Ius Matrimoniale,* n. 613; Cappello, *De Sacramentis,* III, n. 749; Vlaming, *Praelectiones Iuris Matrimonii,* II, n. 682; Vermeersch-Creusen, *Epitome,* II, n. 420; Payen, *De Matrimonio,* III, n. 2161; Triebs, *Handbuch des kanonischen Eherechts,* p. 665; Wanenmacher, *Canonical Evidence in Marriage Cases,* n. 537; Manning, *Presumptions of Law in Marriage Cases,* pp. 92-93.

[193] Benedictus XIV, epist. *"Redditae Nobis,"* 5 dec., 1744—*Fontes,* n. 350.

They do not mention, however, whether a foundling needs a dispensation to receive Holy Orders.[194] The question is mentioned by other authors, of whom some say that a dispensation is necessary in such cases at least *ad cautelam.*[195] Others maintain that a dispensation is not required in such cases [196] Vermeersch holds that those who are doubtfully illegitimate are not irregular.[197] It seems that if the common opinion regarding the legitimacy of foundlings is to be maintained, then one must logically conclude that such a child does not need a dispensation from the irregularity resulting from illegitimacy. In conclusion it may be said that a child whose parents are unknown, but who is not a foundling in the accepted sense of the word, must also be regarded as legitimate.[198]

Part II

LEGITIMATION

Article I. Restrictions Placed Upon Illegitimate Children

Since the definition of legitimation has already been given and the various classes of illegitimate children have been enumerated it is unnecessary to consider these questions again.

It may be said that according to canon law all children who are not conceived or born of a valid or putative marriage are illegitimate. By way of exception those children who are born of parents the use of whose earlier contracted marriage has been denied to them because of solemn profession or Sacred

[194] *De Matrimonio,* II, n. 1114; *De Sacramentis,* III, n. 749.

[195] Wernz-Vidal, *Ius Matrimoniale,* n. 613; Payen, *De Matrimonio,* III, n. 2161.

[196] Vermeersch-Creusen, *Epitome,* II, n. 420; Triebs, *Handbuch des kanonischen Eherechts,* p. 665; Wanenmacher, *Canonical Evidence in Marriage Cases,* n. 537; cf. "Responsum," *Il Monitore Ecclesiastico,* XI (1899), 277.

[197] *Theologiae Moralis Principia,* III, n. 648.

[198] Gasparri, *De Matrimonio,* II, n. 1114; Cappello, *De Sacramentis,* III, n. 749.

Orders are also illegitimate. In canon law illegitimacy has the effect of restricting the capacity of the illegitimate person for certain offices in the Church. Because of the very nature of these offices it is evident that the restrictions of illegitimacy affect men more than women. The following restrictions are placed upon illegitimates in canon law: (1) they are excluded from the Cardinalate, the Episcopacy, and from the office of Abbot or Prelate *Nullius;*[199] (2) They may not become Auditors of the Sacred Roman Rota.[200] (3) They are irregular *ex defectu;*[201] (4) They are not permitted to enter a seminary;[202] (5) They may not be elected to the office of major superior in a religious institute. The prohibition obtains both in the institutes of men and women;[203] (6) By particular law they may be barred from entrance to the religious life;[204] (7) They and their close descendants are ineligible for certain offices in the Papal household.[205]

According to St. Thomas the restrictions which are placed upon illegitimates do not have the nature of a punishment, for, strictly considered, they simply lack the full rights of legitimate children. As the Angelic Doctor observes, it is not a punishment for anyone who is not born the son of a king not to succeed to a kingdom.[206] The view of the nature of the privations of illegitimates as expressed by St. Thomas does not seem to have

[199] Canons 232, § 2, 1°; 331, § 1, 1°; 320, §2.

[200] *Normae S. Romanae Rotae Tribunalis,* 29 iunii, 1934—*AAS,* XXVI (1934), 449 ss.

[201] Canon 984, 1°.

[202] Canon 1363, § 1.

[203] Canon 504.

[204] This provision, it may be observed, is actually found in many constitutions.

[205] . . . a quibusdam muneribus pontificialis domus (e. g. ab advocatis Consistorialis Aulae prohibentur illegitimi eorumque descendentes in proprioribus gradibus—Ciprotti, *Apollinaris,* XII (1939), 492.

[206] . . . Et ideo non dicimus quod sit poena alicui quod non succedit in regno aliquo, per hoc quod non est filius regis. Et similiter non est poena quod alicui qui non est legitimus, non debeantur ea quae sunt legitimorum filiorum.—*Supplementum,* Q. LXVIII, art. 2, ad 1.

been kept always in mind, as can be gathered from various decisions of the Holy See regarding specifically the dispensation requested for an illegitimate to receive Sacred Orders. Thus in one case wherein a son was conceived as a result of sacrilege the dispensation, though actually granted, was opposed by the Consultor on the grounds that the crime was punished in the son that through this the father himself might be punished.[207] In another case in which the son was adulterine the dispensation for the reception of tonsure and minor orders, though finally granted, was opposed by the Consultor on the same grounds as those advanced in the preceding case.[208] In another case, however, the fact that the privations visited upon illegitimates are really not punishments imposed upon the illegitimate person himself was brought out clearly. A dispensation to receive Sacred Orders and to obtain a benefice was sought for a man whose conception had resulted from the two crimes of adultery and incest. The dispensation was granted but in the opinion which was opposed to the granting of the dispensation it was expressly declared that such a son is not punished for the crime of his father.[209]

The doctrine that the privations suffered by illegitimates do not have the nature of punishments did not, of course, originate with St. Thomas. As has been shown before, the same doctrine was held by St. Jerome and St. Augustine.[210] No matter, however, how innocent such children, are their reputation is stained because their birth reflects in them the evil fruit and product of their parents' sin.[211]

[207] Gratia deneganda videtur . . . ob destestationem atque execrationem paterni criminis, quod punitur in filio, ut per hoc puniatur ipsemet pater.—S. C. C., 9 Sept. 1882—*ASS,* XV (1882), 452-455.

[208] S. C. C., 19 Jan. 1884—*ASS,* XVI (1884), 461.

[209] . . . Secundam rationem iampridem expressit, S. Ivo Cartonensis dicens, Quidem Romani Pontifices decreverunt, ne filii presbyterorum assumerentur ad Presbyteratum, non quod personarum acceptio apud Deum alicuius sit momenti; vel natura, quae omnium par est genitrix, ab aliquo possit reprehendi, vel filius pro iniquitate patris condemnari . . . S. C. C., 14 Junii, 1884—*ASS,* XVII (1884), 203-205.

[210] Cf. *supra.* p. 34.

[211] Hostiensis, *Summa Aurea,* lib. I, *de filiis presbyterorum,* n. 3.

To ameliorate the condition of illegitimate children the Church today employs, as it has in the past, various means of effecting legitimation. Legitimation properly so called is permitted according to the present canon law in four ways: (1) by the subsequent marriage of an illegitimate child's parents: (2) by a dispensation from a diriment impediment granted in accordance with the provisions of canon 1051 to enable the parents of children already born or conceived to contract marriage; (3) by the radical sanation of the invalid non-putative marriage of the parents of illegitimate children; (4) by Papal rescript of legitimation. Legitimation in a wide sense, namely, for the purpose only of receiving Sacred Orders, is effected: (1) by solemn Religious Profession; (2) by a Papal Dispensation granted for the specific purpose to enable the recipient to receive Sacred Orders. Although Solemn Profession and Papal Dispensation for Orders do not effect legitimation properly so called, and are not listed among the means of legitimation by most authors, nevertheless, from what has already been said regarding them, it seems that they can be correctly regarded as effecting legitimation in a wide sense.[212]

Article II. Legitimation By Subsequent Marriage

Canon 1116. Per subsequens parentum matrimonium sive verum sive putativum sive noviter contractum sive convalidatum, etiam non consummatum, legitima efficitur proles, dummodo parentes habiles exstiterint ad matrimonium inter se contrahendum tempore conceptionis, vel praegnationis, vel nativitatis.

It may be said that legitimation by the subsequent marriage of the parents is the principal means employed in canon law for the legitimation of children. This must be understood, however, by keeping in mind that in another sense legitimation by

[212] Cf. *supra*. p. 56.

Papal rescript is the widest form of legitimation, since no illegitimate child is excluded from the possibility of such a legitimation.[213] Legitimation by subsequent marriage operates like all other modes of legitimation by a fiction of law. The juridical notion of legitimation by subsequent marriage according to Gasparri is this: a marriage which is celebrated at this moment, or convalidated, is retroactive by a fiction of law, to the time of the conception, or of the gestation, or of the birth of the child which on that account is regarded as if it had been begotten in a valid marriage, and therefore the child is legitimate.[214] The purpose of the Church in permitting legitimation by subsequent marriage is to favor both the children and the institution of marriage. The children are benefitted because they avoid the stigma of someone else's crime; marriage is aided because those persons whose union is not lawful are led by the love of their children to enter upon lawful marriage.[215]

The first requisite for the legitimation of a child by subsequent marriage is that the marriage must take place between the father and the mother of the child. This requirement is evident from the words of the canon which states that the parents in order to effect the legitimation must be capable of contracting marriage between themselves. This condition is apparently taken for granted by many authors as they do not make mention of it; some, however, do mention it expressly.[216]

213 "Ex modis quibus filii non legitimi beneficium legitimationis consequuntur semper aliis potior habitus est contractus subsequentis matrimonii inter parentes."—Vermeersch, "De canone 1116 seu de legitimatione per subsequens matrimonium parentum," *Periodica,* XIX (1930), 26*-28*:

214 *De Matrimonio,* II, n. 1118; The word *"legitimate"* used here by Gasparri cannot, of course, be interpreted to mean that a child legitimated by its parents' subsequent marriage is *"legitimate"* in the sense of canon 1114.

215 Schmalzgrueber, lib. IV, tit. 17, n. 49.

216 Payen, *De Matrimonio,* II, n. 2175; De Smet, *De Sponsalibus et Matrimonio,* n. 290; Ayrinhac-Lydon, *Marriage Legislation,* n. 280; Harrigan, *Radical Sanation,* p. 52; Larraona, "Animadversiones ad Canonem 1116, "*Apollinaris* IV (1931), 57-58; Vermeersch, "De canone 1116 seu de legitimatione per subsequens matrimonium parentum," *Periodica* XIX (1930), 26*-28*; Ciprotti, *Apollinaris,* XII (1939), 498.

Therefore if the child's mother were to marry a man other than the child's father, legitimation would not be effected. In such cases, however, until the contrary is proved, the paternity of the man who marries the mother is presumed. The testimony of the two parties that the man is really the child's father can be accepted as sufficient evidence.[217]

The second requisite for legitimation by subsequent marriage is that the marriage must be contracted after the child's birth. If the parents marry before the child's birth, the child will be legitimate according to the provisions of canon 1114. It is not, however, necessary that the parents' marriage take place immediately after the child's birth. The required condition is fulfilled even when the marriage has been postponed for many years, or when it takes place after one or both of the parents have been previously married to some one else. After such an intermediate marriage (or marriages), the intermarriage of the father and the mother will legitimate the child.[218]

The third requisite for legitimation by subsequent marriage is that such a marriage must be valid or at least putative. Since the requisites for both valid and putative marriage have already been discussed, it is unnecessary to duscuss them further. It suffices to note that this requirement which demands that the marriage be valid or at least putative implicitly exacts good faith on the part of at least one of the parents. Therefore the possibility of legitimation by subsequent marriage is excluded in the case of a child whose parents both knowingly conspire to contract an invalid marriage, even if their sole purpose in entering such a union is to remove the stigma of illegitimacy from the child.

It is not required that the marriage be consummated in order

[217] De Smet, *loc. cit.*, Ayrinhac-Lydon, *loc. cit.;* Payen, *De Matrimonio* II, 2175.

[218] Knecht, *Handbuch des katholischen Eherechts,* p. 679, note 7; Payen, *De Matrimonio,* II, n. 2176; Brennan, *The Simple Convalidation of Marriage.* The Catholic University of America, Canon Law Studies, n. 102 (Washington, D. C.: The Catholic University of America, 1937), pp. 109-110.

to effect legitimation. This can be inferred from the fact that such a marriage is permitted even in the event that one of the parents is in danger of death at the time of the marriage.[219] The reason for this is that the legitimation is effected *non intrinseca vi matrimonii sed Ecclesiae constitutione.*[220] Some writers say that there does not even have to be a possibility that such a marriage may be consummated.[221]

Payen observes that if the marriage has been contracted in good faith by at least one of the parties the antecedent and perpetual impotence of one or of the other party will not hinder the legitimation of the offspring because the marriage is putative.[222]

The canon further states that the subsequent marriage may be either a newly contracted marriage or a convalidated marriage. Regarding legitimation by a newly contracted marriage little comment seems necessary. If two unmarried persons beget a child and actually marry only after the child's birth the marriage will legitimate the child, provided the parents were capable of intermarriage at the time of the child's conception, or during the period of the child's gestation, or at the time of the child's birth. All that the law demands with reference to the marriage itself is that it be valid or at least putative. The child may have been born of fornication or in concubinage.

Regarding the possibility of legitimation by the convalidation of invalid marriages it is obviously beyond the scope of this thesis to consider in detail all the requisites for simple convalidation. This subject has already been treated formally in another work to which the reader is referred.[223] It may be said here that simple convalidation is an act by which a marriage that has been null and void from the beginning is rendered valid by the renewal of consent. It presupposes the removal

[219] Canon 1043.

[220] Cf. *supra*, p. 48.

[221] Payen, *De Matrimonio,* II, n. 2176; Cappello, *De Sacramentis,* III, n. 750; Brennan, *Simple Convalidation,* p. 109.

[222] *Op. cit., loc. cit.*

[223] Brennan, *Simple Convalidation.*

of the cause of the invalidity. The removal qualifies the persons to make a valid act of consent, and the renewal of the consent itself effects the convalidation.[224] The convalidation must take place according to the norms prescribed by law.[225]

Concerning the question of effecting legitimation by the simple convalidation of invalid marriages various possibilities may arise. Thus, if the invalid marriage which is to be convalidated is a putative marriage, there will be no need of legitimation for those children who were born or conceived of such a marriage during the time when the invalidity of the union was unknown to at least one of the parents. Children born or conceived of such a marriage are legitimate according to the norm of canon 1114. If, however, the invalidity of a marriage which is to be convalidated was known to both parties before the conception of any of the children, a distinction must be made. If such a marriage can be convalidated without the aid of a dispensation from a diriment impediment, the convalidation will effect the legitimation of the children already born, provided that all the requisites demanded in such cases by canon 1116 are present. This will be true, for example, in cases wherein the invalidity has resulted from some defect in the marital consent, or on account of the absence of the canonical form, or because of the presence of a diriment impediment which has ceased to exist between the parties at the time of the convalidation of their marriage but which did exist at some time other than at the time either of the conception, or during the period of gestation, or at the time of the birth of the child who is to be legitimated by its parents' convalidated marriage. As will be shown subsequently, it is imperative that the parents, even if a diriment impediment which had existed between them at some time has ceased at the time of the convalidation of their marriage, must have been capable of contracting marriage either at the time of the child's conception, or during the period of its gestation, or at the time of its birth if legitimation in accord-

[224] Brennan, *op. cit.*, p. 2.
[225] Canons 1133-1137.

ance with the provisions of canon 1116 is to be effected without any further authortative act.

If it is necessary to secure a dispensation from a diriment impediment before the marriage may be convalidated, legitimation will not be effected by the convalidation of the marriage, but rather by the granting of a dispensation according to the regulations of canon 1051, which will be treated subsequently.

A convalidated marriage has the same effect with regard to legitimation as a newly contracted subsequent marriage.[226]

Therefore if a child has been born of an invalid and non-putative marriage it will be legitimated when the marriage is convalidated. The same will be true if the parents of a child which has been born outside of wedlock, upon contracting an invalid and non-putative marriage subsequent to the child's birth, later have their invalid union convalidated.

The convalidation must result in a valid or at least a putative marriage. The later possibility can be verified, for example, when a diriment impediment still extant after the attempted convalidation, remains unknown to at least one of the parties, or when the marriage has not actually been convalidated in the proper manner, for example, if in the case when the convalidation takes place before a priest and two witnesses, the priest has no permission to assist validly at the marriage.[227]

If a child is conceived before the convalidation of the parents' invalid marriage but is born after the convalidation has taken place it is legitimate according to the norms of canon 1114, i.e., it is born of a valid marriage.

Finally, the canon demands that the parents must be capable of contracting marriage either at the time of the child's conception, or during the period of its gestation, or at the time

[226] Gasparri, *De Matrimonio,* II, n. 1206; Wernz-Vidal, *Ius Matrimoniale,* n. 614; Cappello, *De Sacramentis,* III, n. 750; Chelodi, *Ius Matrimoniale,* n. 151; Payen, *De Matrimonio,* II, n. 2176; Linneborn, *Grandriss des Eherechts,* p. 362; De Smet, *De Sponsalibus et Matrimonio,* n. 289; Blat, *Commentarium,* III, Pars I, n. 524; Ciprotti, "De prolis legitimatione per matrimonii convalidationem," *Apollinaris,* XI (1938), 126-127.

[227] Cf. Payen, *De Matrimonio, III, n.* 2174-2178.

of its birth. The capacity of the parents to contract marriage is regarded by some canonists to imply the absence of a diriment impediment between the parents at any one of the three points of time mentioned.[228] Other authors give no explanation of the term *habiles.* They state simply that the parents must be capable of contracting marriage at any one of the three times specified in the canon.[229] Ciprotti maintains that the parents are incapable of marriage not only when a diriment impediment exists between them but also when there is lacking in one or both the natural capacity requisite for the contraction of marriage. He enumerates as incapable of marriage insane persons and those who are ignorant of the nature of marriage. He observes that he is not unaware of the fact that there can be dubious cases with reference to defects in consent, for example, when one of the parents could not only under grave fear have entered upon marriage since this fear endured from the time of the conception of the child until the time of its birth. Doubt regarding such cases, he maintains, arises if there is a question of a child to be legitimated by the convalidation of a marriage.[230] Ciprotti's statement that the writers make no mention of the incapacity of the parents to contract marriage as arising from any cause other than the presence of some diriment impediment is not entirely correct. Thus he cites Schönsteiner as one who

[228] De Smet, *De Sponsalibus et Matrimonio,* n. 288; Knecht, *Handbuch des katholischen Eherechts,* p. 679; Triebs, *Handbuch des kanonischen Eherechts,* p. 676; Blat, *Commentarium,* III, Pars I, n. 524; Linneborn, *Grundriss des Eherechts,* p. 362; Ayrinhac-Lydon, *Marriage Legislation,* nn. 280-281; Harrigan, *Radical Sanation,* p. 51; Larraona, "De legitimatione prolis," *Apollinaris* IV (1931), 57-58; Gearin, "Are parents between whom there existed (*"tempore conceptionis, vel praegnationis, vel nativitatis"*) the impediment *"disparitatis cultus"* actually *"habiles"* to contract marriage?" *AER,* LXIII (1920), 504-506; O'Neill, "Legitimacy and Legitimation," *IER,* XXXVII (1931), 520-522.

[229] Wernz-Vidal, *Ius Matrimoniale,* n. 614; Cappello, *De Sacramentis,* III, n. 750; Vermeersch-Creusen, *Epitome* II, n. 421; Chelodi, *Ius Matrimoniale,* n. 151; Gasparri, *De Matrimonio* II, n. 1118; Brennan *Simple Convalidation,* p. 108.

[230] *Apollinaris* XII (1939), 500 and note 9.

mentions only the presence of a diriment impediment as a cause for rendering the parents incapable of marriage.[231]

It is true that Schönsteiner, when discussing the various classes of illegitimate children, refers to "spurious" children as those whose parents are incapable of marriage because of the presence of a diriment impediment between them at the time of their child's conception, during the period of its gestation and at the time of its birth. When he treats the question of the capacity of the parents to marry with reference to the requirements of canon 1116 he expressly mentions that this capacity of the parents means the absence of a diriment impediment or the absence of an essential defect of consent (e.g. insanity).[232]

As has already been observed, many authors give no explanation of the term *habiles*. They simply state that the parties must be capable of marriage. It seems reasonable to maintain that these authors, if questioned as to the meaning of the term, would not insist that a person incapable of contracting marriage for some reason other than the presence of a diriment impediment would be *habilis*. The same may be said of those authors who mention explicitly only a diriment impediment as the cause which renders a person *inhabilis*. It seems very unlikely that they would for a moment maintain, for example, that an insane person or one who is ignorant of the nature of marriage is *habilis,* even if there is no diriment impediment (which these authors mention expressly as rendering a person *inhabilis*) existing between such a person and the other person with whom marriage is contemplated.

The parents are certainly incapable of marriage when a diriment impediment exists between them. The incapacity exists when the diriment impediment is either of divine or merely

[231] *Loc. cit.*

[232] Die Kindeseltern müssen in einem der genanuten drei Zeitpunkte fähig (habiles) gewesen sein, miteinander eine gültige Ehe zu schliesen. Diese Fähigkeit bedeutet: Nichtvorhandensein eines trennenden Ehehindernisses bezw-eines wesentlichen Konsensmangels (z. B. Geistes krankheit). —*Grundriss des kirchlichen Eherechts,* pp. 787-788; cf. also p. 778.

of ecclesiastical law, even if, according to the practice of the Church, the latter type of impediment is readily removable by way of dispensation upon the presentation of canonical causes which merit and obtain this act of ecclesiastical favor.[233] It is not true, therefore, that the parents are incapable of marriage only in those cases wherein the diriment impediment which exists between them cannot be removed by dispensation as is maintained by Schmitz.[234] It seems entirely correct to maintain the opinion that every diriment impediment, whether it can or cannot be removed by dispensation, renders the persons between whom such an impediment exists incapable of marriage. This is so because even if the diriment impediment is one which the Church can and does dispense from the parties bound by such an impediment cannot without a dispensation contract a valid marriage. The fact that a diriment impediment even though it allow of dispensation renders a marriage contracted without a dispensation invalid, indicates clearly that such an impediment really renders the persons between whom it exists incapable of marriage. The incapacity of the persons between whom a diriment impediment exists ceases when the impediment has been removed by dispensation. Thus, if a diriment impediment has existed between the parents at the time of their child's conception, but is removed by dispensation at some time before the child's birth, the parents become capable of marriage at the time the dispensation is granted. If such a dispensation is granted by ordinary power, or by delegated power through a general indult, the provisions of canon 1051 must be kept in mind. The incapacity of the parents may also cease if the impediment itself has ceased to exist between them apart from any dispensation. Such a case would be verified, for example, when one of the parents during the interim between the conception and the birth of the child would have

[233] Triebs, *Handbuch des kanonischen Eherechts,* p. 676; Linneborn, *Grundriss des Eherechts,* p. 362; Ciprotti, *Apollinaris* XII (1939), 501.

[234] *Die Stellung der unehelichen Kinder im geltenden kanonischen Recht* (St. Gabriel, Moedling; Missionsbuchhandlung, 1926), p. 111.

surmounted the earlier deficiency of age for the valid contracting of marriage, or also when an existing marriage, which caused the child to be conceived in adultery, has been dissolved prior to the birth of the child, and has thus, under the supposition that the impediment of crime is not present, left its parents free to enter upon a valid marriage.

It is not required that the parents be capable of contracting marriage at all of the points of time mentioned in canon 1116, namely, at the time of the child's coneption, during the period of gestation, and at the time of the child's birth. It is sufficient for the purpose of effecting legitimation by subsequent marriage, no matter how long after the child's birth the marriage takes place, that the parents should have been able to contract marriage at any one of the three points of time mentioned.[235] The parents' subsequent marriage, therefore, will legitimate a child if a diriment impediment arises between the parties only after the child's conception, though the impediment did not cease until after the child's birth. So also, if the parents were incapable of contracting marriage at the time of the child's conception because of a diriment impediment, which however, ceased before the child's birth, their subsequent marriage will legitimate the child. Again, if the parents were incapable of contracting marriage both at the time of the child's conception and at the time of its birth because of a diriment impediment but were capable of marriage at some time during the period of gestation, the parents' subsequent marriage will likewise legitimate the child. The writer presupposes, of course, that the parents were otherwise capable of contracting marriage at some one of the three points of time specified.

If the continuous incapacity of the parents to contract marriage ceases only after the child's birth, their subsequent marriage will not legitimate the child. It is evident that in such cases

[235] Gasparri, *De Matrimonio,* II, n. 1118; Wernz-Vidal, *Ius Matrimoniale,* n. 614; Cappello, *De Sacramentis* III, n. 750; Payen, *De Matrimonio,* II, n. 2177; Ayrinhac-Lydon, *Marriage Legislation,* n. 280; Brennan, *Simple Convalidation,* p. 109.

the parents have been incapable of marriage at any one of the three points of time mentioned in canon 1116. For this reason the Code Commission declared in an authentic interpretation that the subsequent marriage of the parents does not legitimate a child begotten by them while they were under the impediment of age or disparity of cult, which impediment, however, had ceased at the time of the marriage, but only after the birth of the child.[236]

The declaration of the Commission seems to have been occasioned by an opinion suggested by Vermeersch. He indeed admitted that according to canon 1116 a child which was born before the impediment of age or disparity of cult had ceased to exist between the parents though the impediment had ceased at the time of their marriage, could not be legitimated by the marriage. But he was of the opinion that if the attention of the legislator were drawn to the two impediments mentioned, the conditions demanded in canon 1116 might be relaxed. The reasons he advanced were that under the old law the principle *"malitia supplet aetatem"* was recognized, and that under the old law only adulterine children and those who were the fruit of incest and sacrilege were excluded from the benefits of legitimation by subsequent marriage He also maintained that in a certain sense the condition of those illegitimate children whose parents are rendered capable of contracting marriage without the intervention of a dispensation in view of the naturally lapsed impediment is worse than that of those illegitimate children (excepting adulterine children and those who are the fruit of sacrilege) whose parents require a dispensation to contract marriage in as much as such children can be legitimated by the granting of the necessary dispensation according to the provisions

[236] *AAS,* XXIII (1931), 25; cf. also Payen, *De Matrimonio,* III, n. 2174-8; Brennan, *Simple Convalidation,* p. 109; Ayrinhac-Lydon, *Marriage Legislation,* n. 281; Larraona, "De legitimatione prolis," *Apollinaris,* IV (1931), 57-58; Vermeersch, *"Annotatio ad canonem* 1116," *Periodica,* XX (1931), 148-150; Creusen, "Sur la response de la Commission a le can. 1116," *Nouvelle Revue Theologique,* LVIII (1931), 261; Hilling, "Eine Antwort," *AKKR,* IIC (1918), 306.

of canon 1051. The decision of the Commission settled the question definitively. Vermeersch, commenting on the decision, observed that a more benign interpretation would have avoided difficulties.[237]

From the insistence of the law that the parents be capable of contracting marriage at some one of the periods of time mentioned in canon 1116 it is evident that only a "natural" child may be legitimated by the subsequent marriage of its parents.[238] A "natural" child is one born of parents who were capable of marriage either at the time of the child's conception, or during the period of its gestation, or at the time of its birth. Thus, a child whose conception is, for example, adulterine may be born a "natural" child. If the parents have been incapable of contracting marriage during all the time from the conception of the child until after its birth their subsequent marriage will not legitimate the child. In such a case the retroaction of the marriage to any of the three points of time mentioned in canon 1116 becomes impossible. The authors state with reference to the question of legitimation by subsequent marriage that a marriage cannot be supposed to exist by a fiction of law at a time when the marriage is forbidden by an invalidating law.[239] It must be noted here that the notion of the impossibility of the retroaction of a marriage by a fiction of law to a time when the marriage was prohibited by an invalidating law refers only to the question of legitimation by subsequent marriage. In a radical sanation, as will be shown later, the full juridical effects of a valid marriage are attributed to the marriage which is convalidated The juridical

[237] "De canone 1116 seu de legitimatione per subsequens matrimonium parentum"—*Periodica*, XIX (1930), 26*-28*; cf. also *ibid.*, "Annotatio ad canonem 1116," *Periodica*, XX (1931), 148-150.

[238] . . . Legitima efficitur *omnis* proles naturalis, modo tamen sit vere, non tantum putative naturalis, ac sola proles naturalis—Payen, *De Matrimonio*, II, n. 2177.

[239] Vlaming, *Praelectiones*, II, n. 684; Wernz-Vidal, *Ius Matrimoniale*, n. 614; Cappello, *De Sacramentis*, III, n. 750; Payen, *De Matrimonio*, II, n. 2177; Chelodi, *Ius Matrimoniale*, n. 151; Ayrinhac-Lydon, *Marriage Legislation*, n. 280.

effects are referred back to the moment when marital consent was exchanged. It is not required that the parents be capable of marriage at the time of the child's conception, as was formely maintained by some authors. Thus, if a child is conceived in adultery and the impediment of previous bond ceases before the child's birth. the parents' subsequent marriage will legitimate the child. It is presupposed, of course, that the parents have not incurred the impediment of crime (canon 1075.). If, for example, a married man without any promise of future marriage commits adultery with a single woman from which crime the conception of a child results, and the man's wife dies a week before the child's birth, the subsequent marriage of the parents will legitimate the child as they have been capable of contracting marriage for at least a short time prior to the child's birth, although they were actually prevented from marrying at the time of the child's conception by the diriment impediment of previous bond.[240] Gasparri excludes adulterine children and those born as the result of sacrilege from legitimation by subsequent marriage without any qualification as to the capacity of the parents to marry at any of the points of time specified in canon 1116. He states further that if a child is "spurious," or is begotten *ex damnato coitu,* the retroaction by fiction of law through which subsequent marriage operates is impossible, even though the parents may have been capable of contracting marriage at some one of the times specified in canon 1116.[241]

It has already been demonstrated that if a child has been conceived in adultery by parents who are nevertheless capable of contracting marriage at the time of the child's birth, their subsequent marriage will legitimate the child. On the other hand, if the child has been born before the diriment impediment of previous bond had ceased to exist between the parents their subsequent marriage will not legitimate the child since they

[240] Payen, *De Matrimonio,* II, n. 2177; Cappello, *De Sacramentis,* III, n. 750; Wernz-Vidal, *Ius Matrimoniale,* n. 614, note 56; Ayrinhac-Lydon, *Marriage Legislation,* n. 280; Harrigan, *Radical Sanation,* p. 56.

[241] *De Matrimonio,* II, nn. 1117-1118.

have been incapable of marriage at all the points of time mentioned in canon 1116. The same would be true if any diriment impediment existed between the parents (not only previous bond, Sacred Orders, Solemn Profession as inferred by Gasparri) from the time of the child's conception until some moment following its birth. The statement of Gasparri that the retroaction by fiction of law, through which legitimation is effected in the event of subsequent marriage, is impossible in the case of spurious children whose parents have been capable of marriage either at the time of the child's conception, or during the period of gestation, or at the time of the child's birth cannot be accepted. Canon 1116 states clearly that subsequent marriage does legitimate children provided the parents were capable of marriage at any one of the three points of time specified. The statement of Gasparri which is under consideration contradicts what he himself maintains in explaining the juridical notion of legitimation through subsequent marriage. It is also at variance with his earlier view on the possibility of the retroaction by fiction of law of subsequent marriage in the case of "spurious" children.[242]

Legitimation by subsequent marriage is restricted solely to those children who are "natural" children objectively considered. This is so because canon 1116 expressly demands that the parents be actually *habiles* at some one of the three points of time specified. It does not therefore permit the legitimation of those children who are born to parents one of whom or both of whom think themselves *habiles* at any or at all of the points of time specified, although objectively they are actually incapable of contracting marriage at all of the points of time mentioned.[243]

[242] . . . si enim proles est spuria seu genita ex damnato coitu ita ut parentes nullo ex illis temporibus matrimonium inter se contrahere potuissent, illa fictiva retroactio matrimonii est impossibilis.—*De Matrimonio* (3. ed.), II, n. 1386; Schaaf, "Review of Gasparri's *De Matrimonio*," *AER*, LXXXVIII (1933), 596-598; Harrigan, *Radical Sanation*, p. 56; Ciprotti, *Apollinaris*, XII (1939), 502.

[243] Payen, *De Matrimonio*, II, n. 2177; Cappello, *De Sacramentis*, III, n. 750; Triebs, *Handbuch des kanonischen Eherechts*, p. 676; De Smet,

The importance of the requirement of objective capacity becomes apparent in the case of the subsequent putative marriage of the parents. If the invalidity of the subsequent marriage results from the incapacity of the parents to marry, a child already born will be legitimated by the subsequent marriage only if it is a "natural" child objectively considered, or, in other words, the child of parents capable of marriage at least at one of the points of time specified.[244]

Since it is possible to legitimate a child by the subsequent marriage of its parents when the latter were free to intermarry only at the time of the child's conception it is important to determine whether the parents were free to marry at that time. It has already been shown that the presumption of canon 1115, § 2, may be extended by analogy to apply to all illegitimate children. It is presumed, therefore, that an illegitimate child has been conceived between six and ten months before its birth. Thus, if the parents of an illegitimate child were free to intermarry at any point of time during the four months intervening between the limits of the six-month and the ten-month periods it can be presumed that the child conceived is a "natural" child. This presumption, however, cannot be maintained if it is known certainly that the parents were prohibited to intermarry at the time when the child's conception actually occured.[245]

Finally, since legitimation by subsequent marriage is conceded by the law itself, the attitude either of the parents who contract such a marriage or of the children who are to be legitimated is of no importance. Once the subsequent marriage has been contracted in accordance with the provisions of canon 1116, legitimation is *ipso facto* effected. Thus, even if the legitimation is opposed by anyone concerned, such opposition will not preclude the effects intended by the law. No declaration of legitimation is required.[246]

De Sponsalibus et Matrimonio, n. 288; Schönsteiner, *Grundriss des kirchlichen Eherechts,* p. 789.

[244] Ciprotti, *Apollinaris,* XII (1939), 503.

[245] Cf. Triebs, *Handbuch des kanonischen Eherechts,* p. 670; Ciprotti, *Apollinaris,* XII (1939), 343-344.

[246] Schönsteiner, *Grundriss des kirchlichen Eherechts,* pp. 786, 787; Triebs,

Article III. The Effects of Legitimation by Subsequent Marriage

Canon 1117. Filii legitimati per subsequens matrimonium, ad effectus canonicos quod attinet in omnibus aequiparantur legitimis, nisi aliud expresse cautum fuerit.

It is evident from a consideration of the words of this canon that the Church is most generous towards children who have been legitimated in accordance with the provisions of canon 1116. They are excluded from none of the rights of legitimate children, unless the law expressly states otherwise. The restrictions imposed upon children legitimated by subsequent marriage are actually very few. The law expressly states that they may not become Cardinals, Bishops, Abbots or Prelates *Nullius*.[247] It is to be noted that the restriction placed on such children with regard to becoming Bishops, Abbots or Prelates *Nullius* is a new limitation introduced by the Code of Canon Law. Under the old law, children legitimated by subsequent marriage were hindered only only from becoming Cardinals.[248]

Since the restrictions already mentioned are the only ones expressly stated in the law, it is evident that sons legitmated by their parents' subsequent marriage are not irregular *ex defectu*.[249] Such children are eligible for election to the office of major superior in religious institutes.[250] With regard to the office of major superior it must be noted that the restriction placed on sons legitimated by subsequent marriage as far as their ineligibility for the office of Abbot *Nullius* is concerned must not be extended to the office of Abbot *regiminis,* since the latter office is not expressly forbidden to such children.

Handbuch des kanonischen Eherechts, p. 675; Gasparri, *De Matrimonio,* II, n. 1119; Payen, *De Matrimonio,* II, n. 2175; Cappello, *De Sacramentis,* III, n. 750; Chelodi, *Ius Matrimoniale,* n. 151; Ayrinhac-Lydon, *Marriage Legislation,* n. 280; Brennan, *Simple Convalidation,* p. 110.

247 Canons 232, § 2, 1°; 331, § 1, 1°; 320, § 1.

248 *Supra,* p. 49; Wernz-Vidal, *Ius Matrimoniale,* n. 614.

249 Canon 984, 1°.

250 Canon 504.

Despite the fact that sons legitimated by their parents' subsequent marriage are not expressly forbidden by law to enter a seminary, there was some controversy as to whether such sons could be admitted to a seminary on the authority of the Ordinary alone. The doubt was occasioned by the provisions found in canon 1363, namely, that only legitimate sons can be admitted and, further, that before their admission they must present documents attesting to the legitimacy of their birth.[251] The doubt was finally proposed to the Pontifical Commission for the interpretation of the Code and it declared on July 13, 1930 that sons legitimated by the subsequent marriage of their parents are to be regarded as legitimate for the purpose mentioned in canon 1363, § 1.[252]

The effects of legitimation by subsequent marriage are important for all children who have been legitimated by this means, but in practice the effects of this legitimation are especially important in the case of those who desire to enter the priesthood or to embrace the religious life. It has just been observed that sons legitimated by their parents' subsequent marriage are permitted to enter a seminary; it has been noted before that many institutes today demand that the aspirant to the religious life must be of legitimate birth. If the person has been legitimated by the parents' subsequent marriage, the record of the legitimation should be contained both in the matrimonial and in the baptismal registers. Usually the parish priest of the person who desires either to enter the priesthood or to embrace the religious life is requested to testify in a letter to the character of the person. If the person who requests such a testimonial has been legitimated by subsequent marriage, the parish priest can prudently inform the superiors of the seminary or of the religious institute of the circumstances of the case with the intention that the candidate

[251] Maroto, "Animadversio," *Apollinaris* III (1930), 571-574.

[252] *AAS*, XXII (1930), 365; cf. Haring, "Die Stellung der Legitimierten re c. 1117," *LQS*, LXXV (1922), 317; Vermeersch, "Annotatio ad c. 1363, § 1," *Periodica*, XIX (1930), 345; Vermeersch-Creusen, *Epitome*, II, n. 697; Triebs, *Handbuch des kanonischen Eherechts*, p. 678; Cappello, *De Sacramentis*, III, n. 751; Ayrinhac-Lydon, *Marriage Legislation*, n. 281.

may not be rejected simply because of a possible misunderstanding regarding the person's status. With regard to the question of the admittance to a seminary Maroto maintains that a son legitimated by his parents' subsequent marriage may be given a letter in which it is declared that he is legitimate, because he is made equal in all things before the law (with the exceptions already noted) to a legitimate son. Maroto observes, however, that nothing hinders such a son from presenting a letter describing his exact status as a son legitimated by his parents' subsequent marriage. Vermeersch-Creusen say simply that such a son should present a document of legitimation.[253]

Since it is possible that the person concerned may not know anything about the legitimation, prudence must govern the actions of the parish priest. First of all the parish priest in making out the copies of the person's baptismal record and that of the matrimonial record of the parents should be very careful to note that the parents' subsequent marriage legitimated the person.

It is very possible that a person legitimated by subsequent marriage may have been baptized as an illegitimate in a parish other than that where the parents actually contracted marriage. Consequently, prudence demands that the parish priest of the place of baptism present the copy of the record in a sealed envelope; the parish priest of the place of the parents' marriage should do likewise. This precludes an unfortunate comparison of the respective dates. If the person undertakes to open the envelopes, the responsibility for what may be an unpleasant discovery is entirely his own. If the person's baptism and the parents' marriage have taken place in the same parish where the person actually resides, the parish priest should seal the copies of both records as well as the testimonial which has been requested and in which, as has already been suggested, the parish priest has clearly explained that the person has been legitimated. If the person resides in a parish other than that of his baptism or

[253] *Epitome,* II, n. 697; cf. also Maroto, "De filiis legitimatis: Animadversiones," *Apollinaris,* III (1930), 571-574.

that of the parents' subsequent marriage the testimonial letter of the parish priest in this instance may possibly offer no comment as to the legitimate status of the person who requests the letter. In this event the importance of the annotation of the fact of legitimation on the copies of the person's baptismal record and the matrimonial record of the parents is obvious.

It must be noted that under no pretense of consideration for the feelings of the person concerned may the records of baptism and marriage be changed. The gravity of the punishments for the deliberate falsification of such records indicates the seriousness of the offence.[254]

It sometimes happens that the question, "Are you legitimate?" is found in the questionnaire sent by religious institutes to aspirants. What answer is to be given to this question by one who has been legitimated by subsequent marriage? If the person is ignorant of the fact of legitimation and believes himself legitimate he will answer in the affirmative; on the other hand, if the person already knows that he has been legitimated, the parish priest will be very probably consulted as to the correct answer to be given. Since a person legitimated by his parents' subsequent marriage is made equal to legitimate children in all things, except when the law expressly states otherwise, it seems entirely correct to suggest that the parish priest may properly tell the person to answer the question in the affirmative.

Article IV. Legitimation Granted in Virtue of Canon 1051 and Expressly by Rescript For A Particular Case

Canon 1051. Per dispensationem super impedimento dirimente concessam sive ex potestate ordinaria, sive ex potestate delegata per indultum generale, non vero per rescriptum in casibus particularibus, conceditur quoque eo ipso legitimatio prolis, si qua ex iis cum quibus dispensatur iam nata

[254] Cf. canon 2406.

vel concepta fuerit, excepta tamen adulterina et sacrilega.

The mode of legitimation mentioned in this canon may be said, in a certain sense, to be a new means of legitimation permitted by law. This is so because a dispensation granted in accordance with the provisions of this canon effects legitimation by itself, with no added positive act required once the dispensation has been granted.[255] It may be noted that a dispensation generally implies a relaxation of the law in a particular case: it can be granted by the legislator, by his successor in office, by a superior legislator and by a person delegated by the foregoing.[256]

Specifically, a matrimonial dispensation is a legitimate act of a superior by which the binding force of a law which either prohibits or nullifies the contracting of marriage is relaxed in a particular case.[257] To obtain the effect of legitimation by a matrimonial dispensation it is required, as is evident from the words of the canon, that the impediment which exists between the parties who seek the dispensation be a diriment impediment.[258] From this restriction it is obvious that if the impediment which exists between the parties to a marriage is a prohibitive impediment a dispensation granted in such a case will not effect legitimation.[259] If a prohibitive impediment exists between the parties it is clear from what has been said previously that legitimation can be effected by their subsequent marriage. If a diriment impediment is erroneously thought to exist between the parties and in consequence the grant of a dispensation is secured, the granted dispensation will not effect legitimation, for the dispensa-

[255] Payen, *De Matrimonio*, I, n. 711; De Smet, *De Sponsalibus et Matrimonio*, n. 786, note 2.

[256] Canon 80.

[257] Vermeersch-Creusen, *Epitome*, II, n. 301; cf. O'Keefe, *Matrimonial Dispensations, Powers of Bishops, Priests, and Confessors* (The Catholic University of America, Canon Law Studies, n. 45; Washington, D. C.: The Catholic University of America, 1927), pp. 3-7.

[258] Cf. canon 1036, § 2.

[259] Cf. canon 1036, § 1.

tion cannot be said to remove a diriment impediment which in fact does not exist. If a dispensation from a diriment impediment is actually granted to persons between whom no such impediment exists, then the celebration of marriage becomes a very important factor. Since no diriment impediment exists and legitimation cannot result from the concession of the dispensation, legitimation in such a case will be effected by the parties' subsequent marriage. If a doubtful diriment impediment exists between the parties it is necessary to distinguish whether the impediment is doubtful by reason of a doubt of law or of fact. In the first instance, since no dispensation is required, legitimation must ordinarily be secured by the parties' subsequent marriage; in the second instance, a dispensation *ad cautelam* must be secured. Since such a dispensation will be issued only when the doubt still remains after a diligent inquiry, it seems correct to maintain that a dispensation *ad cautelam* will effect legitimation. In so far as it cannot be said with moral certitude that the diriment impediment does not exist between the parties in such a case, the dispensation granted to them must be regarded, as far as legitimation is concerned, as having the same effect as it would have if a diriment impediment had actually existed between the parties.[260]

It need only be remarked that in the case here contemplated the diriment impediment which exists between the parties must be of a character that allows the granting of a dispensation.

The canon does not attribute the effect of legitimation to every dispensation from a diriment impediment. It is expressly stated that legitimation is effected only when the dispensation is granted by one who has ordinary power, or delegated power in virtue of a general indult.

Since the concepts of ordinary and delegated power have already been treated *ex professo* in another dissertation the reader is referred to that work.[261]

[260] Cf. canon 15; O'Keefe, *Matrimonial Dispensations*, pp. 214-221.

[261] Kearney, *The Principles of Delegation* (The Catholic University of America, Canon Law Studies, n. 55, Washington, D. C.: The Catholic University of America, 1929).

Legitimation is effected in accordance with the provisions of this canon: (1) when the Holy See directly grants a dispensation by a rescript *in forma gratiosa.* This is so because the Holy See acts in virtue of its ordinary power.[262] (2) when an Ordinary or a parish priest grants a dispensation in virtue of the ordinary power conferred by canon 81 and in particular by canons 1043-1045.[263] (3) when a dispensation is granted by one who has delegated power in virtue of a general indult. Any indult, it may be noted, not restricted to one or the other case or to a few determined persons may be called a general indult.[264] Thus, dispensations granted by Apostolic Nuncios, Apostolic Delegates, Bishops, Vicars Apostolic and Prefects Apostolic in virtue either of their quinquennial faculties or of some other general indult which may have been granted to them will effect legitimation.

Legitimation, however, will not be effected if a dispensation is granted in virtue of delegated power through a rescript in a particular case.

It seems that the commentators are not very clear in the explanations they offer concerning the provisions of canon 1051. Vermeersch in discussing the question of legitimation to be obtained in accordance with the provisions of this canon observes that in every dispensation granted by the Holy See either *in forma gratiosa* or through commitment to a local Ordinary for its execution effects legitimation since it is granted by ordinary power. The same cannot be said if the Ordinary is permitted to grant a dispensation in a particular case. In such event the faculty to grant legitimation is not conceded unless it is expressly stated. With reference to a dispensation whose execution when granted by the Holy See is committed to a local Ordinary, Vermeersch notes that he has deliberately avoided the use of the phrase *in forma commissoria,* which is not always employed

262 Cappello, *De Sacramentis,* III, n. 291.

263 Cappello, *loc. cit.*; O'Keefe, *Matrimonial Dispensations,* p. 100; Kearney, *Principles of Delegation,* pp. 55, 56; Harrigan, *Radical Sanation,* p. 55; Brennan, *Simple Convalidation,* p. 111; Gasparri, *De Matrimonio,* I, n. 402; Vermeersch-Creusen, *Epitome,* II, nn. 307, 311.

264 Cappello, *De Sacramentis,* III, n. 245.

in the same sense. The thing that must be kept in mind, he says, is whether the Holy See dispenses *per se* or whether the Ordinary dispenses in virtue of the faculties which he has received.[265]

The different uses of the phrase *in forma commissoria* alluded to by Vermeersch will be apparent from an exposition of the views of various authors. Thus Cappello maintains that dispensation granted *in forma stricte commissoria,* whether by the Holy See or by an Ordinary or by any other person, does not *ipso iure* effect legitimation.[266] De Smet remarks that if an Ordinary grants a dispensation *in forma commissoria* the executor, whether his office be voluntary or necessary, must grant legitimation by an act distinct from the remission of the impediment. Such an act must be performed in virtue of a faculty granted for the purpose by the Ordinary. The same is true, he observes, if the execution of a papal dispensation granted *in forma commissoria* is committed to an Ordinary.[267] Vlaming states that any rescript of the Holy Father granted *in forma commissoria,* and hence any papal dispensation to be conceded through an Ordinary, is a special indult and does not therefore effect legitimation.[268] Ciprotti observes that it seems that a dispensation granted by the Holy See by a rescript *in forma commissoria necessaria* effects legitimation; if however, a dispensation is granted by the Holy See *in forma commissoria libera* it does not effect legitimation.[269] Gasparri is of the opinion that a dispensation granted by delegated power in virtue of a rescript in a particular case cannot effect legitimation unless this faculty was conceded in the rescript of the dispensation.[270] Payen notes that if only the faculty for granting a dispensation is sought from the Holy See, only this faculty will be conceded. Legitimation will not be effected by the

[265] *Theologiae Moralis Principia,* III, n. 705 and note 1.

[266] *De Sacramentis,* III, n. 291.

[267] *De Sponsalibus et Matrimonio,* nn. 786, 876 note 1.

[268] *Praelectiones,* II, n. 454.

[269] *Apollinaris,* XII (1939), 506.

[270] *De Matrimonio,* II, n. 407.

granting of the dispensation.[271] Chelodi maintains that if the power to dispense for a particular case is delegated *in forma stricte commissoria* legitimation will not be effected.[272]

In addition to the various uses of the phrase *in forma commissoria* there is no agreement on the question whether the Holy See, when it grants the faculty to dispense in a particular case, includes the faculty to grant legitimation regardless of whether or not it has been requested to grant such a faculty. Cappello says that the Holy See is accustomed to add the faculty of declaring the legitimation of offspring in a particular case even though such a faculty was not sought.[273]

Payen maintains the same view, but adds that the petitioners should request, at least *ad cautelam,* such a faculty for the executor.[274] Gasparri states that the Congregation of the Sacraments expressly concedes in the rescripts of dispensations the faculty to legitimate the offspring as often as the faculty is expressly sought in the petition. If mention of the desired faculty was omitted in the petition, or if, even though it was included there, the mention of its grant is not contained in the rescript of the dispensation, the offspring remains illegitimate. There must be sought in a new petition the faculty either of declaring the offspring legitimate or of directly effecting the legitimation of the offspring.[275] De Smet observes that it does not seem that the faculty to grant legitimation is contained in rescripts of the external forum unless such a faculty has been expressly sought in the petition.[276]

In view of the authors' conflicting statements which result from their varied use of the phrase *in forma commissoria,* and also in the face of their disagreement over the question whether the Holy See grants the faculty for legitimation, even though it has not been sought, whenever it grants the faculty to dispense

[271] *De Matrimonio,* I, n. 713.

[272] *Ius Matrimoniale,* n. 49.

[273] *De Sacramentis,* III, n. 291.

[274] *De Matrimonio,* I, n. 713.

[275] *De Matrimonio,* I, n. 407.

[276] *De Sponsalibus et Matrimonio,* n. 876, note 1.

from a diriment impediment, an attempt must be made to outline a method of procedure to be observed when legitimation is sought along with the faculty to dispense from a diriment impediment. From the words of canon 1051 there is no doubt that legitimation is effected when a dispensation from a diriment impediment is granted by one who has ordinary power, or delegated power in virtue of a general indult. Since Ordinaries are accustomed to grant dispensations *in forma gratiosa,* there is no need to include a request for legitimation when application is made for a dispensation. Mention may be made of the need of legitimation, not because it is necessary in such a case to include a decree of legitimation in the rescript, but in order that it may be noted in the rescript that legitimation has been effected by the dispensation. The fact of legitimation will then be clear from an authentic document.[277]

On the other hand, it is the practice of the Holy See to issue dispensations *in forma commissoria.*[278] Since this is so, it is evident that when the faculty to grant a dispensation is requested of the Holy See the faculty to grant legitimation, if there be need of it, should also be expressly sought.[279] Gasparri states that the practice of the Congregation of the Sacraments is to add the clause *prolem susceptam legitimam decernat atque declaret* to rescripts of dispensations from any diriment impediment as often as mention has been made of the necessity of legitimation.[280] If the request for legitimation has been expressly mentioned in the petition addressed to the Holy See for the faculty of granting a dispensation it will be evident from the rescript whether the faculty to grant legitimation has been granted or denied.

[277] De Smet, *De Sponsalibus et Matrimonio,* nn. 849, 890; cf. Van Hove, *De Rescriptis* (Mechliniae-Romae: H. Dessain, 1936), n. 130.

[278] Gasparri, *De Matrimonio,* I, n. 407; De Smet, *De Sponsalibus et Matrimonio,* n. 861; cf. also n. 749; Vlaming, *Praelectiones,* II, n. 454.

[279] De Smet, *De Sponsalibus ea Matrimonio,* nn. 786, 849, 876, note 1; Wernz-Vidal, *Ius Matrimoniale,* n. 420, note 79; Vermeersch-Creusen, *Epitome,* II, n. 315.

[280] *De Matrimonio,* I, n. 358.

The Holy See can, of course, dispense directly *in forma gratiosa*. But such a procedure is very rare. De Smet observes that when the Holy See dispenses in this way it handles the whole affair itself, save perhaps the items touching on the verification of the petition. He observes that if there is need of it then such a dispensation will contain a declaration of legitimation. When the dispensation has been granted it is presented to the Ordinary in accordance with the provisions of canon 51.[281] Since a dispensation issued by the Holy See *in forma gratiosa* is granted in virtue of ordinary power, it does not seem necessary as De Smet says, that such a dispensation should contain express mention of the legitimation The canon states explicitly that legitimation is effected by the concession of the dispensation alone. De Smet himself observes that the ordinary power of dispensing does not only denote the power of granting legitimation, but that the very exercise of ordinary power *in forma gratiosa ipso facto* effects legitimation.[282] Other authors state explicitly that if a dispensation is granted in virtue either of ordinary power or of power delegated through a general indult then legitimation is effected even though no mention is made of legitimation either by the petitioners or by the person who dispenses. This is true even though the need of legitimation is unknown.[283] If the Holy See *de facto* does include mention of legitimation in the rescript of a dispensation which it grants *in forma gratiosa,* then the notation will serve as an authentic record of the legitimation.

If a dispensation from a diriment impediment has been granted in virtue either of ordinary power or of power delegated through a general indult, then legitimation is effected at the moment the dispensation is granted. If the dispensation has been granted by a rescript *in forma commissoria* for a particular

[281] *De Sponsalibus et Matrimonio,* n. 861.

[282] *De Sponsalibus et Matrimonio,* n. 786.

[283] Gasparri, *De Matrimonio,* I, n. 407; Wernz-Vidal, *Ius Matrimoniale,* n. 420; Cappello, *De Sacramentis,* III, n. 291; Chelodi, *Ius Matrimoniale,* n. 49; Harrigan, *Radical Sanation,* p. 55; Brennan, *Simple Convalidation,* p. 112; Ciprotti, *Apollinaris,* XII (1939), 508.

case, then legitimation will be effected when the faculty of granting legitimation as contained in the rescript is used. It is presupposed, of course, that the faculty of granting legitimation has been sought along with the faculty to dispense from the diriment impediment. Too much insistence cannot be placed on the necessity of expressly seeking the faculty to grant legitimation when the faculty to grant a dispensation from a diriment impediment in a particular case is sought from the Holy See. If the faculty to grant legitimation is sought expressly then the conflicting opinions of the authors raise no practical difficulty, since the rescript will indicate the faculty to concede legitimation.

The canon states that legitimation is conceded to those children, who have been born to or conceived of the parties who receive a dispensation from the diriment impediment. It is patent that if no child has been born, or at least conceived, there is no need of legitimation. It is required, of course, that the child to be legitimated be the offspring of the man and the woman who have been granted a dispensation.[284] Regarding the case in which a dispensation has been granted to persons after the conception of a child it is necessary to observe that such a child is legitimated by the dispensation granted to the parents. Should the child be born after the parents have contracted marriage it will be legitimate according to the provisions of canon 1114.[285] The possibility not only of legitimation but also of legitimacy in such cases is worthy of consideration. According to the provisions of canon 1051 legitimation is effected by the concession of the dispensation, and not by the marriage of the parents which is made possible by the removal of the diriment impediment which has existed between them. If the parents do not marry after the dispensation has been obtained, the child will nevertheless remain legitimated; if the parents do marry before the birth of the child, it will be legitimate according to the provisions of canon 1114. If the parents marry only

[284] Blat, *Commentarium,* Lib. III, pars. 1, n. 445.

[285] Payen, *De Matrimonio,* I, n. 710; cf. Vlaming, *Praelectiones,* II, n. 454.

after the birth of the child, it will indeed remain legitimated, but in such an event it must be observed that the child is furthermore entitled to the benefits of legitimation which result from the parents' subsequent marriage. Since the diriment impediment existing between the parents was removed before the child's birth it is evident that the parents were capable of marriage at least at the time of the child's birth. The effects of the parents' intermarriage before the birth of the child whose conception occurred at a time when the parents were laboring under a diriment impediment are of the greatest importance to the child. The removal of the parents' impediment before the birth of their child helps to convert the case into one wherein the full benefit of legitimacy accrues to the child in view of its birth from a valid marriage. The full juridical requirement for legitimacy, as stipulated by canon 1114, then stands fulfilled.

If a child has already been born to parents between whom there existed, during all the time from the child's conception until some point of time after its birth, a diriment impediment which is later removed by dispensation the intermarriage of the parents will not render the child legitimate. The child remains legitimated as a result of the dispensation, but it cannot be regarded as legitimate according to the meaning of canon 1114. Since the dispensation itself effects legitimation, such a child will remain legitimated even if the parents do not contract marriage.

Since the dispensation from a diriment impediment, and not the mere cessation of it, effects legitimation, it is evident that legitimation is not effected according to the provisions of canon 1051 if a diriment impediment has ceased for any reason other than the concession of a dispensation. Legitimation by a dispensation from a diriment impediment is impossible when no diriment impediment exists between the parents of an illegitimate child. Thus, it may be observed that with regard to legitimation the condition of a child born of parents between whom there exists a diriment impediment which can be removed by a dispensation is more favorable than that of a child born of parents between whom a diriment impediment has existed but which has ceased at some point of time subsequent to the child's birth. In the first case the child may be legitimated in virtue of canon 1051; in the latter case the child cannot be legitimated through the same means of a granted dispensation for since the impediment has ceased to exist there cannot be any possibility of a dispensation. Moreover, if the diriment impediment which has ceased to exist between its parents had existed from the time of the child's conception until the time of its birth the child cannot be legitimated by the subsequent marriage of its parents.[286]

Canon 1051 excludes two classes of illegitimate children from the benefits of legitimation by dispensation from a diriment impediment, viz., adulterine children and those who are the fruit of sacrilege. As has already been shown, adulterine children are the result of the crime of adultery. They are begotten by parents one of whom or both of whom are already married to another. Children who are the fruit of sacrilege are those begotten of parents one of whom or both of whom are bound by Solemn Vows or whose father is in Sacred Orders from whose obligations he has not been released at the time of the child's conception. These children are regarded as the fruit of sacrilege either if the parents are parties to a vaild marriage the use of which has been denied to them at the time of the conception of the children, or if the parents have attempted marriage after at least one of them has been solemnly professed or the father has received the subdiaconate It must be recalled that by special privilege the simple profession of Jesuit scholistics

[286] "Quo casu, cum, si filius natus sit ante cessatum impedimentum, ipse plerumque (i. e. nisi conceptus sit antequam exoriretur impedimentum) sit spurius neque possit legitimari per subsequens parentum matrimonium, possunt videri minus congruae Codicis normae, utpote quae magis faveant filio si, post eius nativitatem, impedimentum (e. g. aetas vel cultus disparitas), dispensetur, quam si aliter cesset."—Ciprotti, *Apollinaris,* XII (1939), 507; cf. *supra.*

and of the lay coadjutors (brothers) of the Society has a nullifying effect on a subsequent marriage.[287]

With regard to children conceived in adultery it has already been observed that if the impediment of previous bond has ceased before their birth, such children may be legitimated by the subsequent marriage of their parents. If, however, the impediment remains until after their birth, then these children cannot be legitimated by the subsequent marriage of their parents. They are expressly excluded from legitimation by dispensation in accordance with the provisions of this canon. The Church cannot dispense from the impediment of previous bond arising from a ratified and consummated marriage.[288] Ciprotti maintains that adulterine children will not be legitimated by a dispensation from any impediment concurring with the impediment of previous bond for, he states, a dispensation from the impediment of previous bond cannot be granted. Other concurring ecclesiastical impediments can be removed by dispensation, for instance, when the impediment of previous bond has ceased through death or through a dispensation from a non-consummated marriage, or when through the privilege of the faith a new marriage may be contracted. He notes, too, that if a dispensation has been granted for an ecclesiastical impediment concurrent with the impediment of previous bond which latter impediment has ceased before a child's birth, the child may be legitimated by the parents' subsequent marriage, provided of course that no other diriment impediment exists between the parents.[289] It seems that the impediment most probably concurring with the impediment of previous bond in the cases to which Ciprotti refers is the impediment of crime. This seems true for the reason that he is speaking of adulterine children.[290] It must be noted here that the Holy See is not accustomed to grant legitimation to adulterine children even

[287] Vermeersch-Creusen, *Epitome,* II, n. 348.

[288] Canon 1118.

[289] *Apollinaris,* XII (1939), 507 and note 6.

[290] Cf. canons 1075, 1053, 1118, 1119, 1120.

when it grants a dispensation from a diriment impediment. Thus while the Congregation of the Sacraments on December 12, 1924, granted a dispensation from the impediments of consanguinity and crime to parties who had begotten a child in adultery, it was expressly stated in the rescript of the dispensation that the child was not legitimated.[291]

The canon states expressly that children who are the fruit of sacrilege are excluded from legitimation by a dispensation from a diriment impediment. Consequently, even if a dispensation has been granted to the parents of such children, these, if they are already born, will not be legitimated by the dispensation granted to the parents; if such children are born after the dispensation has been granted but before the marriage of their parents they can be legitimated by the subsequent marriage of their parents, since these are capable of marriage at least at the time of the children's birth. If the parents marry before the children's birth these will be legitimate according to the provisions of canon 1114. It is to be noted that the possibility of legitimation, or even of legitimacy, for such children is based not on the dispensation which has been granted to their parents but rather on the capacity of the parents to contract marriage either after or before the birth of the children. This remains true even though it is admitted that the parents are rendered capable of marriage solely because of the dispensation which by reason of the exceptions stated in canon 1051 cannot of itself render the children under discussion legitimated.

The exception of children who are the fruit of sacrilege from the possibility of legitimation in virtue of canon 1051 is restricted to those cases in which the children have been conceived by or born outside of wedlock to persons of whom one or both are bound by solemn vows, or the father is bound by the simple vow which invalidates marriage, or the father is in Sacred Orders. This is so because if Sacred Orders have been received or if solemn profession has been made by a person already

[291] De Smet, *De Sponsalibus et Matrimonio,* n. 849, *in fine,* note 1; cf. Haring, "Eine schwierige Legitimation," *LQS,* LXXXV (1932), 147-148.

married there can be no question of a dispensation from either of these impediments as they did not exist at the time of the marriage.

The authors are not in complete agreement as to the extent of the exception of canon 1051 with reference to children who are the fruit of sacrilege. Thus, for example, Gasparri identifies as the fruit of sacrilege any child begotten by a man in Sacred Orders or begotten by parents one or both of whom have taken a public vow in religion, whether the vow is solemn or simple, final or temporary.[292] Cappello in one place maintains the same view, but adds that the faculty to grant legitimation to such children is sometimes conceded, especially if they have been born of parents one or both of whom are bound only by simple religious profession. In another place he observes that children are the fruit of sacrilege when they are born of parents one or both of whom are bound by a solemn vow of chastity or when the father is in Sacred Orders.[293] Payen states that a child is the fruit of sacrilege if one or the other of the parents is bound by a public vow of chastity, even though it is but a simple vow.[294] From what has already been said regarding the various classes of illegitimate children it can be concluded that the following classes of children are regarded as the fruit of sacrilege with reference to the exception stated in canon 1051: (1) the children begotten by a father who has received at least the Subdiaconate; (2) the children begotten by parents one or both of whom have made solemn religious profession; (3) the children begottent by a father who has taken the simple vow which invalidates marriage.[295] It is to be noted that the children referred to in n. 3 do not come under the exception stated in canon 1114.

With reference to the views of Gasparri, Cappello, and Payen it is to be observed that children who are conceived or born of

[292] *De Matrimonio,* I, n. 358.
[293] *De Sacramentis,* III, nn. 291; 745.
[294] *De Matrimonio,* I, n. 710, note 1.
[295] Cf. Blat, *Commentarium,* Lib. III, pars 1, n. 445.

parents one or both of whom are bound by simple profession must not be regarded as the fruit of sacrilege. It has already been shown that children who are the fruit of sacrilege are classified under "spurious" children, or, in other words, that they are considered the children of parents who cannot validly marry. (The exception of canon 1114 must be kept in mind). Such, however, is not the case of persons who are bound by simple profession. Persons thus bound are, it is true, severely prohibited from marrying, but should they marry in the face of this prohibition their marriage would not be invalid but illicit on the grounds of simple profession.[296] Children then who are begotten by parents one or both of whom are bound by simple vows (with the exception of the simple vow of the Jesuits) are not "spurious" children since their parents are capable of valid marriage. Such children are not to be regarded as the fruit of sacrilege.[297]

The question arises whether the exception stated in canon 1051 with reference to adulterine children and those who are the fruit of sacrilege obtains when a dispensation is granted in accordance with the provisions of canon 1043. The opinion of the great majority of the authors is that the exception is enforced even when one of the parents is in danger of death when the dispensation for the marriage is granted.[298]

With regard to the possibility of legitimation for adulterine children and for those who are the fruit of sacrilege, if their parents are granted a dispensation while in danger of death, the response of the Holy Office to a doubt regarding the scope of

[296] Cf. canons 1058, § 2; 2388, § 2.

[297] Ciprotti, *Apollinaris,* XII (1939), 491, and note 3.

[298] Gasparri, *De Matrimonio,* I, n. 394; Wernz-Vidal, *Ius Matrimoniale,* n. 413; Vlaming, *Praelectiones,* II, n. 401; De Smet, *De Sponsalibus et Matrimonio,* n. 759, note 2; Vermeersch, *Theologiae Moralis Principia,* III, n. 705; Genicot-Salsmans, *Institutiones Theologiae Moralis,* II, n. 523; Blat, *Commentarium,* Lib. III, pars 1, n. 435; Vermeersch-Creusen, *Epitome,* II, n. 305; Leitner, *Lehrbuch des katholischen Eherechts,* p. 324; Ayrinhac-Lydon, *Marriage Legislation,* n. 71; Petrovits, *The New Church, Law on Matrimony,* n. 156.

the faculty granted to Ordinaries by Leo XIII on February 20, 1888, may be cited here. The Holy Office answered the following question on July 8, 1903: "Utrum intelligatur concessa etiam facultas declarandi et nunciandi legitimam prolem spuriam, forsitan . . . susceptam, . . . an contra pro susceptae prolis legitimatione necesse sit novam gratiam a S. Sede postea impetrare?" Responsum: "Affirmative quoad primam partem, *excepta prole adulterina et prole proveniente a personis Ordine sacro aut solemni professione religiosa ligatis.* Quoad secundam partem, provisum in prima." [299] Cappello seems to maintain that adulterine children and those who are the fruit of sacrilege may be legitimated by the concession of a dispensation to the parents while they are in danger of death.[300] From a consideration of the authors whom Cappello cites in support of his opinion it seems that he really maintains the same view as they do, viz., that an Ordinary can dispense with the intention of rendering it more easy to obtain a rescript of legitimation for adulterine children or those who are the fruit of sacrilege.[301]

The question whether an Ordinary may dispense in virtue of canon 1043 when the only cause for granting a dispensation is the legitimation of adulterine children or of those children who are the fruit of sacrilege is discussed at length by O'Keefe. The question, he admits, will hardly ever arise in practice. He observes that most authors hold that since such children cannot be legitimated by a dispensation of this kind, a dispensation cannot be granted for the purpose of granting them legitimation. Other authors, he continues, draw a distinction. While they admit, at least implicitly, that the direct intention of legitimating adulterine children and those who are the fruit of sacrilege, is

299 *Collectanea Sacrae Congregationis de Propaganda Fide*, n. 2171; cf. n. 1685. *ASS*, XXXVI (1903), 118; *Fontes*, n. 1267; cf. n. 1109.

300 "Consulitur proli, sive sit naturalis sive sit incestuosa sive etiam, ut quidam opinantur, adulterina vel sacrilega."—*De Sacramentis*, III, n. 231; cf. Schmitz, *Die Stellung der unehelichen Kinder im geltenden kanonischen Recht*, p. 116.

301 O'Keefe, *Matrimonial Dispensations*, p. 70.

not a sufficient cause for granting a dispensation, they admit that the legitimation of such children can be indirectly a sufficient cause to permit the use of canon 1043. These authors do not deny, he says, that a rescript of legitimation from the Holy See is necessary for the legitimation of such children, but they maintain that such a rescript can be obtained more easily when the parents are already married than when they are unmarried. The greatest difficulty which can be urged against the more liberal opinion is the declaration of the Holy Office on July 8, 1903, to which reference has already been made. This response, O'Keefe maintains, does not consider the point under discussion. According to him all it establishes is that a dispensation granted in the danger of death does not legitimate adulterine children and those who are the fruit of sacrilege; that in such cases a rescript of legitimation from the Holy See is necessary to effect legitimation; and, at most, that the direct intention of legitimating such offspring by the dispensation itself is not a sufficient cause to justify the use of the faculty to grant the dispensation. His conclusion is that since no apodictical argument can be deduced against the milder opinion either from external authority or internal reasoning, and since some grave canonists maintain the more liberal view, it is safe to follow the milder opinion in practice. At the very least, he says, the law restricting the power of the Ordinary in such cases is doubtful. Hence, he maintains, Ordinaries may dispense in such cases until such time as the Holy See shall give an official decision, or the teaching of the canonists renders the opinion improbable.[302]

The canon expressly excludes only adulterine children and those who are the fruit of sacrilege. Consequently, it is necessary to determine if any other classes of "spurious" children may be legitimated according to the provisions of this canon. There is no express mention of those children who are born of parents related in the direct line, because their parents can

[302] *Matrimonial Dispensations,* pp. 67-70.

never be dispensed from this impediment.[303] With regard to children born of parents related within the forbidden degress of consanguinity or affinity in the collateral line it is necessary to draw a distinction. If the parents are related in the first degree of consanguinity there is no possibility of legitimation in accordance with the provisions of this canon, because the parents can never receive a dispensation.[304] If the parents are related within any of the other forbidden degrees of the collateral line a dispensation may be granted and the legitimation of any children will thereby be effected. In view of the exclusion of children born of parents related in the first degree of consanguinity in the collateral line the unqualified statement of Payen that children who are the fruit of incest can be legitimated by a dispensation granted to their parents is not very exact. He does, however, make mention of the exclusion of children born of parents related in the direct line.[305] The same is to be said of the 'statement of Brennan who asserts that children born of parents whose union is invalid because of the impediment of consanguinity in the collateral line are legitimated if a dispensation from the impediment is granted according to the conditions stipulated in the canon.[306] It may be argued, however, that these authors do exclude, at least implicitly, those children who are born of parents related in the first degree of consanguinity in the collateral line—since the parents cannot be dispensed.

Ciprotti excludes from legitimation by dispensation in accordance with the provisions of this canon those children whose parents are otherwise incapable of marriage on account of a perpetual impediment of the divine law. He maintains, however, that if the impediment of the divine law is not perpetual, e.g., insanity, and there is also present an impediment of the ecclesiastical law, a dispensation from the latter, granted after the former

303 Canon 1076, § 1.

304 Canon 1076, § 3.

305 *De Matrimonio,* I, n. 710.

306 *Simple Convalidation,* p. 112.

has ceased, will effect legitimation, unless the child is adulterine or the fruit of sacrilege.[307]

It can be stated now that the following children are excluded either explicity or implicitly from legitimation in virtue of a dispensation granted according to the provisions of this canon: (1) adulterine children; (2) children who are the fruit of sacrilege; (3) children begotten of parents related in the direct line; (4) children begotten of parents who are related in the first degree of consanguinity in the collateral line; (5)) children between whose parents there exists a perpetual impediment of the divine law; (6) "natural" children, excepting the case where a diriment impediment existing between the parents at the time of the conception of such a child is removed by dispensation before the child's birth. With regard to a "natural" child whose parents cannot intermarry at the time of the child's conception, it has already been shown that if the parents do not marry after the dispensation has been granted, the child remains legitimated according to the provisions of canon 1051; if the parents marry before the birth of the child it will be legitimate in accordance with the provisions of canon 1114; if the parents marry after the child's birth the child obtains the benefits of legitimation in accordance with provisions of canons 1116 and 1117. Ciprotti remarks that in such a case the child obtains a fuller legitimation through the marriage itself. This is so because while the effects of legitimation by subsequent marriage are definitely set forth in canon 1117, the same cannot be said of the effects of legitimation granted in virtue of canon 1051.[308]

It has been repeatedly stated in the discussion of this canon that legitimation is effected by the concession of a dispensation and not by the marriage which is made possible by the removal of the impediment. Some authors do not discuss the question of legitimation in the event that the parents do not contract marriage after a dispensation has been granted. Other authors do mention the question. Some say that if the marriage does

[307] *Apollinaris,* XII (1939), 508.
[308] *Apollinaris,* XII (1939), 511.

not take place, through no fault of the parents, after a dispensation has been granted, a child already born or conceived is legitimated. They maintain that if the marriage of the parents is not contracted through their own fault, after the dispensation has been granted the legitimation of the child is disputed. Ayrinhac-Lydon discuss the question and incline to the view that the child will remain legitimated even if the parents through their own fault fail to contract marriage. These authors refer especially to the question of the convalidation of a marriage but their opinion is also applicable to the case in which the marital contract is initially undertaken.[309] Cappello observes that a child remains legitimated if the parents through no fault of their own cannot marry after a dispensation has been granted. With regard to the case when the parties refuse to contract marriage he remarks, as has already been declared, that some authors think the legitimation is inefficacious, since it has been granted in view of the parents' marriage. He maintains, however, that it seems that legitimation must be certainly admitted if a dispensation has been granted either in virtue of ordinary power or through a power delegated by means of a general indult, because in such cases legitimation is granted *ipso iure,* and once it has been granted there is no reason why it should be revoked. Legitimation must be admitted likewise, he continues, if it has been granted in virtue of a particular rescript, unless the rescript expressly contained a restrictive clause. The reasons he advanced for his opinion are: (1) the canons favor the legitimation of offspring as far as possible; (2) legitimation once granted remains until it is revoked by a competent superior; (3) the reason that legitimation is granted only in view of marriage is not to be insisted on too strongly, otherwise it would have to be applied in every case where marriage is not celebrated, inasmuch as legitimation is always granted in view of a future marriage. Gasparri when speaking of legitimation which is granted by the Sacred Congregation of the Sacraments for a particular case in virtue of a clause included in the rescript of a dispensation from a diriment impedi-

[309] *Marriage Legislation,* n. 84.

ment says that if the petitioner dies after the concession of the decree but before marriage can be celebrated, the child remains legitimated. The same is true if the marriage cannot be contracted through no fault of the petitioners. He believes however, that if the petitioner refuses through his own fault to contract marriage the decree of legitimation granted in view of the future marriage has no effect.[310]

The opinion of Ciprotti is that since legitimation is granted by the dispensation itself it does not matter if the parents do not marry afterwards. He maintains that it is of no importance whether the cause which prevents marriage is a just cause or a culpable cause. Whether the cause is culpable or not, since the child is already legitimated, it remains so even if its parents do not contract marriage. He remarks, however, that it is scarcely possible to have a culpable cause on the part of both of the parties dispensed.[311] Ciprotti goes so far as to say that if one or both parents request a dispensation without any intention of contracting marriage, but solely for the purpose of effecting legitimation, this effect will follow unless the dispensation is null either because the truth has been concealed or beause reasons which are untrue have been alleged. He observes further that the lack of the intention to marry does not invalidate a dispensation granted, as is evident from the fact that a dispensation may be granted to persons who are unwilling or ignorant of the concession.[312]

[310] *De Matrimonio,* I, n. 358; Ciprotti correctly maintains that Gasparri, although he expressly mentions canon 1051, speaks here of legitimation which is granted by delegated power in a particular case, and not of legitimation granted in virtue of canon 1051. The passage of Gasparri just referred to is quoted by Ciprotti in his consideration of legitimation by Papal rescript. The question, however, of legitimation in virtue of an express declaration of the Sacred Congregation of the Sacraments as included in the rescript of a dispensation granted in a particular case has already been considered in this thesis along with the question of legitimation according to the provisions of canon 1051.—Cf. *Apollinaris,* XII (1939), 509, note 12; 516, and note 4.

[311] *Apollinaris,* XII (1939), 509.

[312] *Apollinaris,* XII (1939), 509, 510, and note 13; cf. canons 40, 42, 45, 1042, 1054.

In view of the words of canon 1051 itself, and also of the explanations of the authors, that the concession of the dispensation, and not the marriage of the parents, effects legimation, it is correct to maintain that even if the parents do not marry the dispensation does effect legitimation. This view, it may be noted, has been adopted in the foregoing discussion of canon 1051.

The authors who specifically mention this question grant that the legitimation is effected in those cases in which the parents cannot marry. With regard to those cases wherein one or both parents refuse to marry, it seems correct to maintain that legitimation is nevertheless effected by the dispensation, for if all the requisites for the valid granting of the dispensation are present, the granted dispensation (and its effects) cannot be rendered invalid by any action on the part of the dispensed persons.[313] The view that such a dispensation effects legitimation even when there is no intention to marry is absolutely correct in the cases when a dispensation has been granted to remove a minor diriment impediment.[314] With reference to the cases not comprehended under canons 1054 and 1042 it seems correct to maintain also that a granted dispensation does effect legitimation even when there is no intention to marry, as long as the essential conditions for the valid concession of the dispensation have been fulfilled. If it be objected against this view that a dispensation of this kind is granted *intuitu matrimonii* and that consequently the legitimation granted by the dispensation remains inoperative until marriage has actually been contracted, then the objection must also include the case wherein the parents cannot marry as well as the cases wherein one or both of the parents have no intention to marry. This is so because if it is maintained that the legitimation remains inoperative until marriage is contracted, then the nature of

[313] ". . . nam cum obtenta dispensatione, proles iam ipso iure legitimetur, patet subsequentibus eventibus minime legitimationem infirmari, quae iam peracta sit."—Ciprotti, *Apollinaris*, XII (1939), 509.

[314] Cf. canons 1054 and 1042.

the cause which prevents marriage should be of no importance. It has been shown, however, that the authors admit that legitimation is effected by the dispensation when the parents cannot marry. This demonstrates plainly that they do not regard the fact that such a dispensation is granted *intuitu matrimonii* to be of such strict interpretation that the contracting of marriage is demanded as a *conditio sine qua non* for the concession of legitimation It seems correct to argue that if the contracting of marriage is not demanded to make the legitimation effective in the cases wherein the parents cannot marry, the absence of the intention to marry will not render legitimation inoperative provided, of course, that the essential conditions for the valid granting of the dispensation have been fulfilled.

With regard to those cases in which a decree of legitimation is included in the rescript of a dispensation granted by the Sacred Congregation of the Sacraments for a particular case, the opinion of Cappello, that in such cases legitimation is also granted even if the parents cannot or will not marry, seems preferable to the opinion of those authors who deny that the decree of legitimation has any effect in such cases.[315] Thus, the opinion of Gasparri, who believes that the legitimation is inefficacious when the parents refuse to marry, inasmuch as the decree of legitimation is conceded in view of the parents' marriage, cannot be maintained. The view of Gasparri seems to be shared by Ciprotti who quotes the opinion of Gasparri and then cites Sanchez who maintained the same opinion.[316]

It seems that the opinion of the authors who, on the grounds that the decree of legitimation has been granted in view of the parents' marriage, deny the efficacy of legitimation in the cases wherein the parents refuse to marry, is not to be maintained. It does not seem correct to think that the legislator, who, as far as can be deduced from a consideration of canon

[315] These cases, it is true, do not come under the provisions of canon 1051, as has already been observed. Since, however, the question of a dispensation from a matrimonial impediment is concerned, these cases have been considered in the discussion of canon 1051.

[316] Apollinaris, XII (1939), 516, and note 3.

1051, permits legitimation by the granting of a dispensation and not by the marriage, which is made possible by the concession of the dispensation, would be more insistent on the marriage of the parents in the cases wherein legitimation is expressly cleared in the particular rescript of a dispensation issued by the Holy See.

In view of all that has been said regarding the provisions of canon 1051, the opinion of Regatillo, who maintains that legitimation is effected by the subsequent marriage of the parents and not by the concession of the dispensation, cannot be sustained. He proposes what is practically the same argument as that offered by Vermeersch relative to the possibility of legitimation through subsequent marriage for the child of parents between whom there has existed a diriment impediment which, however, ceases at some time subsequent to the child's birth. Regatillo maintains that if legitimation were granted without the subsequent marriage of the parents, "spurious" children would enjoy a more favorable condition than "natural" children. Besides, he observes, it is strange that the Church would grant legitimation without the parents' marriage, for the principal reason which the Church has in granting legitimation by subsequent marriage, namely, the cessation of concubinage, would be frustrated.[317]

The reasons advanced by Ragatillo, while they are admittedly serious, cannot, in view both of the words of canon 1051 itself and of the teaching of the authors, lead one to abandon the opinion that the dispensation, and not the marriage effects legitimation. Regatillo himself admits that his view is contrary to the common opinion of the canonists.[318]

It may be noted here that the legitimation of offspring constitutes a valid canonical cause for the concession of a matrimonial dispensation.[319]

[317] Gonzalez, "Excerptum," *Ius Pontificium,* XIII (1933), 305-306.

[318] . . . Haec argumenta, (ipsius Regatillo), etsi gravia, de iure condendo satius valere possunt, cum perspicuus legis textus non patiatur ut legitimatio quae per dispensationem fieri statuitur, intelligatur per subsequens evenire matrimonium.—Ciprotti, *Apollinaris,* XII (1939), 510.

[319] Octava causa est: "Copula cum consanguinea vel affine vel alia persona

Finally, it is to be noted that the granted dispensation which effects legitimation *ipso iure* in virtue of the provisions of this canon may be a dispensation conceded either to permit the contracting of a new marriage or the convalidation of an already existing invalid marriage. If the marriage to be convalidated is a putative marriage, no legitimation is required; for the offsprng of such a marriage is legitimate according to the provisions of canon 1114.[320]

Article V. Effects of the Legitimation Granted in Accordance With the Provisions of Canon 1051

Although the effects of legitimation by subsequent marriage are expressly stated in the Code, there is no mention there of the effects of the legitimation granted in accordance with the provisions of canon 1051. The authors generally do not discuss the question of the effects of this latter mode of legitimation at all. A few of them do mention the question. Maroto, for example, observes that while the legitimation granted in virtue of this canon is not strictly legitimation by subsequent marriage, it seems that, insofar as its effects are concerned, it is to be regarded as equivalent to legitimation by subsequent marriage.[321] Payen, in referring to the case in which a person has been legitimated by a dispensation granted according to the provisions of this canon, implies that children thus legitimated are, as he expresses it, perfectly legitimated.[322] Blat maintains that the effects of a marriage contracted in virtue of a dispensation granted according to the provisions of canon 1051 are less than those of a subsequent marriage which meets the requirements of canon 1116.[323] Ciprotti observes that the

impedimento laborante praehabita, et praegnantia, ideoque legitimatio prolis, ut nempe consulatur bono prolis ipsius et honori mulieris, quae secus innupta maneret. Haec profecto una est ex ungentioribus causis . . ."—S. C. de Prop. Fide, *Instructio supra Dispensationibus Matrimonialibus,* 9 maii, 1877 —*Collectanea,* n. 1470.

[320] Cf. Brennan, *Simple Convalidation,* pp. 110-113.

[321] *Institutiones,* I, n. 438.

[322] *De Matrimonio,* II, n. 2181.

[323] *Commentarium,* Lib. III, Pars I, n. 445.

effects of this legitimation cannot be stated without difficulty, for although canon 1117 regards those who are legitimated by subsequent marriage as equal generally to legitimate children, it seems that all other legitimated children are not governed by the same norm. He maintains that children legitimated in accordance with the provisions of canon 1051 are not irregular, but still he insists that they cannot enter a seminary or be elected to the office of major superior in religious institutes. These children, he remarks, generally do not have the name of legitimate children unless the law states otherwise. If the foregoing interpretation is admitted, he concludes, the legitimation granted according to canon 1051 would not seem to differ, as far as its effects are concerned, from a dispensation granted from the irregularity of illegitimacy either by the law itself through solemn profession or through a special dispensation.[324]

It seems that for practical purposes the question of the scope of the effects of the legitimation conceded in virtue of canon 1051 is important in two cases: (1) when a dispensation from a diriment impediment has been granted to persons who have already conceived a child but who do not actually marry after the concession of the dispensation; (2) when a dispensation has been granted to persons to whom a child has already been born, in those cases wherein the parents were incapable of intermarriage from the time of the child's conception until some point of time subsequent to its birth. In the first case, if the parents marry before the child's birth, the child will be legitimate in virtue of canon 1114; if they marry at any time after the child's birth, their subsequent marriage will entitle the child to the benefits of legitimation in virtue of canons 1116 and 1117. In the second case the fact of the parents' marriage will have no added effect on the status of the child with regard to the question of legitimation.

It does not seem correct to maintain, as Maroto does, that the effects of the legitimation granted in accordance with the provisions of canon 1051 are the same as the effects of the

[324] *Appollinaris,* XII (1939), 511-512.

legitimation which is conceded by the parents subsequent marriage. There is, for example, no basis in the law for claiming that the children who are legitimated by a dispensation granted in virtue of canon 1051 are regarded as equal to legitimate children in all things, except where the law expressly states otherwise. Children legitimated by their parents' subsequent marriage are declared to be equal to legitimate children as far as the canonical effects of legitimacy are concerned except where the law expressely declares otherwise.[325] On the other hand, it does not seem correct to assert as Ciprotti does, that the legitimation granted according to the provisions of this canon would not seem to differ, as far as its effects are concerned, from a dispensation from the irregularity of illegitimacy granted either by the law itself through solemn profession or through a special dispensation granted for the purpose of receiving Holy Orders. This is so because the legitimation granted in accordance with the provisions of this canon, even though the legislator has not expressly and definitively determined its scope, is legitimation strictly so called and consequently cannot be compared to the removal of the irregularity of illegitimacy either by solemn profession or by a special dispensation. One difference is already apparent in that the effect of solemn profession or of a special dispensation for the reception of Orders is restricted solely to the reception of Orders while the effects of the dispensation granted according to the provisions of canon 1051 are uncertain to say the least.

The statement of Blat that the effects of a marriage contracted in virtue of a dispensation granted according to the provisions of this canon are less than those of a subsequent marriage which has been contracted in accordance with the provisions of canon 1116, would seem to be true with reference to the question of legitimation, if he means that in the latter case legitimation is effected by the marriage itself while in the former case the marriage does not of itself effect legitimation. He seems, however, to have in mind the restriction of canon

[325] Canon 1117.

1051 with reference to adulterine children and those who are the fruit of sacrilege, the marriage of whose parents he contrasts with the subsequent marriage of persons capable of marriage at any of the points of time mentioned in canon 1116.[326]

Since the law itself fails to determine the effects of this legitimation, any statement with regard to its effects, except in those cases where the effects are evident, will be at most a statement of opinion. It is, of course, evident that sons legitimated in this way cannot become Cardinals, Bishops, Abbots or Prelates Nullius.[327] A son legitimated in virtue of canon 1051 is not irregular.[328] It cannot be said with certainty that a son legitimated according to the provisions of this canon can be admitted to a seminary. In view of the fact that such a person is not irregular, it would seem that he could be admitted licitly. It would appear as inconsistent to prevent the entrance of a person who is not irregular from admission to a seminary whose purpose is to prepare men for the reception of Orders. It is not to be denied that in practice such a person might be refused admission, for example, if his parents have never married after they had been granted the dispensation, but in such a case the rejection would probably be based on other grounds.

While it is certain that a person legitimated by subsequent marriage is eligible for election to the office of major superior in religious institutes, the same cannot be said of a person legitimated in accordance with the provisions of this canon. Schaefer, while admitting that a person legitimated by subsequent marriage is eligible for the office of major superior, doesn't

326 ". . . quae exceptio duplex congruit cum canone 1116, ut effectus matrimonii 'per dispensationem' hanc contracti sit minor quam 'per subsequens parentum matrimonium dummodo parentes . . . vel nativitatis,' ac praeter hoc, ut Codex in iuris divini ac religionis honorem iuxta praecedentem disciplinam severior in hac parte se ostendat. . ."—*Commentarium,* Lib. III, pars 1. n. 445.

327 Canons 232, §2, 1°; 331, §1, 1°; 320, §2.

328 Canon 984, 1°.

even mention the eligibility of a person who has been legitimated in virtue of canon 1051.[329]

Despite the uncertainty as to the extent of its effects, it can be concluded that the legitimation granted in view of the provisions of canon 1051 is true legitimation strictly so called. It does not appear to have the same effects as legitimation by subsequent marriage, because at the very least its effects are uncertain as to their extent, while the legitimation through subsequent marriage makes the persons thus legitimated equal to legitimate children in all things except when the law expressly states otherwise. On the other hand, since the legitimation granted in virtue of canon 1051 is legitimation strictly so called its effects must necessarily be greater than the effect of a dispensation granted either by the law itself through solemn profession or by a special dispensation granted for the reception of Sacred Orders. This is so because: (1) it is nowhere stated that the legitimation granted in virtue of canon 1051 has the effect only of removing the irregularity of illegitimacy; (2) both boys and girls can be legitimated in accordance with the provisions of canon 1051, while only the former may receive a dispensation for Sacred Orders or enjoy the effect of solemn profession as far as the removal of the irregularity of illegitimacy is concerned.

In view of the silence of the law with reference to the effects of the legitimation granted when the conditions of canon 1051 are verified, the final, authoritative determination of the effects of this legitimation must be left to the legislator.

Since the question of a dispensation from a diriment impediment, if it be granted by the Holy See in a particular case, has been discussed in connection with the question of a dispensation granted in virtue of canon 1051, a word concerning the effects of the decree of legitimation, which is contained in the rescript of the dispensation granted by the Holy See at the request of the petitioner, may be inserted here. Such rescripts according to Gasparri contain the clause *Prolem susceptam legi-*

[329] *De Religiosis,* n. 115.

timam decernat atque declaret.[330] It appears that this phrase alone does not clearly define the extent of the legitimation granted. It seems, however, that the effects of this legitimation may be compared to the effects of the legitimation granted in virtue of canon 1051 unless, of course, the decree of legitimation contains a qualifying clause showing that the effects intended indicate a restriction or extension of the legitimation granted as compared with the scope of the legitimation granted by the application of canon 1051. The claim that ordinarily the effects of both means of legitimation are the same seems reasonable in view of the fact that legitimation in each instance is granted in connection with a dispensation from a diriment impediment. The legtimation in virtue of canon 1051 is effected by the concession of the dispensation itself; the legitimation in the other case is granted expressly when it is sought along with the dispensation from a diriment impediment. It does not seem unreasonable to maintain that the legislator himself will grant the same legitimation he permits by law, when he himself dispenses in a particular case, unless the circumstances cause him either to grant a fuller or lesser legitimation.

ARTICLE VI. LEGITIMATION BY RADICAL SANATION

Canon 1138, § 1: Matrimonii in radice sanatio est eiusdem convalidatio, secumferens, praeter dispensationem vel cessationem impedimenti, dispensationem a lege de renovanda consensu, et retrotractionem, per fictionem iuris, circa effectus canonicos, ad praeteritum.

§ 1. Convalidatio fit a momento concessionis gratiae; retrotractio vero intelligitur facta ad matrimonii initium, nisi aliud expresse caveatur.

§ 2. Dispensatio a lege de renovando consensu concedi etiam potest vel una tantum vel utraque parte inscia.

[330] *De Matrimonio,* I, n. 358.

It is not intended at this point to enter into a detailed discussion of the notions of, the requisites for, and all the effects of radical sanation. These questions have already been treated *ex professo* in another dissertation to which the reader is referred.[331] There is one aspect of radical sanation which is of interest here, namely, the legitimation of the offspring of persons who have been granted the favor of radical sanation. To understand properly the statements which will be made in this consideration of the legitimation conceded in virtue of radical sanation, it is necessary to review briefly the general notions of radical sanation and its various divisions.

It can be deduced from the words of canon 1138 that, first of all, radical sanation is a means of convalidating marriage. It is, however, an extraordinary means of convalidation which brings with it, in addition to a dispensation from or the cessation of the impediment existing between the parties, a dispensation from the law demanding the renewal of consent. By a fiction of law radical sanation has retroactive force as far as the cononical effects of marriage are concerned. The convalidation of the marriage takes place at the moment the radical sanation is granted; the retroaction is understood to reach back to the beginning of the invalid marriage, unless the contrary is expressly stated. The dispensation from the law demanding a renewal of the consent implies, of course, that marital consent naturally sufficient for marriage has been exchanged by the parties, which consent, however, remained juridically ineffective because of the presence of a diriment impediment of the ecclesiastical law or because of the absence of the canonical form of marriage. The dispensation from the law demanding the renewal of consent does not mean that the Church dispenses from the marital consent itself. This requirement can never be dispensed from nor can it ever be supplied by anyone other than the contracting parties themselves.[332]

While the code refers to radical sanation in general terms,

[331] Cf. Harrigan, *Radical Sanation.*

[332] Canons 1081, 1139, § 1; Harrigan, *Radical Sanation,* p. 8.

the authors have delineated various divisions of it, based on the effects resulting from the particular radical sanation granted. Thus Payen divides it into radical sanation properly so called and radical sanation improperly so called. Radical sanation properly so called is that which results both in the convalidation of marriage and the legitimation of the offspring; radical sanation improperly so called is had when a marriage cannot be convalidated, but the legitimation of the offspring is granted. Radical sanation properly so called is subdivided into perfect or total sanation and imperfect or partial sanation. Perfect radical sanation is that which contains all the elements mentioned in canon 1138, § § 1-3. If any of these elements is lacking, the sanation is imperfect. Thus radical sanation will be imperfect or partial when: 1) the dispensation from an impediment is lacking; 2) the dispensation from the law demanding the renewal of consent is lacking; 3) the retroaction does not extend all the way back to the beginning of the invalid marriage.[333]

The difference between imperfect radical sanation and radical sanation improperly so called must be borne in mind. The first is a division of radical sanation properly so called; the other constitutes at most an extraordinary means of legitimation.[334] It has already been noted that radical sanation was formerly regarded primarily as a means of legitimation and only secondarily as a means of convalidating marriage. A change gradually took place and it has now come to be regarded primarily as a means of convalidating marriage, though its efficacy with regard to legitimation has not been restricted in any way.[335]

As has already been observed, when the favor of a perfect sanation is granted the marriage is convalidated at the time

[333] *De Matrimonio,* II, nn. 2606-2608.

[334] Wernz, *Ius Decretalium,* IV, pars 2, n. 655.

[335] "Antiquiores auctores de ea (viz. de sanatione in radice) vix aliter scribunt quam de plenissima prolis legitimatione: recentiores vero potissimum ut de medio quo occurratur incommodis ex necessitate renovandi consensum orituris; praesertim a parte nullitatis ignara."—Feije, *De Impedimentis et Dispensationibus Matrimonialibus* (3. ed., Lovanii, 1885), n. 765.

of the concession of the favor, but, as far as the canonical effects of marriage are concerned, the marriage, by a fiction of law, is considered as if it had been valid from the beginning, that is, from the moment when a true but juridically ineffective consent was exchanged by the parties.[336] Since one of the principal canonical effects of marriage is the legitimacy of children, the children already born of an invalid marriage which is convalidated by radical sanation are regarded by the Church as if they had been born of a valid marriage provided that they were born after their parents had exchanged a naturally sufficient marital consent.[337]

Since the retroactive force of radical sanation with reference to the canonical effects of marriage is based on a fiction of law it is evident that the legitimation granted in view of the radical sanation is like legitimation in general, based on a fiction of law. The statement of Harrigan who maintains that legitimation by radical sanation confers nothing more than a juridical status of legitimacy, since it is, as he correctly notes, metaphysically impossible that radical sanation confer an absolute legitimacy, or that it restore to a person a status he has never enjoyed—that of objective legitimacy—would be entirely correct if he understands absolute and objective legitimacy as belonging to those children who have been conceived of a valid marriage. However, he further states that according to canon 1114 absolute and objective legitimacy is proper only to those

[336] "Attamen ad effectus canonicos quod attinet, (matrimonium) consideratur tamquam si fuisset validum a praecedenti tempore, id est iidem ipsi tribuuntur effectus, quos haberet si ab illo tempore validum revera fuisset; hoc autem praecedens tempus plerumque incipit ab eo momento quo consensus naturaliter sufficiens ab utroque contrahente expressus est."—Ciprotti, *Apollinaris,* XII (1939), 513.

[337] ". . . proles habetur in eadem condicione, qua esset, si eius parentes inter se valido matrimonio essent coniuncti ab illo momento, ad quod fit retrotractio . . . quapropter proles, quae nata sit post illud momentum, quamvis spuria non est proprie legitimata, sed vere habetur tamquam ab initio legitima, scilicet iuris fictione; seu, ut etiam dici solet, plenissime legitimatur."—Ciprotti, *Apollinaris,* XII (1939), 513; cf. also Harrigan, *Radical Sanation,* p. 58.

who were conceived or born of a valid or putative marriage.[338] It has already been pointed out that absolute, objective, natural legitimacy is proper only to children conceived of a valid marriage. The others mentioned in canon 1114 as legitimate enjoy juridical legitimacy. Since children legitimated by radical sanation are regarded by a fiction of law as if they had been born of a valid marriage the statement by Harrigan that such children enjoy juridical legitimacy may be admitted if it is understood in this sense, namely, that the juridical status these children enjoy is bestowed by the law. It may be mentioned here that if the invalid marriage for which a radical sanation is granted was a putative marriage, the children born or conceived of such a marriage are already legitimate in accordance with the provisions of canon 1114. When their parents' marriage is convalidated by radical sanation these children acquire another title to legitimacy.[339]

Since legitimation is an essential effect of radical sanation there is no necessity for mentioning that legitimation is desired, when the favor of radical sanation is sought. Mention of the need of legitimation should, however, be made, as it constitutes an added reason for the concession of the favor. Legitimation is effected by radical sanation even though the parents, the offspring, or any other person concerned may be unwilling or even positively opposed to the legitimation.[340]

The legitimation granted in virtue of radical sanation is known as *legitimatio plenissima,* in the sense that children thus legitimated are regarded as if they had been born of a valid marriage. The children are regarded as having the same status they would have had if the parents had been validly married from the moment to which the retroaction is effective; if a dispensation has been granted from an impediment it is regarded by a fiction of law as if it had been granted at the moment to which the retroaction is effective.

[338] *Radical Sanation,* p. 71.

[339] Wernz-Vidal, *Ius Matrimoniale,* n. 671.

[340] Gasparri, *De Matrimonio,* II, n. 1231; Harrigan, *Radical Sanation,* p. 58.

It remains now to consider what children may be legitimated by radical sanation. It may be observed, first of all, that only those children already born or conceived by the parties whose union is to be convalidated by radical sanation are legitimated. Any child born or conceived *after* the moment to which the retroaction is effective is regarded by a fiction of law as though it had been always legitimate. The moment to which radical sanation reaches back in its juridical effects is the moment at which the parties have exchanged marital consent. Consequently if a child has been born to the parties *before* they have exchanged a naturally sufficient marital consent it will not be legitimated *per se* by the favor of radical sanation as will be shown presently.

The Church grants a radical sanation when a marriage has been invalid either because of a diriment impediment of the ecclesiastical law, or because of the absence of the canonical form of marriage, provided the marital consent of the parties still perseveres. The Church does not grant a radical sanation for a marriage entered into with an impediment of the divine or the natural law even if the impediment has ceased.[341]

Although the law in canon 1139 states that the Church does not grant a radical sanation for a marriage entered into with an impediment of the divine or the natural law, it does not state that the Church cannot grant a sanation in such circumstances. In fact, such sanations are sometimes granted with retroaction extending to the time when the impediment ceased, provided that very serious reasons have been advanced for the concession of the favor.[342]

In determining which children are legitimated by radical sanation it must be noted first of all that the children of a putative marriage are already legitimate according to canon 1114, but they acquire a second title to legitimacy by the radical sanation of their parents' invalid marriage.[343] In view of the

[341] Canon 1139, §§ 1-2.

[342] Gasparri, *De Matrimonio,* II, nn. 1215-1219; Harrigan, *Radical Sanation,* pp. 96-99; Ciprotti, *Apollinaris,* XII (1939), 515.

[343] Harrigan, *Radical Sanation,* p. 65.

provisions of canon 1139, § 1, it can be said in general that those children whose parents' marriage is invalid because of a diriment impediment of the ecclesiastical law, or because of the lack of the canonical form of marriage, are legitimated by radical sanation. Specifically it may now be stated that radical sanation, unless it is expressly stated otherwise, effects the legitimation of offspring born *after* the moment to which the retroaction of the sanation is extended when the child is: 1) a "natural" child; 2) a "spurious" child, for example, when the impediment of disparity of worship has existed between its parents from the time of the child's conception until some time after its birth; 3) a child which is the result of sacrilege; 4) a child which is the result of incest committeed by persons who may receive a dispensation for marriage.

The question may be asked what effect, as far as legitimation is concerned, does radical sanation have on children who were born *before* the moment to which the retroaction is extended? It can be said that: 1) a "natural" child will be legitimated by the subsequent marriage of its parents. The marriage is regarded as if it had been entered into at the moment to which the retroaction of the sanation extends.[344] Harrigan observes that in such a case there would be no title of legitimation by reason of the sanation, because the sanation would not reach back to the time when the child was born, namely, before the parents exchanged marital consent.[345] 2) A "spurious" child is legitimated in virtue of the provisions of canon 1051 by the dispensation which is granted in the radical sanation, provided the radical sanation is not granted by one who has delegated power for a particular case.[346] 3) A child which is born as the result

[344] "Proles autem, quae ante illud tempus sit nata, legitimatur tamquam per subsequens matrimonium eodem illo initum momento, ad quod fit retrotractio, dummodo ne sit spuria, id est, dummodo adsit requisita parentum habilitas, de qua in canonone 1116."—Ciprotti, *Apollinaris,* XII (1939), 514.

[345] *Radical Sanation,* p. 61.

[346] "Quodsi proles sit spuria, seu desit requisita parentum habilitas, fit legitimatio ex dispensatione ad normam canonis 1051 (nisi sanatio in

of sacrilege, must be legitimated by papal rescript since it cannot be legitimated, in the circumstances under consideration, either by the parents' subsequent marriage or by virtue of a dispensastion granted in accordance with the provisions of canon 1051; 4) a child who has been born of the crime of incest will be legitimated in virtue of the provisions of canon 1051 by the dispensation granted in the radical sanation, unless the favor of radical sanation is granted by one having delegated power for a particular case.

It has been asserted that children born as the result of sacrilege and incest after their parents have exchanged a juri dically ineffective marital consent are legitimated by radical sanation, unless it is expressly stated otherwise. Some further notice must be given to these classes of illegitimate children. The possibility of legitimation by radical sanation exists for those children who are born of an attempted marriage between parents when one or both of them are bound by solemn profession, or when the father is bound either by the obligations of Holy Orders or by the simple vow which invalidates marriage. Harrigan, while admitting that these children can be legitimated by radical sanation, states that this does not mean that the Church is accustomed to extend this favor to such children. Consequently, he maintains, it would seem that for them recourse to the Holy See for direct legitimation is the only alternative.[347] Payen and Ciprotti state that such children are legitimated by radical sanation unless it is expressly stated otherwise in the indult.[348]

The opinion of Payen and Ciprotti is preferable to that of Harrigan. This is so because when the favor of radical sanation is requested in such circumstances, and the need of legitimation (which constitutes a reason for granting a sanation), has been

radice concessa sit ex potestate delegata ad casum particularem), quia dispensatio . . . censetur, per iuris fictionem, concessa statim ante momentum ad quod fit retroactio."—Ciprotti, *Apollinaris,* XII (1939), 514.

[347] *Radical Sanation,* p. 64.

[348] *De Matrimonio,* II, n. 2173; *Apollinaris,* XII (1939), 514.

mentioned it will be evident from the tenor of the rescript whether the legitimation has been expressly denied. If there is no mention of legitimation in the rescript, then legitimation is effected. If mention of the need of legitimation had been omitted in the petition for the sanation, and the favor was actually granted without any mention of legitimation, then legitimation is likewise effected because legitimation is an essential effect of sanation.[349] In reference to those children who are born as the result of incest it must be remembered that in some cases radical sanation is never granted. This is true in those cases in which there is any doubt that the parties are related by consanguinity in any degree of the direct line or in the first degree of the collateral line.[350] Harrigan excludes from legitimation only those children whose parents are related by consanguinity in the direct line. It seems certain, however, from the text of canon 1076, § 3, that children of parents related by consanguinity in the first degree of the collateral line must also be excluded. Outside these cases children who are born as the result of incest are legitimated by radical sanation when this favor is granted to their parents.[351]

Although canon 1139, § 2, expressly states that the Church does not grant a radical sanation for a marriage which is invalid because of a diriment impediment of the natural or the divine law, even from the moment when the impediment has ceased, it has been shown that the Church sometimes does grant a radical sanation for such a marriage if very grave and urgent causes are advanced for the concession of the favor. In such event, however, the sanation granted is not a perfect radical sanation. The Church cannot grant a perfect radical sanation in these cases because when such a sanation is granted, the Church would dispense not only from the law requiring the renewal of consent thus accepting the consent which had been given at the beginning of the invalid marriage which consent still perseveres, but would,

[349] Harrigan, *Radical Sanation*, p. 58.
[350] Canon 1076, § 3.
[351] Cf. *Radical Sanation*, p. 64.

moreover, draw this dispensation back by a fiction of law to the beginning of the marriage, regarding the marriage as if it had been begun without any impediment and consequently as if it had been valid. But the Church cannot, even through a fiction of law, consider as valid a marriage which is prohibited by an impediment of the natural or the divine law which impediment cannot be removed by the Church through a dispensation.[352] It is evident that if a child has been born even after the exchange of a naturally sufficient but juridically ineffective consent by its parents who are laboring under an impediment of the natural or the divine law, an imperfect radical sanation with retroaction to the moment when the impediment has ceased will not cause the child to be regarded as though it had been born in a valid marriage. This is so because the retroaction of the sanation cannot be extended back to the moment when the parties exchanged a true though juridically ineffective consent. For this reason adulterine children have been excluded from the list of children who are legitimated by radical sanation. The Sacred Penitentiary on April 25, 1890, conceded the favor of an imperfect radical sanation for a marriage which had been invalid because of the diriment impediment of previous bond. It expressly declared that the children born of the marriage were legitimated with the exception of those conceived in adultery.[353]

With regard to legitimation by radical sanation it must be remembered that to obtain the *legitimatio plenissima* peculiar to radical sanation all that is required is that the retroactive force of the sanation be extended back to a moment of time prior to the child's birth. The convalidation of the parents' marriage, although it is regarded today as the principal end of the radical sanation, does not have to take place. Thus children can be legitimated by radical sanation when there is no possibility at all of convalidating the parent's invalid marriage through the sanation, for example, when one or both parents have died

[352] Gasparri, *De Matrimonio,* II, nn. 1216 and 1219; Payen, *De Matrimonio,* II, n. 2612; Harrigan, *Radical Sanation,* pp. 98-99.

[353] Wernz-Vidal, *Ius Matrimoniale,* n. 656, note 10.

or become insane. The sanation granted in such cases is radical sanation improperly so called. It constitutes, as has already been noted, an extraordinary means of legitimation. Even though the extraordinary convalidation of marriage is evidently impossible in such cases the Pope can in virtue of a radical sanation cause the marriage, as far as the canonical effects are concerned, to be regarded as though it had been valid from the beginning or from some intermediate point of time. The Pope when he grants such a sanation does nothing more than invalidate the effects which have already followed or are to follow from an ecclesiastical law, which invalidation is within his power.[354] The Church, however, is not accustomed to grant a sanation for an invalid marriage when one or both parties have become insane, especially if the insanity is perpetual.[355]

A case in point occurred in the archdiocese of Mechlin. A Catholic man and a Lutheran woman contracted a civil marriage in the archdiocese. Since the decree *Tametsi* was binding on heretics in Belgium the marriage was invalid. The three children born of the union were baptized and educated as Catholics. The husband later became insane and was confined to an asylum without any hope of being cured. The wife later became a Catholic and petitioned that a radical sanation be granted for the marriage. The Supreme Congregation of the Holy Inquisition replied to the Cardinal Archbishop of Mechlin on Dec. 8, 1889, that it was though inexpedient to grant the radical sanation. It was suggested, however, that the Congregation of the Council should be petitioned to grant a rescript of legitimation. The request was made and on July 12, 1890, the children were legitimated by Papal rescript.[356]

Before proceeding to the consideration of the effects of legitimation granted by radical sanation, the various classes of illegitimate children may be mentioned in reference to the

[354] Ciprotti, "De Sanatione in radice post mortem alterius coniugis. An et quo sensu matrimonium invalidum (hoc in casu) sanari possit," *Apollinaris,* XI (1938), 285-291.

[355] Harrigan, *Radical Sanation,* p. 59.

[356] S.C.C., 12 iulii 1890—*ASS,* XIII (1890), 332-334.

possibility of their legitimation in virtue of this extraordinary favor. The following illegitimate children are legitimated by radical sanation: 1) "natural" children; 2) "merely spurious" children; 3) children who are born of sacrilege; 4) children who are born as the result of incest committed by persons who may be granted a dispensation. The following children cannot be legitimated by radical sanation: 1) adulterine children; 2) children who are born of incest committed by persons related by consanguinity either in any degree of the direct line, or in the first degree of the collateral line, even if the relationship is doubtful.[357]

Article VII. The Effects of Legitimation by Radical Sanation

According to canon 1138, § 1, radical sanation is retroactive, by a fiction of law, to the past as far as the canonical effects of marriage are concerned. Since one of the principal canonical effects of marriage is the legitimacy of the offspring it follows that a child whose parents' marriage has been convalidated by radical sanation is regarded as if it had been born of a valid marriage. The same is true of a child which has been legitimated by radical sanation improperly so called, i.e., when the convalidation of the parents' marriage is impossible, for example, because of the death of one of the parents. The discussion of the effects of the legitimation conferred by radical sanation must necessarily be restricted to the cases wherein the children have been born *after* the parents had exchanged a naturally sufficient though juridically ineffective marital consent, the retroaction of the radical sanation being understood in these cases to extend back to the moment when the consent was given. It has already been shown that children born before the moment to which the retroaction of radical sanation is extended, are not legitimated in

[357] Cf. canon 1076, § 3; cf. Payen, *De Matrimonio,* II, n. 2173; cf. Ciprotti, *De Consummatione Delictorum Attento eorum elemento obiectivo in iure canonico* (Romae: apud Custodiam librariam Pont. Instituti Utriusque Iuris, 1936), pp. 87-88.

virtue of the radical sanation itself, but they are legitimated some other way.

With reference to the extent of the legitimation conferred by radical sanation it can be said that many authors do not discuss this question in any detail. They state only that the children thus legitimated are regarded as though they had been born of a valid marriage. Others authors state that the legitimation conferred by radical sanation renders the children *"habiles quoad omnes effectus canonicos."* [358] De Smet maintains that children legitimated by radical sanation are regarded as if they had been born as legitimate and, as a consequence, they are equal to legitimate children in all things.[359] Cappello, Payen, Ciprotti, and Schmitz state that these children obtain all the canonical effects of legitimacy and they maintain that these children are not bound by the exceptions contained in canon 1117.[360]

Harrigan gives lengthy consideration to the effects of legitimation conferred by radical sanation. His opinion is that children thus legitimated are bound by the exceptions contained in canon 1117. The arguments he advances in support of his opinion which, it may be noted, is contrary to that of the other authors may be set forth briefly: 1) Although it is althogether reasonable to hold fast to the view that legitimation by radical sanation renders the legitimated person *habilis quoad omnes effectus,* inasmuch as he is considered as if he had been born of a valid marriage, nevertheless it does not seem to be in accord with the mind of the legislator to say that such a person is not bound by the exception of canon 1117. For, even granting the fact that *per se* and by its very nature radical sanation is capable of producing the fullest legitimation and therefore of restoring the fullest juridic capacity, it does not follow that the Soverign

[358] Gasparri, *De Matrimonio,* II, n. 1213; Wernz-Vidal, *Ius Matrimoniale,* n. 671.

[359] *De Sponsalibus et Matrimonio,* n. 736, note 1; cf. n. 291, note 6.

[360] Cappello, *De Sacramentis,* III, n. 857; Payen, *De Matrimonio,* II, n. 2600 Ciprotti, *Apollinaris,* XII (1939), 515; Schmitz, *Die Stellung der unehelichen Kinder im geltenden kanonischen Recht,* pp. 101-102.

Pontiff has not acutally limited this effect. The very wording of canon 1117 seems to contain a very clear and explicit declaration of the mind of the legislator on the effect of legitimation and at the same time to set a limit to the extent of eligibility for canonical offices conferred by legitimation. But to say that the limitation of this canon does not apply to those who are legitimated by radical sanation would seem to defeat the very purpose of the limitation therein contained. 2) He appeals not only to the constitution *Postquam* of Sixtus V issued on Dec. 3, 1586,[361] which demanded that those to be promoted to the cardinalate be of legitimate birth, but also to the provisions of canon 6, 3°, to prove that men legitimated by radical sanation are ineligible for promotion to the cardinalate; 3) He maintains that what is true regarding the status demanded of candidates for the cardinalate is true also of candidates for the episcopate.[362]

Before understaking a consideration of the arguments proposed by Harrigan, it seems correct to suggest that the question whether children legitimated by radical sanation are bound by the exceptions stated in canon 1117 is an academic one. This is so because in practice the Holy See investigates thoroughly the candidates proposed for promotion to any of these dignities. Whether the Holy See would actually reject a candidate solely on the grounds that he has been legitimated by radical sanation is a question which only the Holy See can answer.

Harrigan maintains that even granting the fact that *per se* and by its very nature radical sanation is capable of producing the fullest legitimation it does not follow that the Soverign Pontiff has not actually limited this effect. The answer to this argument is that any restriction of the effects of the legitimation conferred by radical sanation has to be proved. This contention seems reasonable in view of the fact that the legitimation conferred by radical sanation has always been regarded as *legitimatio plenissima*. The further statement of Harrigan that canon 1117 seems to contain a very clear and explicit declaration of the mind of

[361] *Fontes*, n. 159.

[362] *Radical Sanation*, pp. 67-71.

the legislator on the effect of legitimation and at the same time to set a limit to the extent of the eligibility for canonical offices conferred by legitimation seems unwarranted in view of the fact that the legislator can grant legitimation which is more complete or less complete than that resulting from subsequent marriage, e.g., by Papal rescript. To say that the mind of the legislator regarding the effects of the legitimation granted by radical sanation is to be determined from canon 1117 does not seem correct in view of the provisions of canon 20. This canon states that a norm of action is to be taken from laws given in similar cases if there is no explicit provision concerning some matter either in the general or particular law. It seems then that recourse to canon 1117 could be had only if there were no explicit provisions of the law relative to the effects of legitimation by radical sanation. The law, however, in canon 1138, § 1, states expressly and without any qualification that radical sanation by a fiction of law is retroactive to the past as far as canonical effects are concerned.

The constitution *Postquam* seems to constitute the strongest argument advanced by Harrigan for restricting men legitimated by radical sanation from the dignity of the cardinalate. It would be futile to ignore the fact that Sixtus V demanded a legitimate status on the part of those who were to be chosen for this high office.[363] At first sight it would appear from the words of Sixtus V that there was no possibility for a man legitimated by radical sanation to become a cardinal. There are, however, various arguments which may be advanced against their exclusion

[363] "Praeterea qui cardinales creandi erunt, legitimis sint exorti natalibus, neque ulla prorsus labe aut illegitimorum natalium suspicione quovis modo laborent . . . Ideo ut puriori dignitati puriores natales respondeant . . . quoscumque illegitime natos . . . etiam genitos ex soluto, et soluta, inter quos tunc Matrimonium constare poterat, ac postea per subsequens Matrimonium, etiam rite, et solemniter in facie Ecclesiae contractum, vel alias legitimatos, et quomodolibet habilitatos, et natalibus restitutos, . . . nihilominus praedictae cardinalatus dignitatis prorsus incapaces, et ad eam obtinendam perpetuo inhabiles decernimus ac declaramus."—Sixtus V, const. *Postquam*, 3 dec. 1586, § 12—*Fontes*, n. 159.

from the cardinalate: 1) Those legitimated by radical sanation are regarded in law as though they had been born of a valid marriage. This is the universal doctrine which has always been taught regarding the legitimation effected by radical sanation. If this teaching be admitted, then persons legitimated in this way can be included logically and juridically among those born as legitimate and as a consequence eligible for the cardinalate; 2) There is no express mention of the exclusion of persons legitimated by radical sanation. Apropos of this Harrigan remarks that Pope Sixtus V certainly was not unaware or unmindful of the operation and effects of radical sanation when he published his constitution. Yet he concedes no particular privilege and makes no specific grant in favor of this mode of legitimation. On the contrary he seems definitely to exclude all classes of legitimated persons.[364] The fact that Pope Sixtus V was aware of the extraordinary effects of radical sanation and yet did not even mention it seems very strange, especially when it is recalled that when he published his constitution *Postquam* radical sanation, as Harrigan himself admits, was regarded primarily as a means of legitimation. Radical sanation came only later—around the beginning of the seventeenth century—to be regarded primarily as a means of convalidating marriage.[365] If it be contended that the primary conception of radical sanation as a means of legitimation was giving way gradually to the notion of radical sanation as a means intended primarily for convalidating marriage and only secondarily for producing legitimation, even at the time Sixtus V wrote his constitution, there is still much cause for wonder regarding his silence concerning it either as a means of producing legitimation or of convalidating marriage.

It is certain that Sixtus V contrasted the legitimate status of those who are born of a valid marriage with the legitimated status of those whose legitimation had been effected by their parents' subsequent marriage or in any other way. In treating the question of the legitimacy he demanded of those to be promoted to the

[364] *Radical Sanation,* p. 69.
[365] *Op. cit.,* p. 23.

cardinalate and in distinguishing between their status and that of legitimated persons he makes no mention at all of the extraordinary effects of the legitimation conferred by radical sanation. It seems reasonable to suggest that if the Pope wished to exclude also those who were legitimated by radical sanation he would have contrasted the legitimacy possessed by those who are born of a valid marriage with the *legitimatio plenissima* conferred by radical sanation rather than with the *legitimatio plena* granted by subsequent marriage. If he wished to exclude all legitimated persons without exception its seems that he would have mentioned those legitimated by radical sanation and would have declared that even the legitimation conferred in this way was not sufficient to make candidates eligible for the cardinalate. It is true that the Pope conceded no particular privilege and made no specific grant in favor of those legitimated by radical sanation, but it does not follow necessarily from this, that those who were legitimated in this way were excluded from the possibility of attaining to the dignity of the cardinalate.

The words *"alias legitimatos, et quomodolibet habilitatos, et natalibus restitutos"* are certainly very strong and would seem to exclude even those who are legitimated by radical sanation. It seems, however, that these words do not necessarily have to be interpreted to include those who are legitimated by radical sanation. This is so because, as has already been observed, those who are legitimated by radical sanation are regarded in law as enjoying the juridical effects of legitimacy. Ciprotti goes as far as to say that a person legitimated in this manner must be regarded absolutely as legitimate.[366] If it be asserted that, even granting the extraordinary character of the effects of radical sanation, persons legitimated in this way have *de facto,* been legitimated, it does not seem unreasonable to suggest that the words *alias legitimatos etc.* are insufficient in themselves to be understood of persons legitimated by radical sanation in view of the fact that those who are legitimated in this extraordinary way are regarded in law as enjoying the juridical effects of

[366] *Apollinaris,* XII (1939), 515.

legitimacy. It would seem that to exclude those who are legitimated by radical sanation a specific declaration of their ineligibility should have been included. It appears that recourse to canon 6, 3°, is of no avail in this instance, because it has not been definitively established, nor has Harrigan proved conclusively, nor has any author even mentioned that men legitimated by radical sanation are excluded from the cardinalate according to the provisions of the constitution *Postquam.* This constitution is cited in the footnotes to canon 232 which outlines the qualifications demanded of those who are to be promoted to the cardinalate. It is also found in the *Fontes* of the Code of Canon Law. In view of this the phrase *"etiamsi per subsequens matrimonium fuerint legitimati"* employed in the canon is of special interest. According to the literal meaning of the words used, all illegitimates are excluded *even if* they have been legitimated by subsequent marriage. There is no mention of those who have been legitimated by radical sanation, which confers a fuller legitimation than does subsequent marriage.[367]

Since radical sanation confers a fuller legitimation than subsequent marriage, one cannot consider the phrase *"etiamsi per subsequens matrimonium fuerint legitimati"* of canon 232 to exclude from the cardinalitial dignity those who enjoy the fullest kind of legitimation. Radical sanation confers *legitimatio plenissima;* subsequent marriage effects *legitimatio plena.* The phrase in question, moreover, because of its restrictive character must be interpreted strictly.[368] Not one commentator consulted makes any mention of the exclusion of men legitimated by radical sanation. The authors do, it is true, exclude legitimated persons, but it must be borne in mind that those who are legitimated

[367] "Legitimatio prolis per sanationem in radice peculiari fit ratione, et ideo praesertim a ceteris distinguitur, quia pleniores habet effectus, cum saepe proles non proprie legitimetur, sed legitima omnino fiat per sanationem."—Ciprotti, *Apollinaris,* XII (1939), 512.

[368] Cf. canon 19; cf. also Harrigan, *Radical Sanation,* pp. 65-66.

by radical sanation are regarded juridically as if they had been born of a valid marriage.[369]

Augustine remarks that the parents of a man to be promoted to the cardinalate must have lived in lawful wedlock at the birth of the candidate.[370] A man legitimated by radical sanation, however, is, as has been repeatedly mentioned, regarded through a fiction of law as if he had been born of a valid marriage.

It is evident from a comparison of Wernz's consideration of the effects of radical sanation and his discussion of the status demanded in candidates for the cardinalitial dignity that he did not consider men legitimated by radical sanation as excluded from this high dignity in virtue of the constitution *Postquam.*[371]

It seems that men legitimated by radical sanation are not ineligible for promotion to the Cardinalitial dignity. Consequently the opinion of Harrigan cannot be maintained. This assertion is substantiated because: 1) in the constitution *Postquam* there was no express mention of the

[369] Vermeersch-Creusen, *Epitome,* II, n. 349; Ayrinhac, *Constitution of the Church in the New Code of Canon Law* (2. ed., New York: Longmans, Green and Co., 1930), p. 43, n. 24; Augustine, *A Commentary,* II (6. ed., 1936), 233; Woywood, *A Practical Commentary on the Code of Canon Law* (5. ed., 2 vols., New York: Joseph F. Wagner, 1939), I, 88; Coronata, *Institutiones Iuris Canonici* (5 vols., [vols. I et II, 2. ed.], Taurini: Marietti, 1933-1939), I, n. 322; Chelodi, *Ius de Personis* (Tridenti: Libr. Edit. Tridentum, 1922), n. 157; Pruemmer, *Manuale Iuris Canonici* (4. et 5. ed., Friburgi Brisgoviae: Herder, 1927), p. 133; Claeys Bouuaert-Simenon, *Manuale Iuris Canonici* (2. ed., Gandae et Leodii: apud Auctores, 1926), n. 393; Bargilliat, *Praelectiones Iuris Canonici* (2 vols., 37. ed., ad Canones novi Codicis redacta, Parisiis: Apud Baston, Berche, et Pagis, 1923), I, n. 507.

[370] *Loc. cit.*

[371] ". . . proles reputabitur ita legitima, ac si parentes inde a primis nuptiis legitimi coniuges fuissent. Quae legitimatio prolis per sanationem matrimonii in radice plenissma est quoad omnes effectus spirituales sive ecclesiasticos, v.g., quoad ordines sacros vel beneficia ecclesiastica, uti constat ex indubitata et communi doctorum sententia."—*Ius Decretalium,* IV, pars II, n. 664; "Illegitimi etiam per subsequens matrimonium legitimati aut super defectu natalium auctoritate apostolica dispensationem consecuti inhabiles sunt."—*op. cit.,* II, pars II, n. 626.

exclusion of those who were legitimated by radical sanation. The reasons proposed by Harrigan to show that no specific mention of radical sanation was necessary have been opposed by other more cogent reasons to show the reasonableness of insisting that radical sanation should have been mentioned specifically; 2) the words *alias legitimatos etc.* are not in themselves sufficient to include those who are legitimated by radical sanation since they are regarded in law as if they had been born of a valid marriage In view of the extraordinary favor bestowed on such persons it seems reasonable to insist that any restriction placed upon them should be explicitly stated. Their exclusion from the cardinalate in virtue of the provisions of the constitution *Postquam* has not been certainly proved. Their exclusion is at the most very doubtful; 3) Canon 232, § 2, 1°, excludes illegitimates from the cardinalate *even if* they have been legitimated by subsequent marriage, but makes no mention at all of those who have been legitimated by radical sanation which admittedly confers a fuller legitimation than does subsequent marriage; 4) Canon 1117 cannot serve as a norm in determining the effects of legitimation by radical sanation because the effects of radical sanation (including legitimation) are expressly stated in canon 1138, § 1; 5) The authors do not expressly mention as excluded from the cardinalate those who have been legitimated by radical sanation; 6) Legitimation is a favor and must be given the widest possible interpretation consistent with the law. The only possible restriction up to the present time would be from the constitution *Postquam*. However, the exclusion from the cardinalate on the part of those who have been legitimated by radical sanation has not certainly been proved and would be very doubtful. Hence it seems correct to say that since the exclusion of these persons is doubtful at most, they are not ineligible for promotion to the cardinalate.[372]

Harrigan maintains that those who are legitimated by radical sanation are ineligible for the office of Bishop, Abbot, and Prelate *Nullius*. His argument regarding their exclusion from

[372] Cf. canon 15.

the Episcopate is based on the assumption that it is very unlikely that the legislator would enhance the juridical prestige of the Cardinalate, which is of ecclesiastical institution, to the possible relative detriment of the innate dignity of the Episcopate, which is of divine foundation. He also employs the argument that the legislator formerly demanded absolute legitimacy of those who were to be appointed to offices lower in dignity than the offices of bishop and inferior prelates.[373] He maintains that it is therefore reasonable to assume that the same status was demanded of bishops and inferior prelates.[374] It has already been shown that prior to the promulgation of the Code those who had been legitimated by subsequent marriage were excluded only from the Cardinalate.[375] Consequently, it is evident that before the Code men legitimated by subsequent marriage and, *a fortiori,* by radical sanation could become bishops and inferior prelates. Since the Code, men legitimated by subsequent marriage have been excluded from the office of bishop, abbot, and prelate *nullius,* but there is no express provision in the law which excludes men legitimated by radical sanation.

It seems correct, then, to maintain that those who are legitimated by radical sanation are not bound by the exceptions of canon 1117. Legitimation conferred by radical sanation is admittedly a fuller legitimation than that conferred by subsequent marriage. If its effects were exactly the same as those of legitimation by subsequent marriage it would be futile to distinguish between *legitimatio plenissima* and *legitimatio plena.* What purpose, moreover, would it serve to regard a man in law as if born of a valid marriage and then deny him the rights which flow from birth in a valid marriage? It seems reasonable to maintain that the extraordinary nature of the legitimation conferred by radical sanation should also be seen in the extraordinary effects which it has for the persons legitimated.

[373] Cf. Gregorius XIV, const. *"Onus Apostolicae,"* 15 maii 1591—*Fontes,* n. 171.

[374] *Radical Sanation,* pp. 70, 71.

[375] Wernz, *Ius Decretalium,* IV, pars II, n. 686, note 52.

It can be said here that the question whether the Pope can legitimate children, as far as civil effects are concerned, outside of his temporal jurisdiction is of little practical moment today. Accordingly, the treatment already given this question in the historical section will suffice.

Article VIII. Legitimation by Papal Rescript

There is no specific mention of this means of legitimation in the Code. Consequently, recourse must be had to the old law, to the teaching of the canonists, and to the practice of the Roman Curia.[376] It may be said that this means of legitimation is the most extensive method of conferring legitimation in the sense that the Soverign Pontiff can legitimate any illegitimate child in this way whether the child is "natural" or "spurious". A Papal rescript of legitimation may be granted in connection with a dispensation from a matrimonial impediment, or it may be granted separately from any other dispensation. This question of the legitimation granted by Papal rescript in connection with a matrimonial dispensation has already been treated along with the question of the legitimation granted in accordance with the provisions of canon 1051. It is necessary here only to add that legitimation by Papal rescript is granted usually in connection with the concession of a matrimonial dispensation.[377] Although this is ordinarily the case, there is no reason why an illegitimate person may not petition the Holy See for a rescript of legitimation when there is no question of a dispensation to be granted for the convalidation of the parents' marriage. Theoretically the Pope can confer the fullest legitimation when he confers legitimation by rescript. In practice, however, he is not accustomed to legitimate any one fully by rescript, i.e., by rendering the legitimated person capable of all ecclesiastical dignities. Besides, in granting such legitimation the Pope does not intend to prejudice the acquired rights of a third party, nor does he

[376] Schönsteiner, *Grundriss des kirchlichen Eherechts,* p. 791; Triebs, *Handbuch des kanonischen Eherechts,* p. 680.

[377] Wernz-Vidal, *Ius Matrimoniale,* n. 615.

intend to abrogate any special right.[378] Unless it is expressly stated otherwise in the rescript, it must be presumed that the legitimation conferred is not to militate against the rights of other persons.[379] To determine the effects of the legitimation conferred by Papal rescript it is necessary to consult the rescript issued in each case.[380]

While the Soverign Pontiff can legitimate all classes of illegitimate children by rescript, it does not follow that he does actually extend this favor to all the various classes of those children. In practice the Pope rarely grants legitimation to adulterine children and to those born of parents related by consanguinity in the direct line; he hardly ever grants this favor to those children who are born as the result of sacrilege.[381] Gasparri, moreover, maintains that children born as the result of sacrilege are never legitimated by the Roman Pontiff.[382] The fact that the Pope is not accustomed to grant legitimation to certain classes of illegitimates should not deter an illegitimate person, no matter what his status may be, from petitioning for a rescript of legitimation. This legitimation depends solely on the will of the Pope and it is reasonable to assume that in certain circumstances he will graciously confer the favor of legitimation even upon those to whom he usually denies this favor.

Outside those cases which pertain to the Congregation for the Oriental Church and to the Congregation for the Propagation of the Faith recourse must be had to the Congregation of the Sacraments for a Papal rescript of legitimation which is to

[378] Wernz, *Ius Decretalium,* IV, pars II, n. 687.

[379] "Si adsint filii legitimi, illegitimus factus legitimus per rescriptum Principis non admittitur in successionem bonorum paternorum, nisi adsit haec clausula 'non obstante quod adsint filii legitimi'."—Santi, *Praelectiones Iuris Canonici,* IV, pp. 166-167, n. 15.

[380] Wernz, *Ius Decretalium,* IV, pars II, n 687; Gasparri, *De Matrimonio,* II, n. 1121.

[381] Ciprotti, *Apollinaris,* XII (1939), 517; cf. S.C.C., 17 aug. 1884—*ASS,* XVI (1884), 428; S.C.C., 12 iulii 1890—*ASS,* XXIII (1890), 332; Haring, "Eine schwierige Legitimation," *LQS,* LXXXV (1932), 147-148.

[382] *De Matrimonio,* II, nn. 1121, 1231.

be valid in the external forum. The Sacred Penitentiary grants such rescripts for the internal forum.

Finally, it must be noted that a Papal rescript of legitimation is not the same as a Papal dispensation for the reception of Holy Orders.

Article IX. Solemn Religious Profession

A summary treatment may be accorded to this topic as well as to the one which will be considered next, namely, that of Papal dispensation. It need only be noted that the removal of the irregularity of illegitimacy in virtue of solemn profession does not constitute legitimation strictly so called. Canon 984, 1°, distinguishes between those who have been legitimated and those who have made solemn profession. The removal of the irregularity of illegitimacy by solemn profession enables one to receive Holy Orders, but it does not render him capable of election to the office of major superior inasmuch as he still remains illegitimate.[383] Since the law provides for the automatic removal of the irregularity of illegitimacy by solemn profession, it follows that an illegitimate may be admitted to a clerical institute of solemn vows without having first obtained a dispensation from his irregularity.[384] It must be noted, however, that this is true only of clerical institutes of solemn vows wherein solemn profession is made before the reception of clerical tonsure and of orders.[385]

Article X. Papal Dispensation

A Papal dispensation from the irregularity of illegitimacy does not constitute legitimation strictly so called. It enables the person thus dispensed to receive Holy Orders, including that of the priesthood. The Soverign Pontiff, however, can

[383] Payen, *De Matrimonio,* II, n. 2171; Schönsteiner, *Grundriss des kirchlichen Eherechts,* p. 792.

[384] Voltas, "Irregularitas," *Commentarium Pro Religiosis,* II (1921), 368; Coronata, *Institutiones Iuris Canonici,* I, n. 571.

[385] "Irregularitas ex defectu natalium non obstat, si ante susceptionem ordinum solemnis professio emittenda sit."—Chelodi, *Ius de Personis,* n. 265, note 3. In law the term *ordo* is applied to first tonsure—canon 950.

grant a dispensation which renders a man eligible for election to the episcopate or even to the cardinalate. It is to be noted that if a dispensation has been granted to a man enabling him to be elevated to the episcopate such a dispensation is not sufficient to render him eligible for the cardinalate.[386] No class of illegitimate children is absolutely excluded from the possibility of receiving such a dispensation for the reception of Holy Orders. The Pope can and has granted dispensations to practically all the various class of illegitimates for the purpose of receiving Holy Orders. This can be inferred from various examples of the concession of this dispensation. On September 9, 1882, such a dispensation was granted to man who had been born as the result of sacrilege. It was stipulated that he be transferred after ordination to some part of the diocese where the circumstances surrounding his birth were absolutely unknown.[387] On January 19, 1884, a "natural" child was given a dispensation. It was noted in the concession of the dispensation that the petitioner had promised his ordinary in writing that he would remain for a time in another diocese to avoid the danger of scandal.[388] On June 14, 1884, a dispensation was granted to a man whose birth had resulted from the double crime of adultery and incest. The ordinary of the petitioner had declared that he needed priests. The dispensation was granted provided that no scandal resulted, the bishop being charged in conscience to verify this condition.[389] It is to be noted that the present practice of the Holy See is to issue such dispensations privately. The reasons for the granting of this dispensation are given by the Holy See in the text of the dispensations cited above. These reasons are: 1) the necessity of priests; 2) the good character of the person who was to receive the dispensation; 3) the talents possessed by such a person.

[386] Coronata, *Institutiones Iuris Canonici,* I, n. 322; Vermeersch-Creusen, *Epitome,* II, n. 349; Ayrinhac, *Constitution of the Church,* p. 43, n. 24.

[387] S.C.C., 9 sept. 1882, *ASS,* XV (1882), 452-455.

[388] S.C.C., 19 ian. 1884, *ASS,* XVI (1884), 461.

[389] S.C.C., 14 iunii 1884, *ASS,* XVII (1884), 203.

The granting of a dispensation for first tonsure and all orders both minor and major is reserved today to the Roman Pontiff.[390] Formerly, bishops could dispense for first tonsure and the four minor orders.[391] The Sovereign Pontiff can, of course, delegate the power to dispense for the reception of orders, as he actually had done since the promulgation of the Code, e.g., in an indult which was granted for use in Spain.[392]

A word may be added here regarding the possibility of the admission of illegitimates to seminaries without a Papal dispensation. Canon 1363, § 1, states that only legitimate persons are to be admitted to seminaries. This is understood to comprehend also those who have been legitimated. It may be said with certainty that those who have been legitimated by radical sanation, by subsequent marriage, or by papal rescript—provided it is not expressly stated in the rescript that admission to a seminary is forbidden—may be admitted to a seminary.[393] Those who have been legitimated in virtue of the provisions of canon 1051 probably can be admitted to a seminary, as has already been observed, since such persons are not irregular. Schaefer and Larraona both state that the legitimation granted in virtue of the provisions of canon 1051 is equal to that conferred by subsequent marriage but they offer no arguments in support of their opinion.[394] Coronata and Vermeersch-Creusen state simply that legitimated persons may be admitted.[395] With reference to those who are illegitimate it must be said that they

[390] Cappello, *De Sacramentis,* III, n. 752; Payen, *De Matrimonio,* n. 2171, note 1, (p. 494) ; Schönsteiner, *Grundriss des kirchlichen Eherechts,* p. 792.

[391] Wernz, *Ius Decretalium,* IV, pars II, n. 688.

[392] ". . . Indultum quoad dispensationem ab irregularitate et ab impedimento affinitatis et criminis. 1) Exsecutor harum litterarum Apostolicarum possit dispensare . . . nec non super irregularitate ex legitimorum natalium defectu, dummodo de adulterinis vel sacrilegis non agatur ad effectum suscipiendi primam clericalem tonsuram et sacros Ordines usque ad Presbyteratum inclusive . . ."—De Bulla *"Cruciata"* ad Alphonsum XIII Hispaniarum regem catholicum—*AAS,* XXI (1929), 17.

[393] Vermeersch, "Annotatio ad c. 1363, § 1,"—*Periodica,* XIX (1930), 345.

[394] *De Religiosis,* p. 243, n. 115; *CpR,* VII (1926), 296-297.

[395] *Institutiones Iuris Canonici,* II, n. 940; *Epitome,* II, n. 697.

require a Papal dispensation for admission. The words *"ne admittantur"* are clearly preceptive and not merely directive. A strong argument in support of this view can be deduced from the text of the faculty granted by the Sacred Consistorial Congregation to Nuncios, Internuncios, and Apostolic Delegates on June 16, 1920, which permitted them under certain conditions, to grant admission to seminaries to illegitimates with the obligation of having recourse later to the Holy See for a dispensation relative to the reception of Orders.[396] Haring proposed an opinion which was also favored by Janssens, namely, that illegitimates do not require a Papal dispensation for admission to seminaries. The arguments advanced by Haring were ably refuted by Hilling, who insists that a dispensation must be sought before any illegitimate may be admitted.[397] Finally, it must be noted that the admission to a novitiate of those persons who are laboring under an irregularity or any other canonical impediment is illicit if such persons intend to become priests.[398] Consequently, an illegitimate should obtain a dispensation to enter the novitiate of a clerical institute licitly. This is true of those illegitimates who enter either the novitiate of a clerical

[396] "Permittendi ingressum in Seminarium illegitimis, dummodo non agatur de adulterinis aut sacrilegis, si de coetero conditiones ad ingressum in pium locum necessariae habeantur, et firma obligatione recurrendi ad S. Sedem pro eorum sacra ordinatione."—Hilling, *Codicis Iuris Canonici Supplementum Praecipua Acta Summorum Pontificum et sacrarum Congregationum Codicem Iuris Canonici Illustratum* (Friburgi Brisgoviae: Herder, 1925), p. 39; Bouscaren, *Canon Law Digest,* I, 186. The faculty (n. 21) as expressed in the list granted to the Apostolic Delegate to the United States is the same as the one here mentioned, but adds "de qua obligatione (i.e., recurrendi ad S. Sedem pro eorum sacra ordinatione) explicite monendi sunt tum Ordinarii locorum, tum parentes illegitimorum."

[397] Haring, "Bedürfen Illegitimi bei Aufnahme in ein Seminar einer päpstlichen Dispensation?"—*LQS,* LXXVI (1923), 691-692; Janssens, "L'irregularité pour cause d'illegitimité,"—*Nouvelle Revue Theologique,* LI (1924), 47-48; Hilling, "Aufnahme der Illegitimi in das Seminar,"—*AKKR,* CV (1925), 191-194; cf. Haring, "Bedürfen Illegitimi bei Aufnahme in ein Seminar einer päpstlichen Dispensation?"—*LQS,* LXXIX (1926), 152.

[398] Canon 542, 2°.

institute of simple vows, or the novitiate of a clerical institute of solemn vows, wherein solemn profession is made only after the reception of the clerical tonsure and of minor orders. It has already been shown that illegitimates do not require a dispensation to enter the novitiate of a clerical institute of solemn vows, wherein solemn profession is made before the reception of the clerical tonsure. The dispensation, however, which is granted to an illegitimate to enter a novitiate licitly does not necessarily have to be either a rescript of legitimation or a formal dispensation from the irregularity of illegitimacy. A dispensation to enter the novitiate cannot be interpreted as a virtual dispensation from the irregularity. Usually such a dispensation according to Vermeersch will declare expressly that the person dispensed may receive the clerical tonsure and the minor orders. For major orders it is necessary to have recourse to the Holy See for a further dispensation.[399]

A general dispensation to receive Orders is valid also for major orders and the one dispensed can obtain non-consistorial benefices, even those to which the care of souls is attached, but he cannot become a cardinal, bishop, abbot or prelate *nullius,* nor a major superior in clerical exempt institutes.[400]

Though the question is one which is not connected necessarily with the question of a Papal dispensation for the reception of Orders, it is not out of place here to note that local ordinaries may dispense, in virtue of their quinquennial faculties, from the obstacle of illegitimacy in as far as such a dispensation is made necessary by the constitutions of the institute which an illegitimate person wishes to enter. Three conditions must be verified: 1) the superiors of the institute must request that the dispensation be granted; 2) the illegitimate person must not be the offspring of a sacrilegious union; 3) the person dispensed must be excluded from the office of major superior in accordance with canon 504.[401]

[399] Vermeersch, "Canon 542, 2°„ et dispensatio ab irregularitate,"—*Periodica,* XX (1931), 136*-137*; Gonzalez, "Licetne recipere in novitiatum filios illegitimos vel parentis ignoti?"—*Ius Pontificium,* XV (1935), 318.

[400] Canon 991, § 3.

[401] Bouscaren, *Canon Law Digest,* I. 67.

Chapter IV

THE BAPTISMAL RECORD OF ILLEGITIMATE CHILDREN

Canon 777. § 1. Parochi debent nomina baptizatorum, mentione facta de ministro, parentibus ac patrinis, de loco ac die collati baptismi, in baptismali libro sedulo et sine ulla mora referre.

§ 2. Ubi vero de illegitimis filiis agatur, matris nomen est inserendum, si publice eius maternitas constet, vel ipsa sponte sua scripto vel coram duobus testibus id petat; item nomen patris, dummodo ipse sponte sua a parocho vel scripto vel coram duobus testibus id requirat, vel ex publico authentico documento sit notus; in ceteris casibus inscribatur natus tanquam filius patris ignoti vel ignotorum parentum.

It may be observed first of all that the solemn baptism of an illegitimate child is reserved by law to the pastor of the place where the mother of the child possesses either a domicile or a quasi-domicile.[1] Cappello maintains that if the father of an illegitimate child is known and his name is found in the baptismal register the child follows the domicile or quasi- domicile of the father.[2] Ciprotti, however, correctly maintains that such a child follows the domicile or quasi-domicile of the mother. He states, too, that once the juridical place of origin has been fixed it is not changed by the subsequent legitimation of the child.[3]

The question of the registration of the baptism of illegitimate children has its difficulties. No procedure can be outlined which will be found completely satisfactory in all the possible

[1] Cf. canons 90, §1; 94; 738; Fanfani, *De Iure Parochorum ad Normam Codicis Iuris Canonici* (2. ed., Taurini-Romae: Marietti, 1936), nn. 79, 244.

[2] *Summa Iuris Canonici* (2. ed., 3 vols., Romae: Apud Aedes Universitatis Gregorianae, 1932-1936), I, n. 192.

[3] *Apollinaris,* XII (1939), 493.

circumstances which may arise concerning the registration of the baptism of these children. The existence of the difficulties to be encountered in various cases was recognized by the Pontifical Commission for the Interpretation of the Code when it declared on July 14, 1922, that the names of the parents are to be inserted in such a way that all occasions of the loss of good repute will be avoided and that in particular cases recourse should be had to the Sacred Congregation of the Council.[4] Although the existence of difficulties in particular cases is admitted, nevertheless something may be said regarding the provisions of canon 777, § 2, so that the regulations outlined there may be properly obeyed. The canon states that the name of the mother of an illegitimate child is to be inserted in the baptismal register: 1) when the fact of her motherhood is known publicly, or when she requests of her own accord either in writing or in the presence of two witness that her name be inserted. There is usually no difficulty regarding the insertion of an unmarried mother's name, as the fact of her motherhood is generaly well known. It can be said that the fact that an unmarried woman is the mother of an illegitimate child is public if it has already been divulged, or if the circumstances are such that it can be judged prudently that it can and must easily become known.[5] If these conditions are verified, that mother's name is to be inserted even if she requests that it be omitted. The canon states that mother's name must be inserted when the fact of her motherhood is public knowledge.

If the fact that an unmarried mother has given birth to a child is not publicly known and it cannot be judged prudently that it can and must easily become public knowledge, her name may not be inserted in the baptismal register without her permission. This is so even if the pastor has received reliable information of a private character that a particular woman is the mother of an illegitimate child brought to him for baptism. If the fact of her motherhood is unknown publicly and is unlikely

[4] *AAS,* XIV (1922), 528.

[5] Cf. canon 2197, 1°; Blat, *Commentarium,* III, pars I, n. 68.

to become known, the mother's name may be inserted if she requests either in writing or in the presence of two witnesses that this be done. It would seem that there is no prohibition for the pastor to explain to the mother, when the fact of her motherhood is not known publicly, that he cannot enter her name in the baptismal register unless she requests that this be done. It is very unlikely that a woman would be acquainted with the provisions of this canon. Consequently, it seems unlikely that a request would be made either in writing or before two witness to have one's name inserted unless the provisions of the canon have been explained.[6] Should the mother refuse to have her name entered even after she has been made aware of the law, her refusal must be respected, provided the fact of her motherhood is not publicly known or likely to become known easily. On the other hand, if the mother in such circumstances requests either in writing or before two witnesses that her name be entered in the register, this request must be complied with. The mother's request must be made of her own accord, personally.[7] When such a request is made in writing the document should be preserved in the parochial archives.[8] It seems that the existence of such a document should be indicated clearly in the baptismal register itself; otherwise it could possibly happen that all traces of it would be lost and its existence become unknown to succeeding pastors of the parish.

If the mother's request is made orally in the presence of two witnesses, it should be accepted by the pastor only when he is morally certain that the witnesses are trustworthy.[9] Otherwise they might possibly deny later the fact that they had witnessed to the mother's request. The names of the witnesses should, of course, be recorded. If the witnesses are the child's sponsors, it seems that a notation in the baptismal register itself in declaration of their witnessing the mother's request will be sufficient;

[6] Cf. "The Baptismal Record of Illegitimates"—*AER,* LXII (1920), 91.
[7] Blat, *Commentarium,* III, pars I, n. 68.
[8] Canon 470, § 4.
[9] Blat, *Commentarium,* III, pars I, n. 68.

if the witnesses are not the child's sponsors, their names can be inserted in the register or, if this cannot be done, their names should be recorded in the parochial archives with a notation made in the baptismal register explaining where the names of the witnesses may be found. The names of the witnesses to the mother's request may be entered in the baptismal register itself because once the mother has requested that her name be inscribed in the register there is no longer any question of the unjust loss of her good repute.

The father's name is to be inserted in the register: 1) when he makes a request either in writing or in the presence of two witnesses that his name be entered; 2) when the fact of his paternity is known from an authentic public document. It is to be noted that while the mother's name must be inscribed in the register if the fact of her motherhood is publicly known, the same rule does not obtain with reference to the father's name. The fact that a particular man is reputed publicly to be the father of an illegitimate child is not sufficient warranty to permit the insertion of his name in the register. The father's name is to be inserted when he requests either in writing or in the presence of two witnesses that this be done. What has already been said regarding such a request made by the mother will apply also to the request made by the father. If the father's paternity is known from an authentic public document, his name must be inserted. Such a document may be either ecclesiastical or civil.[10] Thus, if a man has been convicted on a paternity charge. a properly certified copy of the sentence will be regarded as an authentic public document and the man's name must be inscribed in the baptismal register even against his will. If a man has made an affidavit acknowledging that he is the father of the child, this of itself will not suffice to enter his name. An affidavit is a private document and hence does not meet the requirements of this canon. Of course if a man adds to the affidavit a request that his name be entered, then the entry must be made. An affidavit by an unmarried mother that a

[10] Blat, *Commentarium,* III, pars I, n. 68; cf. canon 1813, §§ 1-2.

particular man is the father of her child is not to be recognized at all for the purpose of registering the man named as the father of the child.[11] Once the father has requested that his name be entered in the register, there is no longer any question of the possibility of the loss of his good repute.[12]

The canon states that if the father's name cannot be entered and the mother's name alone is inscribed, the child must be described as having been born of an "unknown father". It seems, therefore, that the practice of leaving a blank space where the father's name is ordinarily inserted or even of drawing a line through this space is not in conformity with the law. The canon expressly commands that the child in such circumstances must be designated as having been born of an "unknown father." If neither the father's name nor the mother's can be inserted according to the provisions of the canon, it is stated that the child is to be designated as having been born of "unknown parents". It seems that regarding the inscription which is to be made of a child as having been born of "unknown parents" a distinction ought to be made on the one hand, between a child which is certainly known to be illegitimate and in whose case the names of neither of its parents can legally be inserted in the register, and on the other hand a child which is not certainly known to be illegitimate, for example, a foundling. It could be argued that if the pastor knows certainly that the child is illegitimate, but cannot legally enter the name of either parent, he should add a note declaring that the child is illegitimate. This would cause no loss of reputation to the parents since their names will not be found in the register, and at the same time it will establish the fact of the child's illegitimacy. The correct procedure, however, is to enter the name of the child which is known to be illegitimate, though the names of the parents cannot be inserted according to the provisions of this canon, simply as having been born of "unknown parents." If a child

[11] "Recording the Baptism of Illegitimate Children"—*AER,* LXXIX (1928), 191-196.

[12] Blat, *Commentarium,* III, pars I, n. 68.

is a foundling the record of its baptism must contain mention of the date and place of its finding, the person who found it, and an estimate of its probable age.[13] If the regulations of the Ritual are properly observed [14] it will be immediately evident that a child registered *simply* as having been born of "unknown parents" is actually illegitimate, in so far as the record then offers no indication of the child's condition as a foundling.

It may be observed here that since it is not usual for the mother to accompany the sponsors and the child to baptism, and since it is likewise very improbable that the father of an illegitimate child will be present, great caution must be exercised by the officiating priest with regard to the question of the child's parentage.[15] If a woman is publicly known as the mother, her name is to be inserted immediately in the register; if she is not publicly known as the mother, her name is not to be inserted unless she requests that this be done. The father's name is not to be inserted unless he requests that this be done, or unless his paternity is known from an authentic public document.

From what has been said it can be deduced that there is never any occasion to mention expressly in the register that a child of an unmarried mother is illegitimate. This is so because: 1) when the mother's name alone is mentioned and the words of an "unknown father" are found in the space for the father's name the child's status is evident; 2) when the father's name is mentioned there will be found a reference to the request he has made to have his name inserted; 3) when a child is described simply as having been born of "unknown parents" it will also be known to be illegitimate, for the record then does nothing to identify the child as a foundling.

Thus far reference has been made only to the registration of the baptism of the child of an unmarried woman. This restriction was employed because if the mother of a child brought for

[13] *Rituale Romanum* (editio juxta Typicam, Romae: Desclée et Socii, 1939), Tit. XII, c. II.

[14] Cf. canon 2.

[15] Cf. *Rituale Romanum,* Tit. II, c. I, n. 69.

baptism is married, the name of her husband is always inserted as the father of the child. It has already been seen that if the child has been born at least six months after the mother's marriage or within ten months of the dissolution of conjugal life it is presumed by a presumption of law that the child's conception occurred during marriage and that consequently the child is legitimate according to the provisions of canon 1115, § 2. If the child has been born within six months of the day of the mother's marriage it is legitimate according to the provisions of canon 1114. There is a human presumption in such cases that the father of the child has married the mother. Should the mother's husband declare that he is not the child's father, then his name nevertheless must be inserted in the baptismal register according to canon 777, § 1. His name is to remain in the register as that of the father of the child until such time when he has proved to the competent ecclesiastical or civil authorities that he could not have been the child's father. Even if such proof is given, the pastor may not change the record until he has been ordered to do so by the competent ecclesiastical authorities. It is not within the pastor's province to judge in any dispute as to paternity. Should the mother admit, or even swear, that she has been unfaithful and should the other guilty party even corroborate her testimony, the husband's name is nevertheless to be inserted as that of the father of the child. As has already been shown, the strength of the presumption that a husband is the father of his wife's child is so great that it cannot be overthrown except by evident proof to the contrary. It is extremely difficult to prove that the husband of the mother is not the father of her child when the two cohabited at the time with which the conception of the child may be connected as a probable or even possible occurrence.

If a woman has given birth to a child within ten months of the dissolution of her conjugal life, then her former husband's name is to be inscribed in the baptismal register as that of the father of the child. If the child is born more than ten months after the dissolution of her conjugal life, then it must not be immediately concluded that the child is illegitimate. As has already been shown, it is possible in extraordinary cases that the period of gestation may be prolonged. In such a case, however, if more than ten months have passed since the dissolution of the mother's conjugal life, there is no presumption of law in favor of the child's legitimacy. The mother must prove with the aid of expert medical testimony (i.e., concerning the prolonged period of gestation) that her husband could have been the child's father. She must also adduce, insofar as possible, indications that her husband was actually the child's father. If these proofs cannot be advanced, or if only inconclusive proofs are offered, then it seems correct to maintain that the husband's name must not be entered in the baptismal register as that of the father of the child.

It may be asked what procedure is to be followed in recording the baptism of a child whose parents have been married civilly or before a non-Catholic minister. Woywod observes that special caution is necessary in baptizing a child whose parents are married lawfully in the eyes of the civil law, but invalidly in the eyes of the Church. The priest, he says, may not make a note to the effect that the child is illegitimate, but he may note that the parents were married only before a non-Catholic minister or a civil magistrate. This is stating a fact for which nobody can accuse the pastor of libel.[16] Beste states that if the parents have been married civilly, the record of their child's baptism is to be made out in the usual way with added mention of the parent's civil marriage, but without any express intimation of the child's illegitimacy.[17] Vermeersch-Creusen remark that when the child has been born of an adulterous civil marriage the inscription of this fact will not add any infamy, but it may be scandalous. In such a case, they maintain, the pastor should make no entry until he has consulted the Ordinary.[18] One writer states simply that the baptismal record of a child born

[16] *A Practical Commentary,* I, n. 677.

[17] *Introductio in Codicem* (Collegeville, Minn.: St. John's Abbey Press, 1938), p. 483.

[18] *Epitome,* II, n. 55.

of a civil marriage should contain the notation *"ex contractu civili."*[19] Another writer, observing that some pastors add the remark at the entry of the child's baptism that its parents are married only civilly, maintains that while this remark will not lay the pastor open to prosecution in civil law, it will inform those who understand the law of the Church on the point of the implication of the child's illegitimacy in the eyes of the Church. But even such a note, he contends, is superfluous and unwarranted.[20]

Because of the possibility of the presence of good faith and its consequent effect upon the status of the child it does not seem correct in all such cases either to add simply in the baptismal register that child has been born of a civil marriage or, on the other hand, to omit all mention of the fact of the existence of such a marriage. The legitimacy of a child can be deduced ordinarily from a comparison of the marimonial and baptismal registers, but it is obvious that such a deduction cannot be made if there is no record in the matrimonial register of a marriage between the parents. Justice demands that if the civil marriage of the parents is actually a putative marriage then the fact of the legitimacy of the child must be safeguarded. It seems that this can best be done by adding a note to the effect that the child has been born of a putative marriage. The following possible cases may be mentioned: 1) If two Catholics have knowingly and deliberately neglected the canonical form of marriage the baptismal record of their child should contain mention of the fact that the child has been born of parents who are married only civilly, the implication being that the child is illegitimate; 2) If two Catholics have married without observing the canonical form, but at least one of them was ignorant of the necessity of its observance and the good faith remained at the time of the child's conception, the register

[19] Van Acken, "Das uneheliche Kind im Lichte des Glaubens und der Erbbiologie,"—*LQS,* XCII (1939), 432.

[20] "Recording the Baptism of Illegitimate Children,"—*AER,* LXXIX (1928), 191-196.

should contain mention of the fact that the parents are married civilly with added mention of the fact that their marriage was of a putative character at the time of the child's conception.[21] 3) If the child was born of parents one of whom is a non-Catholic it is very possible that the non-Catholic parent is in good faith. If this condition is verified, it should be noted in the register that the child was born of a putative marriage.[22] If the child, however, was born of an adulterous civil marriage, then the case, according to the opinion of Vermeersch-Creusen already referred to, should be submitted to the judgment of the Ordinary.

It is evident that if the baptism of a child takes place in a parish where the fact that its parents are married only civilly is absolutely unknown, their marriage being commonly regarded as valid, the child will be inscribed in the baptismal register as legitimate, unless the parents themselves disclose the fact that they are married only civilly. This will be so because, although the form prescribed by the Roman Ritual for the registration of the baptism of a legitimate child includes mention of the parents as being married, it appears that the pastor is to seek only the names of the parents and is not to inquire further regarding the validity of their marriage.[23] It is not out of place here to note the reflection of Woywod. He declares that when some of the widely used baptismal and matrimonial registers are examined in the light of the regulations of the Ritual, it would appear that these books are very incomplete and inadequate for the proper satisfaction of the regulations.[24]

[21] Cf. "Answer,"—*AER,* LXXXVII (1932), 521-523.

[22] "Putative Marriage,"—*Homiletic and Pastoral Review, The,* XXVII (1926-1927), 519-520.

[23] Anno Domini . . ., die . . . mensis . . ., ego N. Parochus huius ecclesiae S. N., civitatis vel loci N., in ecclesia S. N. baptizavi infantem natum vel natam die . . . ex N. et N. *coniugibus* huius paroeciae vel paroeciae S. N., civitatis vel loci N.; cui impositum est nomen N. Patrini fuerunt N., filius N., ex paroecia seu loco N., coniux N., filia N., ex paroecia seu loco N.—Tit. XII, c. II; cf. Tit. II, c. I, n. 69; Eaton, "Baptismal Register,"— *Irish Ecclesiastical Record,* XXVIII (1926), 418.

[24] *A Practical Commentary,* I, n. 675.

Reference has already been made to the reply of the Commission for the Interpretation of the Code to the question whether the word *"illegitimi"* in canon 777, § 2, includes obsolutely all illegitimate children, even those who are born of adulterous or sacrilegious unions, and other spurious children, so that it is allowed to inscribe the names of their parents in the record of their baptisms. The Commission answered that the names of the parents are to be inserted in such a way that all occasion of the loss of good repute will be avoided; and that in particular cases recourse should be had to the Sacred Congregation of the Council.[25] The reply of the Code Commission should be borne in mind whenever there is a question of the registration of the baptism of any illegitimate child which is not simply a "natural" child. If the mother of a "spurious" child is unmarried, e.g., when a single woman has begotten a child in adultery, it seems that any occasion of infamy can be avoided if the circumstances surrounding the birth of the child are not expressed. Thus it seems that the fact that a child is adulterine or otherwise "spurious" should not be expressly mentioned. The record, if the parents have requested that their names be mentioned, should merely contain their names without any notation that the child belongs to one of the various classes of "spurious" children.[26] It appears, however, that in some circumstances the name of a parent is not to be inserted immediately by the pastor even if it has been requested that this be done.[27] If the mother of the child brought for baptism is married, the name of her husband is to be inserted as that of the father. If it is proved that the child is adulterine, then the record must be changed in accordance with the provisions of law.

[25] *AAS,* XIV (1922), 528; ". . . ad S.C. Concilii recurrendum dicitur. Etenim, cum non agatur iam de ipsa sacramenti collatione sed de praecepta eius annotatione, res non ad S. C. de Sacramentis, verum ad S. C. Concilii pertinet."—Vermeersch, "Annotatio baptismi,"—*Periodica,* XI (1922), 170.

[26] Vermeersch, *loc. cit.;* Vermeersch-Creusen, *Epitome,* II, n. 55.

[27] "Verum fieri potest ut alia ex annotatione timenda sint detrimenta, v.g., religioni, si audax sacrilegus sacerdos velit ut pater pueri designari."—Vermeersch, "Annotatio baptismi," *Periodica,* XI (1922), 170.

It may be noted here that the registration of the baptism of a child born of a marriage of conscience is to be made in a special book to be preserved in the secrete archives of the diocesan curia. Hilling observes that difficulties can arise in practice regarding the registration of the baptism of a child born of such a marriage, for example, if the pastor of the place of baptism knows nothing of the marriage. In such a case, he maintains, the pastor is absolutely justified and obligated to record the name of the child. In such a case the pastor is to proceed in accordance with the provisions of canon 777, § 2.[28]

With regard to the family name to be given to an illegitimate child in the baptismal record, the pastor must not become a party to any possible injustice. Thus, if the father of an illegitimate child has not requested that his name be inscribed in the register, and his paternity cannot be proved from any authentic public document, then a request by the mother that the name of the man whom she accuses of being her child's father be inserted in the register must be ignored absolutely. If the mother wishes the child to be called, for example, John "Doe" Brown, "Doe" being the name of the man whom she maintains to be the father, the pastor must omit all mention of the reputed father's name.[29]

Finally, it must be noted that if an illegitimate child is later legitimated a notation must be made of this fact. If the child is legitimated by a Papal rescript a notation of this fact in the baptismal register will suffice. If the child has been legitimated by radical sanation, by subsequent marriage, or by a dispensation granted in accordance with the provisions of canon 1051, then a notation of the legitimation should be made both in the matrimonial and in the baptismal registers.[30] It seems that if a matrimonial dispensation has been granted by the Holy See

[28] "Eherechtliche Kontroversen und Probleme,"—*AKKR,* CV (1925), 108-111.

[29] "The Baptismal Name of an Illegitimate Child,"—*AER,* LXXIX (1928), 648-649.

[30] Payen, *De Matrimonio,* II, n. 2179; cf. Vlaming, *Praelectiones Iuris Matrimonii,* II, n. 686.

by a rescript in a particular case with an added decree of legitimation, mention of the legitimation should be made in the matrimonial register as well as in the baptismal register. It is true that the legitimation in such cases is regarded as having been conceded by a Papal rescript, but it is evident that the rescript which contains both a dispensation and a decree of legitimation is not exactly the same as a simple Papal rescript of legitimation granted when there is no question of the marriage of the parents.

In view of the different effects produced by the various modes of legitimation, it appears correct to insist that it should be expressly noted how the legitimation was effected, for example, by subsequent marriage. The opinion of Payen on this question does not seem altogether correct.[31]

[31] "Ne tamen nimis premas hoc verbum *expresse*, Satis enim est, quandoque referre in paroeciales libros: aut subsequens matrimonium, aut dispensationem concessam ad normam can. 1051, aut sanationem in radice. *In usu*, addatur prolem esse legitimatam: nam sic constabit eam potuisse, aut prima, aut secunda, aut tertia via legitimari,"—*De Matrimonio*, II, n. 2179.

APPENDIX

Legitimacy and Legitimation in the Common Law and in the Modern American Law

Common Law may be defined as the general Anglo-American system of legal concepts and the traditional legal technique which forms the basis of the law of the States which have adopted it.

Though Common Law is strictly a system of unwritten law, various compilations have been made of its subject matter. The first compilation of this kind was made in 878 during the reign of King Alfred the Great (871-901) and was known as the *Liber Iudicialis.* Another such collection was made in 1065 under Edward the Confessor (1042-1066). This was known as the *Leges Confessoris.* For practical purposes, however, it can be said that the history of the Common law of England dates from 1215, when the constitutive elements of the Common Law were summed up in the *Magna Carta.* These constitutive elements were: 1) Germanic law, which was the principal element; 2) Roman law; 3) Feudal law; 4) Ancient Canon law.[1]

In the absence of the statutes, American law in most jurisdictions is interpreted according to the principles and maxims of the common law. This makes it advisable here to give a summary consideration to the common law on marriage and legitimacy. It must be kept in mind, of course, that many American jurisdictions have enacted statutory laws on these two questions. These statutes, as will be shown presently, contain provisions contrary to the common law. Since, however, some jurisdictions have no statutes governing all the questions concerning marriage and legitimacy, and since the statutes which do exist are interpreted according to the common law, it is necessary to see what the common law is regarding the questions of marriage and legitimacy.

Common law considers marriage merely as a civil contract.

[1] Alford, *Ius Matrimoniale Comparatum* (New York: P. J. Kenedy and Sons, 1938), nn. 39-41.

The holiness of the matrimonial state is a factor which is relegated entirely to the ecclesiastical law. The courts do not consider unlawful marriage as a sin, but purely as a civil inconvenience.[2]

The parties to a common law marriage must be able and willing to enter the marriage.[3] Strictly considered, no form of celebration was demanded by the common law. If there were no impediments present, then a contract *per verba de praesenti* or *per verba de futuro cum copula* was sufficient. In 1753, however, a statute was enacted in England demanding a religious ceremony according to the Anglican ritual. This statute had no effect on the common law in America.[4]

In England this law caused considerable hardship to Catholics as only Quakers and Jews were exempted. The question was not settled finally until the passage of the Marriage Act of 1836, which placed all Dissenters, including Catholics, on the same footing as the Quakers and the Jews.[5]

The invalidating impediments recognized by common law were: 1) prior marriage; 2) want of age; 3) insanity; 4) absence of the contract *per verba de praesenti* or *per verba de futuro cum copula*. The following impediments rendered a marriage voidable at common law: 1) precontract, 2) consanguinity; 3) affinity; 4) certain corporal infirmities.[6]

At common law only those children who were born during the marriage of their parents are considered legitimate.[7] The strict common law declared the issue of every married woman

[2] Blackstone, *Commentaries on the Laws of England* (2 vols., from the nineteenth London edition, Philadelphia: 1889), I, n. 433.

[3] Blackstone, *op. cit.*, I, n. 434.

[4] May, *Marriage Laws and Decisions in the United States* (New York: Russell Sage Foundation, 1929), pp. 9-12.

[5] Trappes-Lomax, *Bishop Challoner* (London: Longmans, Green and Co., 1936), pp. 123-131.

[6] Blackston, *Commentaries,* I, nn. 434-440.

[7] Blackstone, *op. cit.*, I, n. 446; Schouler, *A Treatise of the Law of Marriage, Divorce, Separation, and Domestic Relations* (3 vols., 6. ed., Albany: Bender and Co., 1921), I, § 695.

legitimate except in the two special cases of the impotence of the husband and his absence from the realm.[8] For a very long time no proof was admitted against this presumption if the husband was "within the four seas." Gradually limitations were introduced, so that if it could be proved that the husband had been imprisoned, afflicted with a grievous illness, impotent, or the wife unfaithful at the time of conception, the child was presumed illegitimate.[9] If a child was born more than nine months or forty weeks after the husband's death it was deemed illegitimate. On the other hand, if it was born before the expiration of nine months after the husband's death it was regarded as legitimate.[10] The legitimacy of children was presumed when their father and mother lived openly as man and wife.[11] At common law the children of marriages declared null and void were on general principles necessarily illegitimate.[12]

In England the temporal courts followed the canon law rule on putative marriage until about 1340. After that a harsher rule prevailed. If a marriage was dissolved by reason of consanguinity, affinity or precontract, the children were *ipso facto* bastardized.[13] It may be noted here that at common law all illegitimates are called bastards.[14] A bastard at common law is a child not born in wedlock, or born under circumstances which were such that the husband of the mother could not be the father of the child, or also whenever the marriage of its supposed parents was void.[15]. It can be stated here that the word "bastard" is of reputedly Saxon origin, being derived from the Saxon words signifying "base start." The most significant disabilities of an illegitimate child at common law are that he has no inheritable

[8] Schouler, *op. cit.,* I, § 696.

[9] Brydall, *Lex Spuriorum* or *The Law of Bastardy* (London, 1703), pp. 83-87.

[10] Brydall, *op. cit.,* p. 94.

[11] Schouler, *A Treatise of the Law of Marriage,* I, § 706.

[12] Schouler, *op. cit.,* I, § 700.

[13] Joyce, *Christian Marriage,* p. 82, note 2.

[14] Brydall, *Lex Spuriorum,* p. 6.

[15] Schouler, *A Treatise of the Law of Marriage,* I, § 705.

blood; that he is incapable of becoming heir, either to his reputed father or to his mother, or to anyone else; that he can have no heirs but those of his own body, i.e., that he cannot transmit a family inheritance.[16] On the other hand, the rights of the bastard are very few at common law, for the children born outside of a legal marriage have been from the earliest times stigmatized with shame, and made to suffer through life the reproach which was rightfully visited upon those who brought them into being.[17]

At common law neither the reputed father nor the mother of an illegitimate child had any exclusive right of guardianship. The common law rule in the absence of statutes is that the reputed father is under no legal liability to support his illegitimate offspring, and a statute providing for the punishment of any person who shall neglect his child has no application to illegitimate children, but the mother will generally be bound to support her illegitimate child.[18]

Strict common law recognized only one method of legitimation, viz., an act of Parliament.[19] One famous instance of such legitimation may be cited. John of Gaunt, the Duke of Lancaster, had four children before marriage by Katherine Swinford. After a petition by their father the children were legitimated by King Richard II (1377-1399), with the consent of Parliament in the twentieth year of his reign. One restriction was placed on the legitimated children. They or their descendants could not succeed to the throne of England.[20]

At the Parliament of Merton in 1236 the Lords absolutely refused to recognize and follow the provision of canon law to effect legitimation of children by the parents' subsequent

[16] Schouler, *op. cit.*, I, § 711.
[17] *Ibidem*, § 704.
[18] Schouler, *op. cit.*, §§ 707-709.
[19] Brydall, *Lex Spuriorum*, p. 42.
[20] Brydall, *op. cit.*, p. 38. It may be noted that John of Gaunt was an uncle of King Richard II. This fact gives the reason for the restriction here mentioned relative to succession to the throne of England.

marriage.[21] It may be noted here that in England legitimation can now be effected in various ways in virtue of the Legitimacy Acts passed in 1858 and 1926.[22]

Under American law the harsh treatment accorded the illegitimate child at common law has been greatly mitigated by statutory provisions. These provisions, it must be noted, are not at all uniform in all the American jurisdictions and leave much to be desired as the writers on civil law themselves admit.[23] It is intended here to show in a general way the provisions of American law with regard to the questions of legitimacy and legitimation, so that a comparison may be made between the provisions of American law and those of canon law. No detailed enumeration then of the statutes of the various jurisdictions will be undertaken. In practice, should a question arise concerning either legitimacy or legitimation in American law, it is necessary to seek expert legal advice regarding the provisions of the law in the jurisdiction where the question arises.[24]

It need only be mentioned that under American law the children of a valid marriage are legitimate. Some jurisdictions have provisions codifying the common law presumption that a child born in wedlock is legitimate. A few jurisdictions have statutes providing for the legitimacy of children born within ten months of the dissolution of the parents' conjugal life. In a few states the presumption that the chidren of a wife cohabiting with her husband who is not impotent are legitimate, is regarded as indisputable. In some jurisdictions the presumption of legiti-

[21] Brydall, *op. cit.*, p. 42 sq.; Joyce, *Christian Marriage*, p. 231; Schouler, *A Treatise of the Law of Marriage*, I, § 697.

[22] Breckinridge, *The Family and the State* (Chicago: The University of Chicago Press, 1934), p. 439.

[23] Cf. Freund, *Illegitimacy Laws of the United Statess Analysis and Index* (U. S. Department of Labor, Children's Bureau, Washington: Government Printing Office, 1919), pp. 55-56.

[24] It may be noted that a detailed listing of the laws on legitimacy and legitimation of the various jurisdictions enacted up to and including 1938 can be found in Vernier, *American Family Laws* (5 vols. and Supplement, Stanford University, California: Stanford University Press, 1931-1938).

macy can be disputed only by the husband and the wife or the descendant of one or both of them. In Louisianna the husband must contest the legitimacy of a child within a month, or in some cases two months, or else lose all rights to object to the legitimacy of the child. The Louisiana Code establishes the presumption that a child conceived in wedlock is legitimate. If a child is born within 180 days after marriage it is not presumed legitimate. In such a case the husband may not object if he knew of the wife's pregnancy at the time of marriage or if he signed the birth or baptismal register.[25]

It has already been shown that at common law the children born of marriages which are void or annulled are regarded as illegitimate. In American law wherever there is no statutory provision to the contrary the common law principle still prevails. Forty-three jurisdictions have statutory provisions which modify the common law rule in some particulars. The most generally adopted statutory policy, and also the most liberal principle, is that enacted to the effect that the children born of marriages null in law shall be legitimate. Such legislation has been enacted in twenty-eight jurisdictions.[26] Other more specific rules are embodied in the statutes of the twenty-eight jurisdictions just referred to and in the statutes of other less liberal jurisdictions. In many jurisdictions the statutes declare that only the children born of marriages null on account of the disabilities expressly mentioned in the statutes, for example, insanity, force or duress, etc., are legitimate.[27]

Various jurisdictions have a statute which declares in effect that when parties have contracted a marriage which is void because a former marriage exists undissolved the offspring of such a second marriage shall be legitimate if the second marriage

[25] Vernier, *American Family Laws,* IV, section 241.

[26] Vernier, *American Family Laws,* I, section 48; *ibidem, Supplement,* section 48; Alford, *Ius Matrimoniale Comparatum,* n. 259, note 9.

[27] It may be noted that Connecticut, Delaware, Maryland, Mississippi, North Carolina, Pennsylvania, Tennessee, and Washington have no statutes regarding the legitimacy of children born of a marriage which is null.—Vernier, *op. cit., loc. cit.*

was entered into in good faith, or on a reasonable belief that no disability existed. On the other hand, some jurisdictions declare legitimate the offspring of marriages null on account of bigamy without expressly requiring good faith of the parties.[28]

Thirty-four jurisdictions have statutes concerning the effect of divorce on the legitimacy of children. In some of these jurisdictions the statutory rule is that divorce in itself does not affect the legitimacy of any child of the marriage. In other jurisdictions there are other special statutory rules. In a few states the offspring is bastardized if the wife is divorced for ante-nuptial pregnancy attributable in cause to a man other than her husband. Some jurisdictions have special rules regarding legitimacy when the divorce is granted for adultery. In a few jurisdictions it is provided that when a divorce is granted because of a prior undissolved marriage the children of the second shall be illegitimate; in others it is declared that if the second marriage was contracted in good faith, and with the full belief that the former husband or wife was dead, the offspring of such a second marriage begotten before suit for divorce is commenced shall be deemed the legitimate child of the parent who at the time of the marriage was capable of contracting.[29]

It can be said that generally considered a marriage which is valid in canon law is valid also in American law. Hence the children born of a marriage valid in canon law will be as a rule recognized *de facto* as legitimate in American law also. There are exceptions, however, to this general norm. A marriage which is recognized as valid in canon law may be regarded as void by the law of various jurisdictions which at the same time declare the children of such a marriage illegitimate. This is true in some jurisdictions with regard to marriages prohibited on account of the difference in race, color, etc. Since such differences do not constitute a diriment impediment in canon law, it is evident that marriages contracted between persons of different race, color, etc., would be recognized as valid in canon law and the children of such marriages would be legitimate.

[28] Vernier, *op. cit.,* I section 48.

[29] Vernier, *op. cit.,* II, section 94; *Supplement,* section 94.

Difficulties may arise concerning the question of the legitimacy of children born of putative marriages. It has already been shown that according to canon law an invalid marriage is considered to be a putative marriage, no matter what diriment impediment stands in the way, as long as the good faith of one of the parties remains. On the other hand, it has been noted that some American jurisdictions do not regard the children of every void marriage as legitimate. They declare legitimate only those children who are born of parents laboring under the disabilities expressly mentioned in their statutes. Some jurisdictions demand that both parties to a void marriage be in good faith to effect the legitimacy of the children; others do not demand that either party be in good faith. It is evident then that the statutes of the various jurisdictions regarding the legitimacy of children born of void marriages are not in agreement with the canon law concept of putative marriage. In practice, however, it will often be the case that a marriage which is putative in canon law will be actually valid in American law. On the other hand, if a marriage, though putative in canon law, is regarded as void in American law and the legitimacy of the children is not admitted because not both of the parties are in good faith, or because the impediment existing between the parties is one the presence of which according to the civil law renders the children illegitimate, it seems that the children of such marriages will be legitimate in canon law and illegitimate in civil law.

In all American jurisdictions there are found some means of effecting the legitimation of children. Forty-eight jurisdictions permit legitimation by subsequent marriage; nineteen require an acknowledgment by the father in addition to the marriage. In twenty-four jurisdictions an acknowledgment of the child by the father is ordinarily sufficient to legitimate the child. In some jurisdictions the acknowledgment must be in writing; in others it suffices that it be by oral declaration or by the conduct of the father towards the child. In a few jurisdictions provision is made for a court process wherein the child, upon petition by the father, may be declared legitimate.[30] Legitimation by the parents' subsequent marriage is recognized in all American jurisdictions with the exception of Arizona, Kansas, and Tennessee. Some jurisdictions provide that if the mother and the "reputed" father intermarry, the child is legitimated. It has been held that such a provision does not require that the man marrying the mother be in fact the father of the child.[31] In those jurisdictions which demand an acknowledgment of the child in addition to the parents' marriage, the acknowledgment by the father is ordinarily sufficient. Some jurisdictions, however, demand that such an acknowledgment be made both by the father and by the mother. A few require an acknowledgment which is regarded as an "adoption into the father's family" in order to give the child certain rights of inheritance. A curious statute is found in one state (Nebraska) which demands besides subsequent marriage and the acknowledgment of the child that the parents have other children after marriage in order to legitimate a child born before their marriage. In another state (Louisiana) adulterine children are not legitimated by subsequent marriage. This view has been adopted in some other jurisdictions, but most courts permit the legitimation of such children.[32]

It can be said that a child legitimated in canon law by its parents' subsequent marriage will be recognized *de facto* as legitimated in American law also in those jurisdictions which require only that the parents intermarry. In those jurisdictions which require an acknowledgement by one or both parents or "an adoption into the father's family" or any other formality, such requirements should be complied with to safeguard the child's status before the civil law. As was noted in the introduction to the commentary, legitimation is not an inseparable effect of marriage. Hence the State acts within its proper sphere of competence when it decrees that certain reasonable requirements

[30] Vernier, *American Family Laws,* IV, section 242; Long, *A Treatise on the Law of Domestic Relations* (St. Paul: 1905), p. 206.

[31] Vernier, *op. cit.,* IV, section 243.

[32] Vernier, *op. cit., loc. cit.*

must be complied with to effect legitimation. It is evident that the statutes of those jurisdictions which have been interpreted as permitting legitimation by the subsequent marriage of the mother and a man who is not the child's father are not in harmony with the canon law concept of legitimation by subsequent marriage, which demands that the father of the child must marry the mother to effect the child's legitimation.

Legitimation is permitted in American law by acknowledgment. This acknowledgment, it must be noted, is not the same as that demanded by some jurisdictions in connection with the parents' subsequent marriage. Legitimation by acknowledgment is, of course, not recognized in canon law.[33]

A few jurisdictions have statutes providing for legitimation in other ways. They declare that upon petition by the father the civil court may decree the child legitimate. In Louisiana the "natural" father or mother may legitimate a "natural" child by an act executed before a notary and two witnesses.[34]

With regard to the effects of legitimation granted by the various American jurisdictions it may be said that the statutes usually declare that the child is legitimated for all purposes. It is expressly stated in some statutes that the legitimation effected through subsequent marriage is valid for all purposes. In other statutes, while the effects are not expressly stated, it seems that it is intended that the legitimation is to be valid for all effects. A few statutes restrict the effects of the legitimation to inheritance rights.

In some of the jurisdictions which provide for legitimation by acknowledgment without a written document the statutes expressly declare that the legitimation is for all purposes. In others the effects are limited to inheritance rights. The statutes which provide for legitimation by acknowledgment in writing limit the effects of the legitimation to the right to inherit. The one exception is the statute of Michigan.

Some of the jurisdictions which permit legitimation by a court

[33] Vernier, *American Family Laws,* IV, section 244.

[34] Vernier, *op. cit.,* IV., section 245.

process apparently legitimate the child for all purposes. In others which permit legitimation in this way the intention of the legislature is obscure, but the effect of the statute is probably confined to inheritance rights.[35]

Finally, it can be observed that according to Madden the legitimacy of a child, not only for the purpose of determining when he can inherit, but for all other purposes, is to be determined by the law of the place where he was born and where the parents were domiciled. A child, therefore, that is legitimate in the place of its birth is legitimate everywhere. On the other hand, a child that is illegitimate in the place of its birth is illegitimate everywhere, and is incapable of inheriting in another state, though he would have been capable of inheriting if he had been born in the latter state. Whether an illegitimate child is legitimated by the subsequent marriage of its parents, or by acknowledgment, or by any other legal means, is determined, he maintains, by the law of the domicile of the father at the time of the attempted legitimation. If an illegitimate child has been rendered legitimate by the subsequent marriage of his parents or in some other way it will be recognized as legitimate for all purposes in any other state in which there is no such statute.[36] It appears, however, that despite the assertions of Madden there is a serious conflict as to whether the *lex domicilii descendentis,* the *lex rei sitae,* or the *lex fori* should be applied in cases of legitimation.[37]

[35] Vernier, *op. cit.,* IV, section 246.

[36] *Handbook of the Laws of Persons and Domestic Relations,* p. 347.

[37] Cf. "Legitimation, Legitimacy, and Recognition in the Conflict of Laws,"—18 *Canadian Bar Review,* Oct. 1940, pp. 589-629; "The Status of Children in the Conflict of Laws," — 8 *University of Chicago Law Review,* Dec. 1940, pp. 42-62.

CONCLUSIONS

1. Only those children who are conceived of the use of a valid marriage are legitimate according to the natural law.

2. Children born of a marriage contracted *coram Deo* and *in facie Ecclesiae* (according to the various meanings the latter term enjoyed in the history of canon law) have always been regarded as legitimate.

3. The legislation of the Church on legitimation was greatly influenced by similar legislation in Roman law. The Church, however, has provided other means of legitimation unknown to Roman law, viz., radical sanation and the dispensation granted in virtue of the provisions of canon 1051.

4. Children conceived of the use of a previously contracted marriage by a father who subsequently has taken a simple vow which invalidates marriage are not regarded as the fruit of sacrilege according to canon 1114.

5. Since the promulgation of the Code there is a *dubium iuris* regarding the necessity of observing the canonical form of marriage in order to render an invalid marriage putative.

6. The term *legitimi* in canon 1114 has not exactly the same significance which it has in canon 1115, § 2.

7. Children whose conception has resulted from artificial fecundation are legitimate provided that the "father" and the mother are united in a valid or putative marriage.

8. The legal presumption of paternity found in canon 1115, § 1, applies only in those cases wherein a child has been conceived in a valid or putative marriage.

9. Blood tests in their present stage of development are not acceptable as conclusive proof of paternity.

10. The months mentioned in canon 1115, § 2, are to be computed as consisting of 30 days each.

11. A dispensation granted in accordance with the provisions of canon 1051 effects legitimation even if the parents for any

reason whatsoever do not marry. The same is true in those cases in which a decree of legitimation is included in the rescript of a dispensation granted for a particular case.

12. Those persons who have been legitimated by radical sanation are not bound by the restrictions of canon 1117.

BIBLIOGRAPHY

Sources

Acta Apostolicae Sedis, Commentarium Officiale, Romane, 1909—

Acta Sanctae Sedis, 41 vols., Romae, 1865-1908.

Bullarium Diplomatum et Privilegiorum Sanctorum Romanorum Pontificum Taurinensis Editio, 25 vols., Augustae Taurinorum, 1857-1872.

Canones et Decreta Sacrosancti Oecumenici Concilii Tridentini, Parisiis, 1856.

Codex Iuris Canonici Pii X Pontificis Maximi iussu digestus Benedicti XV auctoritate promulgatus, Romae: Typis Polyglottis Vaticanis, 1917.

Codex Theodosianus, quem recognovit P. Krueger, Berolini, 1923.

Codicis Iuris Canonici Fontes cura Emi. Petri Card. Gasparri editi, 9 vols., Romae (postea Civitate Vaticana) : Typis Polyglottis Vaticanis, 1923-1939 (vols. VII, VIII, IX *ed. cura et studio Emi. Iustiniani Card. Serédi*).

Collectanea Sacrae Congregationis de Propaganda Fide, 2 vols., Romae: Typographia Polyglotta S. C. de Propaganda Fide, 1907.

Corpus Iuris Canonici, Editio Lipsiensis II (Richter-Friedburg), 2 vols., Lipsiae, 1922.

Corpus Iuris Civilis, 3 vols., Berolini, 1928-1929.

Institutiones, quas recognovit et retractavit P. Krueger.

Digesta, quae recognovit et retractavit P. Krueger.

Codex Iustinianus, quem recognovit et retractavit P. Krueger.

Novellae, quas recognovit R. Schoell, et absolvit G. Kroll.

Decretales D. Gregorii Papae IX, una cum Glossis Restitutae, Romae, 1582.

Decretum Gratiani, una cum Glossis Gregorii XIII Pont. Max. iussu editum, Romae, 1582.

Fontes Iuris Romani Ante-Iustiniani, ed. S. Riccobono, J. Bavierra, C. Ferrini, Florentiae, 1909.

Harduin, Jean, *Acta Conciliorum et Epistolae Decretales ac Constitutiones Summorum Pontificum,* 12 vols., Parisiis, 1715.

Hefele, Carl, *Conciliengeschichte,* 9 vols., 2 ed., Freiburg im Breisgau, 1873-1890.

Journel, M. J. Rouet de, *Enchiridion Patristicum,* Freiburg im Breisgau: Herder, 1929.

Mansi, Ioannes, *Sacrorum Conciliorum Nova et Amplissima Collectio,* 53 vols., Parisiis, 1901-1927.

Migne, Jacques Paul, *Patrologiae Cursus Completus, Series Latina,* 221 vols., Parisiis, 1844-1864.

Moyle, J. B., *Imperatoris Iustiniani Institutiones,* 5. ed., Oxford: Clarendon Press, 1923.

Muirhead, James, *The Institutes of Gaius and the Rules of Ulpian,* Edinburgh, 1904.

Pflugk-Harttung, J. von, *Acta Pontificum Romanorum Inedita,* 3 vols., Tuebingen, 1881-1886.

Poste, Edward, *Gai Institutiones,* Oxford, 1904.

Rituale Romanum Pauli V Pontificis Maximi iussu editum Sanctissimi D. N. Pii Papae XI ad Normam Codicis Iuris Canonici accomodatum, Editio iuxta Typicam, Romae: Desclée et Socii, 1939.

S. Romanae Rotae Decisiones seu Sententiae quae . . . prodierunt anno 1909-1932, 24 vols., Romae: Typis Vaticanis, 1912-1940

Thesaurus Resolutionum Sacrae Congregationis Concilii, 167 vols., Romae, 1718-1908.

Authors

Alford, Culver B., *Ius Matrimoniale Comparatum,* New York: P. J. Kenedy and Sons, 1938.

Aquinas, St. Thomas, *Summa Theologica,* 6 vols., ed. De Rubeis, Billuart et Aliorum, Taurini: Marietti, 1932.

Ayrinhac, H. A., *Constitution of the Church in the New Code of Canon Law,* 2. ed., New York: Longmans Green and Co., 1930.

Ayrinhac-Lydon, *Marriage Legislation in the New Code of Canon Law,* revised edition, New York: Benziger Brothers, 1936.

Bachofen, Charles Augustine, *A Commentary on the New Code of Canon Law,* 8 vols., Vol. V, 5. ed., St. Louis: Herder, 1935.

Bargilliat, M., *Praelectiones Iuris Canonici,* 2 vols., 37. ed., ad canones novi Codicis redacta, Parisiis: apud Baston, Berche, et Pagis, 1923.

Benedictus XIV, *De Synodo Diocesana,* Romae, 1806.

Bernardus Papiensis, *Summa Decretalium,* ed. Ern. Laspeyres, Ratisbon, 1860.

Beste, Udalricus, *Introductio in Codicem,* Collegeville, Minn.: St. John's Abbey Press, 1938.

Blackstone, Sir William, *Commentaries on the Laws of England,* 2 vols., from the nineteenth London edition, Philadelphia, 1889.

Blat, Albertus, *Commentarium Textus Codicis Iuris Canonici,* 6 vols., Romae: Ex Typographia Pontificia in Instituto Pii IX, 1921-1927.

Bouscaren, T. Lincoln, *The Canon Law Digest,* 2 vols., Milwaukee: Bruce, 1934-1937, *Supplement,* 1938.

Breckinridge, Sophonisba, *The Family and the State,* Chicago: The University of Chicago Press, 1934.

Brennan, James H., *The Simple Convalidation of Marriage,* The Catholic University of America, Canon Law Studies, N. 102, Washington, D. C.: The Catholic University of America, 1937.

Brydall, John, *Lex Spuriorum* or *The Law of Bastardy,* London, 1703.

Buckland, William Warwick, *Elementary Principles of the Roman Private Law,* Cambridge, 1912.

—— *The Main Institutions of Roman Private Law,* Cambridge: Cambridge University Press, 1931.

—— *A Textbook of Roman Law from Augustus to Justinian,* 2. ed., Cambridge: Cambridge University Press, 1932.

Cappello, Felix M., *Summa Iuris Canonici,* 2. ed., 3 vols., Romae: Apud Aedes Universitatis Gregorianae, 1932-1936.

—— *Tractatus Canonico-Moralis de Sacramentis,* Vol. III, *De Matrimonio,* 4. ed., Romae: Apud Aedes Universitatis Gregorianae, 1939.

Carberry, John J., *The Juridical Form of Marriage,* the Catholic University of America, Canon Law Studies, N. 84, Washington, D. C.: The Catholic University of America, 1934.

The Catholic Encyclopedia, 15 vols., New York, 1907-1913.

Chelodi, Ioannes, *Ius Matrimoniale Iuxta Codicem Iuris Canonici,* 3. ed., Tridenti: Libr. Edit. Tridentum, 1921.

—— *Ius de Personis Iuxta Codicem Iuris Canonici,* Tridenti: Libr. Edit. Tridentum, 1922.

Cicognani, Amleto, *Canon Law,* authorized English Version by J. O'Hara and F. Brennan, 2. ed., Philadelphia: Dolphin Press, 1935.

Ciprotti, Pius. *De Consummatione Delictorum Attento Eorum Elemento Obiectivo in Iure Canonico,* Romae: Apud Custodiam Librariam Pontificis Instituti Utriusque Iuris, 1936.

Claeys-Bouuaert, F. et Simenon, G., *Manuale Iuris Canonici,* 2. ed., Gandae et Leodii, 1926.

Corbett, Percy Elwood, *The Roman Law of Marriage,* Oxford: Clarendon Press, 1930.

Coronata, Mattheus Conte a, *Institutiones Iuris Canonici,* 5 vols. (Vols. I et II, 2. ed.), Taurini: Marietti, 1933-1939.

Creusen, Joseph, *Religious Men and Women in the Code,* (third English edition by Adam C. Ellis, first translation by Edward F. Garesche), Milwaukee: The Bruce Publishing Co., 1940.

DeBecker, Julius, *De Sponsalibus et Matrimonio,* Bruxellis, 1896.

DeRoskovany, Augustinus, *Coelibatus et Breviarium,* 3 vols., Pestini, 1861.

DeSmet, Al., *Tractatus Theologico-Canonicus De Sponsalibus et Matrimonio,* 4. ed., Brugis: Car. Beyaert, 1927.

Esmein, A., *Le Mariage en Droit Canonique,* 2 vols., Paris, 1891.

—— *Le Mariage en Droit Canonique,* 2. ed., 2 vols., Paris: Recueil Sirey, 1929-1935.

Fanfani, Ludovicus, *De Iure Parochorum ad Normam Codicis Iuris Canonici,* 2. ed., Taurini-Romae: Marietti, 1936.

Feije, Henricus, I., *De Impedimentis et Dispensationibus Matrimonialibus,* 3. ed., Lovanii, 1885.

Ferraris, F. Lucius, *Prompta Bibliotheca, Canonica, Iuridica, Moralis, Theologica, nec non Ascetica, Polemica, Rubristica,* ed. Migne, 8 vols., Parisiis, 1860-1863.

Freisen, Joseph, *Geschichte des Canonischen Eherechts,* 2. ed., Paderborn, 1893.

Freund, Ernst, *Illegitimacy Laws of the United States Analysis and Index,* U. S. Department of Labor, Children's Bureau, Washington, D. C.: Government Printing Office, 1919.

Funk, Francis X., *A Manual of Church History,* 2 vols., trans. P. Perciballi, London: Burns, Oates and Washbourne Ltd., 1931.

Gasparri, Petrus, *Tractatus Canonicus de Matrimonio,* 3. ed., 2 vols., Parisiis, 1904.

—— *Tractatus Canonicus de Matrimonio,* ed nova, ad mentem Codicis I. C., 2 vols., Romae: Typis Polyglottis Vaticanis, 1932.

Genestal, R., *Histoire de la Legitimation des Enfants Naturels en Droit Canonique,* Paris, 1905.

Genicot, Eduardus, *Institutiones Theologiae Moralis,* 12. ed., (5. post Codicem Iuris Canonici), 2 vols., quam recognovit I. Salsmans, Bruxellis: Alb. Dewit, 1931.

Girard, Paul Frederic, *Manuel Elementaire de Droit Romain,* 7. ed., Paris: Rousseau et Cie., 1924.

Harrigan, Robert J., *The Radical Sanation of Invalid Marriages,* The Catholic University of America, Canon Law Studies, N. 116, Washington, D. C.: The Catholic University of America, 1938.

Hilling, Nicolaus, *Codicis Iuris Canonici Supplementum Praecipua Acta Summorum Pontificum et Sacrarum Congregationum Codicem Iuris Canonici Illustr.,* Friburgi-Brisgoviae: Herder, 1925.

Hinschius, Paul, *Das Kirchenrecht der Katholiken und Protestanten in Deutschland,* 6 vols., Berlin, 1869-1897.

Hostiensis, Cardinalis (Henricus de Segusio), *Summa Aurea,* Venetiis, 1570.

Jacobs, A. C., *Cases and Other Materials on Domestic Relations,* 2. ed., Chicago: The Foundation Press, Inc., 1939.

Ioannes Andreae, *In Sex Decretalium Libros Novella Commentaria,* 6 vols. in 5, Venetiis, 1581.

Joyce, George Hayward, *Christian Marriage,* Heythrop Theological Series, I, London: Sheed and Ward, 1933.

Kearney, Raymond A., *The Principles of Delegation,* The Catholic University of America, Canon Law Studies, N. 55, Washington, D. C.: The Catholic University of America, 1929.

Knecht, August, *Handbuch des katholischen Eherechts,* Freiburg im Breisgau: Herder, 1928.

Kutschker, Johann, *Das Eherecht der katholischen Kirche nach seiner Theorie und Praxis,* 5 vols., Wien, 1856-1857.

Leage, R. W., *Roman Private Law,* 2. ed., by C. H. Ziegler, London: Macmillan and Co. Ltd., 1937.

Leitner, Martin, *Lehrbuch des katholischen Eherechts,* 3. ed., Paderborn: Ferdinand Schoeningh, 1920.

Linneborn, Johannes, *Grundriss des Eherechts nach dem Codex Iuris Canonici,* 2. and 3. ed., Paderborn: Ferdinand Schoeningh, 1922.

Lombardus, Petrus, *Libri IV Sententiarum,* 2. ed., 2 vols., Collegium S. Bonaventurae, ad Claras Aquas prope Florentiam: Ex Typographia Collegii S. Bonaventurae, 1916.

Long, Joseph, *A Treatise on the Law of Domestic Relations,* St. Paul, 1905.

Madden, Joseph, *Handbook of the Law of Persons and Domestic Relations,* St. Paul: West Publishing Co., 1931.

Manning, John J. *Presumptions of Law in Marriage Cases,* The Catholic University of America, Canon Law Studies, N. 94, Washington, D. C.: The Catholic University of America, 1935.

Maroto, Philippus, *Institutiones Iuris Canonici,* 2 vols., Romae, 1919.

May, Geoffrey, *Marriage Laws and Decisions in the United States,* New York: Russell Sage Foundation, 1929.

Merkelbach, Ben. H., *Quaestiones de Embryologia et de Ministratione Baptismatis,* 2. ed., Liege: La Pensee Catholique, 1928.

Meyer, Paul, *Der Roemische Konkubinat,* Leipzig, 1895.

Miaskiewicz, Francis S., *Supplied Jurisdicton According to Canon* 209, The Catholic University of America, Canon Law Studies, N. 122, Washington, D. C., The Catholic University of America Press, 1940.

McCurdy, William E., *Cases on the Law of Persons and Domestic Relations,* 3, ed., Chicago: Callaghan and Co., 1939.

Ojetti, B., *Commentarium in Codicem Iuris Canonici,* 4 vols., Romae: Apud Aedes Universitatis Gregorianae, 1927-1931.

O'Keefe, Gerald M., *Matrimonial Dispensations, Powers of Bishops, Priests, and Confessors,* The Catholic University of America, Canon Law Studies, N. 45, Washington, D. C.: The Catholic University of America, 1927.

O'Neill, William H., *Papal Rescripts of Favor,* The Catholic University of America, Canon Law Studies, N. 57, Washington, D. C.: The Catholic University of America, 1930.

Ostheimer, Anthony L., *The Family,* The Catholic University of America, Philosophical Studies, vol. 50, Washington, D. C.: The Catholic University of America, 1939.

Ottaviani, Alaphridus, *Institutiones Iuris Publici Ecclesiastici,* 2. ed., 2 vols., Romae: Typis Polyglottis Vaticanis, 1935-1936.

Panormitanus, Abbas (Nicolaus de Tudeschis), *Commentaria in Quinque Libros Decretalium,* 5 vols. in 7, Venetiis, 1588.

Payen, G., *De Matrimonio in Missionibus ac Potissimum in Sinus Tractatus Practicus et Casus,* 2. ed., 3 vols., Zi-ka-wei: in typrographia T'Ou-Sè-Wè, 1935-1936.

Petrovits, Joseph, *The New Church Law on Matrimony,* The Catholic University of America, Canon Law Studies, N. 6, Philadelphia: John Joseph McVey, 1919.

Pruemmer, Dominicus M., *Manuale Iuris Canonici,* 4. et 5. eds., Friburgi-Brisgoviae: Herder, 1927.

—— *Vademecum Theologiae Moralis,* 2. ed., Friburgi-Brisgoviae: Herder, 1923.

Reiffenstuel, Anacletus, *Ius Canonicum Universum,* 6 vols., Romae, 1831-1833.

Santi, Franciscus, *Praelectiones Iuris Canonici,* 5 books in 2 vols., Ratisbon, 1886.

Schaefer, Timothus, *De Religiosis ad Normam Codicis Iuris Canonici,* 3. ed., Roma: S.A.L.E.R., Rappresentante Della Casa Editrice Herder, 1940.

Schmalzgrueber, Franciscus, *Ius Ecclesiasticum Universum,* 5 vols. in 12, Romae, 1843-1845.

Schmitz, P., *Die Stellung der unehelichen Kinder im geltenden kanonischen Recht,* St. Gabriel, Moedling: Missionsbuchhandlung, 1926.

Schoensteiner, Ferdinand, *Grundriss des kirchlichen Eherechts,* 2. ed., Wien: Verlag der Buchhandlung Ludwig Auer, 1937.

Schouler, James, *A Treatise on the Law of Marriage, Divorce, Separation, and Domestic Relations,* 6. ed., 3 vols., Albany: M. Bender and Co., 1921,

Sherman, Charles, *Roman Law in the Modern World,* 2. ed., 3 vols., New York: Baker, Voorhis and Co., 1924.

Sohm, Rudolph, *Institutes of Roman Law,* trans. James Ledlie, 3. ed., Oxford, 1907.

Trappes-Lomax, Michael, *Bishop Challoner,* London: Longmans, Green and Co., 1936.

Triebs, Franz, *Praktisches Handbuch des geltenden kanonischen Eherechts in Vergleichung mit dem deutschen staatlichen Eherecht,* Breslau: Ostdeutsche Verlagsanstalt, 1933.

Van Hove, A., *Commentarium Lovaniense in Codicem Iuris Canonici,* Vol. I, Tom. I, *Prolegomena ad Codicem Iuris Canonici,* Mechliniae-Romae: H. Dessain, 1928.

Vol. I, Tom. II, *De Legibus Ecclesiasticis,* Mechliniae-Romae: H. Dessain, 1930.

Vol. I, Tom. IV, *De Rescripts,* Mechliniae-Romae: H. Dessain, 1936

Vol. I, Tom. V, *De Privilegiis—De Dispensationibus,* Mechliniae-Romae: H. Dessain, 1939.

Vermeersch, Arthurus, *Theologiae Moralis Principia—Responsa-Consilia,* 3. ed., 4 vols., Roma: Università Gregoriana, 1933.

Vermeersch, Arthurus, et Creusen, Josephus, *Epitome Iuris Canonici,* 3 vols., (Vol. I, 6. ed., Vols. II et III, 5. ed.) Mechliniae-Romae: H. Dessain, 1934-1937.

Vernier, Chester G., *American Family Laws,* 5 vols., Stanford University, California: Stanford University Press, 1931-1937; *Supplement,* 1938.

Vlaming, Th. M., *Praelectiones Iuris Canonici ad Normam Codicis Iuris Canonici,* 3. ed., 2 vols., Bussum in Hollandia: Sumptibus Societatis Editricis Anonymae olim Paulus Brand, 1919.

Wahl, Francis X., *The Matrimonial Impediments of Consanguinity and Affinity,* The Catholic Uiversity of America, Canon Law Studies, N. 90, Washington, D. C.: The Catholc University of America, 1934.

Wanenmacher, Francis, *Canonical Evidence in Marriage Cases,* Philadelphia: The Dolphin Press, 1935.

Wernz, Franciscus X., *Ius Decretalium,* 2. ed., 6 vols., Romae et Prati, 1906-1913.

Wernz, Franciscus X., et Vidal, Petrus, *Ius Canonicum ad Codicis Normam Exactum,* 7 vols., in 9, Vol. V, *Ius Matrimoniale,* 2. ed., Romae: Apud Aedes Universitatis Gregorianae, 1928.

Whalen, Donald, *The Value of Testimonial Evidence in Matrimonial Procedure,* The Catholic University of America, Canon Law Studies, N. 99, Washington, D. C.: The Catholic University of America, 1935.

Woywood, Stanislaus, *The New Canon Law,* 3. ed., New York, 1918.

—— *A Practical Commentary on the Code of Canon Law,* 5. ed., 2 vols., New York: Joseph F. Wagner, 1939.

Periodicals

Apollinaris, Romae, 1928—

Archiv fur katholisches Kirchenrecht, Vols. I-VI (1857-1861), Innsbruck; Vols. VI— (1862-), Mainz.

Canadian Bar Review, The, Toronto, 1923—

Commentarium pro Religiosis (later *Commentarium pro Religiosis et Missionariis),* Romae, 1920—

Ecclesiastical Review, The (originally *The American Ecclesiastical Review),* Philadelphia, 1889—

Homiletic and Pastoral Review, The, New York, 1900—

Irish Ecclesiastical Record, Dublin, 1864—

Ius Pontificium, Romae, 1921—

Monitore Ecclesiastico, Il, Romae, 1876—

Nouvelle Revue Théologique, Paris, 1869—

Periodica de Re Canonica et Morali utili praesertim Religiosis et Missionariis, Bruges, 1905—

Theologisch-praktische Quartalschrift, Linz, 1832—

University of Chicago Law Review, Chicago, 1933—

Principal Articles

Ciprotti, Pius, "An per matrimonii convalidationem legitimetur proles ex matrimonio irrito nata,"—*Apollinaris,* XI (1938), 126-127.

——— "De prole legitima vel illegitima in iure canonico vigenti,"—

Apollinaris, XII (1939), 329-347; 490-519.

——— "De sanatione in radice post mortem alterius coniugis an et quo sensu matrimonium invalidum (hoc in casu) sanari possit,"—*Apollinaris,* XI (1938), 285-291.

Haring, Johann, "Bedürfen Illegitimi bei Aufnahme in ein Seminar einer päpstlichen Dispensation?"—*LQS,* LXXVI (1923), 691-692.

——— "Eine schwierige Legitimation,"—*LQS,* (1932), 147-148.

Hilling, Nicolaus, "Aufnahme der Illegitmi in das Seminar,"—*AKKR,* CV (1925), 191-194.

——— "Eherechtliche Kontroversen und Probleme,"—*AKKR,* CV (1925), 108-111.

Kelly, Gerald, "The Morality of Artifical Fecundation,"—*AER,* CI (1939), 109-118.

Kinane, J., "Illegitimacy and the Religious Life,"—*IER,* XIX (1922), 540-541.

Larraona, Arcadius, "Canon 504 (interpretatio textus),"—*CpR,* VII (1926), 296-297

Maroto, Philippus, "An filii legitimati per subsequens parentum matrimonium habendi sint uti legitimi ad effectum de quo in canone 1363, § 1,"—*Apollinaris,* III (1930), 571-574.

Meister, Oskar, "Die Bedeutung der Blutprobe für die Seelssorge,"—*LQS,* LXXX (1927), 314-318.

Mocnik, Vinko, "Legitimation unhelicher Kinder durch die nachfolgende Ehe,"—*LQS,* XCI (1938), 691-696.

O'Neill, P., "Legitimacy and Legitimation,"—*IER* XXXVIII (1931), 520-522.

Schaaf, Valentine, "Review of the new edition of Gasparri's *De Matrimonio,*"—*AER,* LXXXVIII (1933), 596-598.

Stumberg, G. W., "The Status of Children in the Conflict of Laws,"—8 *University of Chicago Law Review,* Dec. 1940, 42-62.

Taintor, Charles W., "Legitimation, Legitimacy, and Recognition in the Conflict of Laws,"—18 *Canadian Bar Review,* Oct. 1940, 589-629.

Van Acken, B., "Das uneheliche Kind im Lichte des Glaubens und der Erbbiologie,"—*LQS,* XCII (1939), 427-441.

Vermeersch, Arthurus, "Canon 542, 2°, et dispensatio ab irregularitate,"—*Periodica,* XX (1931), 136*-137*.

"Recording the Baptsm of Illegitimate Children,"—*AER,* LXXIX (1928), 191-196.

Abbreviations

AAS—*Acta Apostolicae Sedis.*
AER—*American Ecclesiastical Review.*
AKKR—*Archiv fur katholisches Kirchenrecht.*
ASS—*Acta Sanctae Sedis.*
C.—*Codex Imperatoris Iustiniani.*
CpR—*Commentarium pro Religiosis et Missionariis.*
D.—*Digesta Imperatoris Iustiniani.*
Fontes—*Codicis Iuris Canonici Fontes cura . . . Gasparri editi.*
Harduin—*Acta Conciliorum* etc.
Hefele—*Concilengeschichte.*
IER—*Irish Ecclesiastical Record.*
Inst—*Institutiones Imperatoris Iustiniani.*
LQS.—*Theologisch-praktische Quartalschrift* (Linz).
Mansi—*Sacrorum Conciliorum Nova et Amplissima Collectio.*
Nov—*Novellae Imperatoris Iustiniani.*
Periodica—*Periodica de Re Canonica et Morali utili praesertim Religiosis et Missionariis.*
S.C.C.—*Sacra Congregatio Concilii.*

BIOGRAPHICAL NOTE

Gilbert Joseph McDevitt was born in Philadelphia, Pennsylvania, August 24, 1911. He attended Our Mother of Sorrows parochial school and the West Philadelphia Catholic High School for Boys, from which he graduated in June, 1928. On September 3, 1928, he entered St. Charles Borromeo Seminary, Overbrook, Pennsylvania, where he received the A. B. degree in June, 1934. He was ordained to the Sacred Priesthood on May 26, 1938, and enrolled in the School of Canon Law of the Catholic University in September, 1938. He received the degree of the Baccalaureate in Canon Law in June, 1939, and the degree of the Licentiate in Canon Law in June, 1940.

ALPHABETICAL INDEX

CANON LAW STUDIES

1. Freriks, Rev. Celestine A., C.PP.S., J.C.D., Religious Congregations in Their External Relations, 121 pp., 1916.
2. Galliher, Rev. Daniel M., O.P., J.C.D., Canonical Elections, 117 pp., 1917.
3. Borkowski, Rev. Aurelius L., O.F.M., J.C.D., De Confraternitatibus Ecclesiasticis, 136 pp., 1918.
4. Castillo, Rev. Cayo, J.C.D., Disertacion Historico-Canonica sobre la Potestad del Cabildo en Sede Vacante o Impedida del Vicario Capitular, 99 pp., 1919 (1918).
5. Kubelbeck, Rev. William J., S.T.B., J.C.D., The Sacred Pentitentiaria and Its Relations to Faculties of Ordinaries and Priests, 129 pp., 1918.
6. Petrovits, Rev. Joseph J.C., S.T.D., J.C.D., The New Church Law On Matrimony, X-461 pp., 1919.
7. Hickey, Rev. John J., S.T.B., J.C.D., Irregularities and Simple Impediments in the New Code of Canon Law, 100 pp., 120.
8. Klekotka, Rev. Peter J., S.T.B., J.C.D., Diocesan Consultors, 179 pp., 1920.
9. Wanenmacher, Rev. Francis, J.C.D., The Evidence in Ecclesiastical Procedure Affecting the Marriage Bond, 1920 (Printed 1935).
10. Golden, Rev. Henry Francis, J.C.D., Parochial Benefices in the New Code, IV-119 pp., 1921 (Printed 1925).
11. Koudelka, Rev. Charles J., J.C.D., Pastors, Their Rights and Duties According to the New Code of Canon Law, 211 pp., 1921.
12. Melo, Rev. Antonius, O.F.M., J.C.D., De Exemptione Regularium, X-188 pp., 1921.
13. Schaaf, Rev. Valentine Theodore, O.F.M., S.T.B., J.C.D., The Cloister, X-180 pp., 1921.
14. Burke, Rev. Thomas Joseph, S.T.D., J.C.D., Competence in Ecclesiastical Tribunals, IV-117 pp., 1922.
15. Leech, Rev. George Leo, J.C.D., A Comparative Study of the Constitution, "Apostolicae Sedis" and the "Codex Juris Canonici," 179 pp., 1922.
16. Motry, Rev. Hubert Louis, S.T.D., J.C.D., Diocesan Faculties According to the Code of Canon Law, II-167 pp., 1922.
17. Murphy, Rev. George Lawrence, J.C.D., Delinquencies and Penalties in the Administration and Reception of the Sacraments, IV-121 pp., 1923.
18. O'Reilly, Rev. John Anthony, S.T.B., J.C.D., Ecclesiastical Sepulture in the New Code of Canon Law, II-129 pp., 1923.

19. Michalicka, Rev. Wenceslas Cyrill, O.S.B., J.C.D., Judicial Procedure in Dismissal of Clerical Exempt Religious, 107 pp., 1923.
20. Dargin, Rev. Edward Vincent, S.T.B., J.C.D., Reserved Cases According to the Code of Canon Law, IV-103, pp., 1924.
21. Godfrey, Rev. John A., S.T.B., J.C.D., The Right of Patronage According to the Code of Canon Law, 153 pp., 1924.
22. Hagedorn, Rev. Francis Edward, J.C.D., General Legislation on Indulgences, II-154 pp., 1924.
23. King, Rev. James Ignatius, J.C.D., The Administration of the Sacraments to Dying Non-Catholics, V-141 pp., 1924.
24. Winslow, Rev. Francis Joseph, A.F.M., J.C.D., Vicars and Prefects Apostolic, IV-149 pp., 1924.
25. Correa, Rev. Jose Servelion, S.T.L., J.C.D., La Potestad Legislativa de la Iglesia Catolica, IV-127 pp., 1925.
26. Dugan, Rev. Henry Francis, A.M., J.C.D., The Judiciary Department of the Diocesan Curia, 87 pp., 1925.
27. Keller, Rev. Charles Frederick, S.T.B., J.C.D., Mass Stipends, 167 pp., 1925.
28. Paschang, Rev. John Linus, J.C.D., The Sacramentals According to the Code of Canon Law, 129 pp., 1925.
29. Pointek, Rev. Cyrillus, O.F.M., S.T.B., J.C.D., De Indulto Exclaustrationis necnon Saecularizationis, XIII-289 pp., 1925.
30. Kearney, Rev. Richard Joseph, S.T.B., J.C.D., Sponsors at Baptism According to the Code of Canon Law, IV-127 pp., 1925.
31. Bartlett, Rev. Chester Joseph, A.M., LL.B., J.C.D., The Tenure of Parochial Property in the United States of America, V-108 pp., 1926.
32. Kilker, Rev. Adrian Jerome, J.C.D., Extreme Unction, V-425 pp., 1926.
33. McCormick, Rev. Robert Emmett, J.C.D., Confessors of Religious, VIII-266 pp., 1926.
34. Miller, Rev. Newton Thomas, J.C.D., Founded Masses According to the Code of Canon Law, VII-93 pp., 1926.
35. Roelker, Rev. Edward G., S.T.D., J.C.D., Principles of Privilege According to the Code of Canon Law, XI-166 pp., 1926.
36. Bakalarczyk, Rev. Richardus, M.I.C., J.U.D., De Novitiatu, VIII-208 pp., 1927.
37. Pizzuti, Rev. Lawrence, O.F.M., J.U.L., De Parochis Religiosis, 1927. (Not printed).
38. Bliley, Rev. Nicholas Martin, O.S.B., J.C.D., Altars According to the Code of Canon Law, XIX-132 pp., 1927.
39. Brown, Mr. Brendan Francis, A.B. LL.M., J.U.D., The Canonical Juristic Personality with Special Reference to Its Status in the United States of America, V-212 pp., 1927.

40. Cavanaugh, Rev. William Thomas, C.P., J.U.D., The Reservation of the Blessed Sacrament, VIII-101 pp., 1927.
41. Doheny, Rev. William J., C.S.C., A.B., J.U.D., Church Property: Modes of Acquisition, X-118 pp., 1927.
42. Feldhaus, Rev. Aloysius H., C.PP.S., J.C.D., Oratories, IX-141 pp., 1927.
43. Kelly, Rev. James Patrick, A.B., J.C.D., The Jurisdiction of the Simple Confessor, X-208 pp., 1927.
44. Neuberger, Rev. Nicholas J., J.C.D., Canon 6 or the Relation of the Codex Juris Canonici to the Preceding Legislation, V-95 pp., 1927.
45. O'Keefe, Rev. Gerald Michael, J.C.D., Matrimonial Dispensations, Powers of Bishops, Priests and Confessors, VIII-232 pp., 1927.
46. Quigley, Rev. Joseph A.M., A.B., J.C.B., Condemned Societies, 139 pp., 1927.
47. Zaplotnik, Rev. Johannes Leo, J.C.D., De Vicariis Foraneis, X-142 pp., 1927.
48. Duskie, Rev. John Aloysius, A.B., J.C.D., The Canonical Status of the Orientals in the United States, VIII-196 pp., 1928.
49. Hyland, Rev. Francis Edward, J.C.D., Excommunication, Its Nature, Historical Development and Effects, VIII-181 pp., 1928.
50. Reinmann, Rev. Gerald Joseph, O.M.C., J.C.D., The Third Order Secular of Saint Francis, 201 pp., 1928.
51. Schenk, Rev. Francis J., J.C.D., The Matrimonial Impediments of Mixed Religion and Disparity of Cult, XVI-318 pp., 1929.
52. Coady, Rev. John Joseph, S.T.D., J.U.D., A.M., The Appointment of Pastors, VIII-150 pp., 1929.
53. Kay, Rev. Thomas Henry, J.C.D., Competence in Matrimonial Procedure, VIII-164 pp., 1929.
54. Turner, Rev. Sidney Joseph, C.P., J.U.D., The Vow of Poverty, XLIX-217 pp., 1929.
55. Kearney, Rev. Raymond, A., A.B., S.T.D., J.C.D., The Principles, of Delegation, VII-149 pp., 1929.
56. Conran, Rev. Edward James, A.B., J.C.D., The Interdict, V-163 pp., 1930.
57. O'Neil, Rev. William H., J.C.D., Papal Rescripts of Favor, VII-218 pp., 1930.
58. Bastnagel, Rev. Clement Vincent, J.U.D., The Appointment of Parochial Adjutants and Assistants, XV-257 pp., 1930.
59. Ferry, Rev. William A., A.B., J.C.D., Stole Fees, V-135 pp., 1930.
60. Costello, Rev. John Michael, A.B., J.C.D., Domicile and Quasi-domicile, VII-201 pp., 1930.
61. Kremer, Rev. Michael Nicholas, A.B., S.T.B., J.C.D., Church Support in the United States, VI-1930,

62. Angulo, Rev. Luis, C.M., J.C.D., Legislation de la Iglesia sobre la intencion en la application de la Santa Misa, VII-104 pp., 1931.
63. Frey, Rev. Wolfgang Norbert, O.S.B., A.B., J.C.D., The Act of Religious Profession, VIII-174 pp., 1931.
64. Roberts, Rev. James Brendan, A.B., J.C.D., The Banns of Marriage, XIV-140 pp., 1931.
65. Ryder, Rev. Raymond Aloysius, A.B., J.C.D., Simony, IX-151 pp., 1931.
66. Campagna, Rev. Angelo, Ph.D., J.U.D., Il Vicario Generale del Vescovo, VII-205 pp., 1931.
67. Cox, Rev. Joseph Godfrey, A.B., J.C.D., The Administration ot Seminaries, VI-124 pp., 1931.
68. Gregory, Rev. Donald J., J.U.D., The Pauline Privilege, XV-165 pp., 1931.
69. Donohue, Rev. John F., J.C.D., The Impediment of Crime, VII-110 pp., 1931.
70. Dooley, Rev. Eugene A., O.M.I., J.C.D., Church Law On Sacred Relics, IX-143 pp., 1931.
71. Orth, Rev. Raymond Clement, O.M.C., J.C.D., The Approbation of Religious Institutes, 171 pp., 1931.
72. Pernicone, Rev. Joseph M., A.B., J.C.D., The Ecclesiastical Prohibition of Books, XII-267 pp., 1932.
73. Clinton, Rev. Connell, A.B., J.C.D., The Paschal Precept, IX-108 pp., 1932.
74. Donnelly, Rev. Francis B., A.M., S.T.L., J.C.D., The Diocesan Synod, VIII-125 pp., 1932.
75. Torrente, Rev. Camilo, C.M.F., J.C.D., Las Processiones Sagradas, V-145 pp., 1932.
76. Murphy, Rev. Edwin J., C.PP.S., J.C.D., Suspension Ex Informata Conscientia, XI-122, pp., 1932.
77. Mackenzie, Rev. Eric F., A.M., S.T.L., J.C.D., The Delict of Heresy in its Commission Penalization, Absolution, VII-124 pp., 1932.
78. Lyons Rev. Avitus E., S.T.B., J.C.D., The Collegiate Tribunal of First Instance, XI-147 pp., 1932.
79. Connolly, Rev. Thomas A., J.C.D., Appeals, XI-195 pp., 1932.
80. Sangmeister, Rev. Joseph V., A.B., J.C.D., Force and Fear as Precluding Matrimonial Consent, V-211 pp., 1932.
81. Jaeger, Rev. Leo A., A.B., J.C.D., The Administration of Vacant and Quasi-vacant Episcopal Sees in the United States, IX-229 pp., 1932.
82. Rimlinger, Rev. Herbert T., J.C.D., Error Invalidating Matrimonial Consent, VII-79 pp., 1932.
83. Barrett, Rev. John D.M., S.S., J.C.D., A Comparative Study of the Third Plenary Council of Baltimore and the Code, IX-221 pp., 1932.

84. Carberry, Rev. John J., Ph.D., S.T.D., J.C.D., The Juridical Form of Marriage, X-177 pp., 1934.
85. Dolan, Rev. John L., A.B., J.C.D., The Defensor Vinculi, XII-157 pp., 1934.
86. Hannan, Rev. Jerome D., A.M., S.T.D., LL.B., J.C.D., The Canon Law of Wills, IX-517 pp., 1934.
87. Lemieux, Rev. Delisle A., A.M., J.C.D., The Sentence in Ecclesiastical Procedure, IX-131 pp., 1934.
88. O'Rourke, Rev. James J., A.B., J.C.D., Parish Registers, VII-109 pp., 1934.
89. Timlin, Rev. Bartholomew, O.F.M., A.M., J.C.D., Conditional Matrimonial Consent, X-381 pp., 1934.
90. Wahl, Rev. Francis X., A.B., J.C.D., The Matrimonial Impediments of Consanguinity and Affinity, VI-125 pp., 1934.
91. White, Rev. Robert J., A.B., LL.B., S.T.B., J.C.D., Canonical Ante-Nuptial Promises and the Civil Law, VI-152 pp., 1934.
92. Herrera, Rev. Antonio Parra, O.C.D., J.C.D., Legislation Ecclesiastica sobra el Ayuno y la Abstinencia, XI-191 pp., 1935.
93. Kennedy, Rev. Edwin J., J.C.D., The Special Matrimonial Process in Cases of Evident Nullity, X-165 pp., 1935.
94. Manning, Rev. John J., A.B., J.C.D., Presumption of Law in Matrimonial Procedure, XI-111 pp., 1935.
95. Moeder, Rev. John M., J.C.D., The Proper Bishop for Ordination and Dismissorial Letters, VII-135 pp., 1935.
96. O'Mara, Rev. William A., A.B., J.C.D., Canonical Causes For Matrimonial Dispensations, IX-155 pp., 1935.
97. Reilly, Rev. Peter, J.C.D., Residence of Pastors, IX-81 pp., 1935.
98. Smith, Rev. Mariner T., O.P., S.T.L., J.C.D., The Penal Law For Religious, VII-169 pp., 1935.
99. Whalen, Rev. Donald W., A.M., J.C.D., The Value of Testimonial Evidence in Matrimonial Procedure, XIII-297 pp., 1935.
100. Cleary, Rev. Joseph F., J.C.D., Canonical Limitations on the Alienation of Church Property, VIII-141 pp., 1936.
101. Glynn, Rev. John C., J.C.D., The Promoter of Justice, XX-337 pp., 1936.
102. Brennan, Rev. James H., S.S., A.M., S.T.B., J.C.D., The Simple Convalidation of Marriage, VI-135 pp, 1937.
103. Brunini, Rev. Joseph Bernard, J.C.D., The Clerical Obligations of Canons, 139 and 142, X-121 pp., 1937.
104. Connor, Rev. Maurice, A.B., J.C.D., The Administrative Removal of Pastors, VIII-159 pp., 1937.
105. Guilfoyle, Rev. Merlin Joseph, J.C.D., Custom, XI-144 pp., 1937.
106. Hughes, Rev. James Austin, A.B., A.M., J.C.D., Witnesses in Criminal Trials of Clerics, IX-140 pp., 1937.

107. Jansen, Rev. Raymond J., A.B., S.T.L., J.C.D., Canonical Provisions for Catechetical Instruction, VII-153 pp., 1937.
108. Kealy, Rev. John James, A.B., J.C.D,, The Introductory Libellus in Church Court Procedure, XI-121 pp., 1937.
109. McManus, Rev. James Edward, C.SS.R., J.C.D., The Administration of Temporal Goods in Religious Institutes, XVI-196 pp., 1937.
110. Moriarity, Rev. Eugene James, J.C.D., Oaths in Ecclesiastical Courts, X-115 pp., 1937.
111. Rainer, Rev. Eligius George, C.SS.R., J.C.D., Suspension of Clerics, XVII-249 pp., 1937.
112. Reilly, Rev. Thomas F., C.SS.R., J.C.D., Visitation of Religious, VI-195 pp., 1938.
113. Moriarty, Rev. Francis E., C.SS.R., J.C.D., The Extraordinary Absolution from Censures, XV-334 pp., 1938.
114. Connolly, Rev. Nicholas P., J.C.D., The Canonical Erection of Parishes, X-132 pp., 1938.
115. Donovan, Rev. James Joseph, J.C.D., The Pastor's Obligation in Prenuptial Investigation, XII-322 pp., 1938.
116. Harrigan, Rev. Robert J., M.A., S.T.B., J.C.D., The Radical Sanation of Invalid Marriages, VIII-208 pp., 1938.
117. Boffa, Rev. Conrad Humbert, J.C.D., Canonical Provisions for Catholic Schools, X-211 pp., 1939.
118. Parsons, Rev. Anscar John, O.M. Cap., J.C.D., Canonical Elections, XII-236 pp., 1939.
119. Reilly, Rev. Edward Michael, A.B., J.C.D., The General Norms of Dispensation, X-156 pp., 1939.
120. Ryan, Rev. Gerald Aloysius, A.B., J.C.D., Principles of Episcopal Jurisdiction, XII-172 pp., 1939.
121. Burton, Rev. Francis James, C.S.C., A.B., J.C.D., A Commentary on Canon 1125, X-222 pp., 1940.
122. Miaskiewicz, Rev. Francis Sigismund, J.C.D., Supplied Jurisdiction according to Canon 209, XII-340 pp., 1940.
123. Rice, Rev. Patrick William, A.B., J.C.D., Proof of Death in Prenuptial Investigation, VIII-156 pp., 1940.
124. Anglin, Rev. Thomas Francis, M.S., J.C.L., The Eucharistic Fast.
125. Coleman, Rev. John Jerome, J.C.L., The Minister of Confirmation.
126. Downs, Rev. John Emmanuel, A.B., J.C.L., The Concept of Clerical Immunity.
127. Esswein, Rev. Anthony Albert, J.C.L., Extrajudicial Penal Powers of Ecclesiastical Superiors.
128. Farrell, Rev. Benjamin Francis, M.A., S.T.L., J.C.L., The Rights and Duties of the Local Ordinary Regarding Congregations of Women Religious of Pontifical Approval.

129. Feeney, Rev. Thomas John, A.B., S.T.L., J.C.L., Restitutio in Integrum.
130. Findlay, Rev. Stephen William, O.S.B., A.B., J.C.L., Canonical Norms Governing the Deposition and Degradation of Clerics.
131. Goodwine, Rev. John, A.B., S.T.L., J.C.L., The Right of the Church to Acquire Property.
132. Heston, Rev. Edward Louis, C.S.C., Ph.D., S.T.D., J.C.L., The Alienation of Church Property in the United States .
133. Hogan, Rev. James John, S.T.L., J.C.L.,, Judicial Advocates and Procurators.
134. Kealy, Rev. Thomas M., A.B., Litt. B., J.C.L., Dowry of Women Religious.
135. Keene, Rev. Michael James, O.S.B., J.C.L., Religious Ordinaries and Canon 198.
136. Kerin, Rev. Charles A., S.S., M.A., S.T.B., J.C.L., The Privation of Christian Burial.
137. Louis, Rev. William Francis, M.A., J.C.L., Diocesan Archives.
138. McDevitt, Rev. Gilbert Joseph, A.B., J.C.L., Legitimacy and Legitimation.
139. McDonough, Rev. Thomas Joseph, A.B., J.C.L., Apostolic Administrators.
140. Meier, Rev. Carl Anthony, A.B., J.C.L., Penal Administrative Procedure Against Negligent Pastors.
141. Schmidt, Rev. John Rogg, A.B., J.C.L., The Principles of Authentic Interpretation in Canon 17 of the Code of Canon Law.
142. Slafkosky, Rev. Andrew Leonard, A.B., J.C.L., The Canonical Episcopal Visitation of the Diocese.
143. Swoboda, Rev. Innocent Robert, O.F.M., J.C.L., Ignorance in Relation to the Imputability of Delicts.
144. Dubé, Rev. Arthur Joseph, A.B., J.C.L., The General Principles for the Reckoning of Time in Canon Law.
145. McBride, Rev. James T., A.B., J.C.L., Incardination and Excardination of Seculars.

www.ingramcontent.com/pod-product-compliance
Lightning Source LLC
LaVergne TN
LVHW050251080826
844660LV00012B/624

9780813223278